A MEASURE OF DANGER

A Measure of Danger

MEMOIRS OF
A BRITISH WAR CORRESPONDENT

Michael Nicholson

HarperCollins
An Imprint of HarperCollins*Publishers*

First published in Great Britain in 1991
by HarperCollins Publishers,
77/85 Fulham Palace Road,
Hammersmith, London W6 8JB

9 8 7 6 5 4 3 2 1

BRITISH LIBRARY CATALOGUING IN PUBLICATION DATA

Nicholson, Michael
A measure of danger: memoirs of a british war correspondent.
1. British war correspondents, history
I. Title
070.433092

ISBN 0 00 215386 6

Photoset in Itek Janson by Ace Filmsetting Ltd, Frome, Somerset
Printed and bound in Great Britain by
Hartnolls Limited, Bodmin, Cornwall

CONTENTS

LIST OF ILLUSTRATIONS

This book is dedicated to

NEIL DAVIS
1934–1985

JOURNALIST AND COMBAT CAMERAMAN

and to all those who remember him

Introduction

'. . . That feeling of exhilaration which a measure
of danger brings to a visitor with a return ticket'
                              – Graham Greene, *Ways of Escape*

THE WORST MOMENT in a war was my fear I should not be sent to it.
The expectation, the sight and sound of gunfire never failed to
exhilarate. Risk spiced my life, but then I had the return ticket, the
paper promise to lift me alive and away from the killing fields and
dangerous living. There was only ever one answer to the repeated
question why did I go to war: it was because I wanted to. I could not
otherwise have gone so often to so many – thirteen war zones in all,
returning to some many times over. It was easily done because,
except the once, it never occurred to me I would not come back.

In my generation the same newsmen went to war, the regulars,
who missed one only by accident or if they were dead. You were
bound to see the same faces at one or other end of the flight. We
were an eccentric club of privileged globe-trotters who held our
meetings in the most bizarre places. When we were together was
the only time we talked of our wars, and even then warily. Our
adventures seemed so unlikely in retrospect.

Was it machismo or masochism that encouraged us so compul-
sively and repeatedly to risk our lives? Probably both, but there was
really no choice. Having done it once we had to do it again. You
went up the road simply because the others went too and, like the
others, you believed that survival was anyway a fluke. You lived
with a colossal and comforting fatalism, like the GIs in Vietnam,
who boasted they worried only about the bullet with their name on
it.

Correspondents who travel the world, especially war correspondents and the select cameramen and photographers who do the
same, suffer from an overdose of everything. They become

saturated in the world's woes, and it is sometimes difficult to separate the cynicism and black humour from the caring conscience they sometimes have. A story is told of a British reporter and his photographer who were covering the famine in Ethiopia. At the end of the day the photographer told his colleague how he had been followed around the refugee camp by a woman, frail and sticklike and barely able to carry the baby in her arms. Disease and malnutrition had made her so horribly deformed, even her own people rejected her. For hours she had hobbled behind him, whispering, begging, touching his arm, appealing. 'What did you give her?' asked the reporter. The photographer answered: '125th at F/8. It's a great picture!'

Yet such is the contradiction of the trade that we could not do it if we did not care. If we were troubled, it was because it was sometimes hard to know what it was that separated the observer from the participant; to distinguish how you thought from how you felt and to know the difference between what you thought you saw and what you knew you had to say. And to resist the temptation not simply to report the story but to assume a role in it.

War reporting has been described as the contemporary man's duel: when a newsman comes back from up the road, from the challenge of enemy fire, he feels the pounding in his blood like any corny soldier. Whether to go up the road was always the first decision in every working day at war; for many it was the last decision they ever had to make. Newspaper or magazine reporters, of course, did not need to go to find the war every day and some even persuaded themselves they need not go at all. So many of the day's events could be picked up on a bar-stool from other, braver souls who had chanced their luck. Some simply rewrote agency copy. One of the most vivid first-person testimonies describing the fall of Saigon was written by a British newspaper reporter who was in Hongkong at the time.

Television people, though, have always to make that journey, have always to be where it is happening, day after day for as long as it is light, for as long as the satellite is beckoning. Our editors and news producers have a voracious and frantic appetite – nympholepsy is the word I found tucked away in the dictionary that best describes them. It means an ecstasy or frenzy caused by the desire for the unattainable. They also have an insatiable passion for violence. They are bemused by it. The bloodier the offensive, the bigger the coverage; the worse the atrocity, the bigger the by-line. The news agenda has become bloodier and bloodier. At times, it almost borders on titillation.

I once complained to an anonymous face over a large whisky in the Hotel Royale in Saigon: 'Once the bosses were satisfied with a corpse. Now they must have people dying in action. But when they really do get something that shows what a mortar does to a man, when they see how shrapnel tears the flesh and the blood explodes, they get squeamish. They want it just so. They want TV to be cinema.'

I had in mind one particular sequence we had filmed in Vietnam. We flew with the Medivacs (the Medical Evacuation helicopters), dropping right in among heavy fighting to pick up the wounded and, more often than not, the dying, and flying them to a field hospital. There we filmed a boy, he was barely nineteen, who had stepped on a mine. His face was grey with morphine; towels, six deep, which had been laid across his middle were sodden with blood and he was shivering uncontrollably with shock. When finally he was still and they took the towels away, there was little left between his stomach and his thighs. But on the coloured screen, blood is a very sobering red and television will not transmit such horrors. That is its Catch 22. Fascinated by it themselves, programme editors filter out what they consider viewers should not see. They contrive a surrogate war, where much of the suffering is deleted. They help to sanitise war; they almost make it acceptable.

When I returned from the Falklands I was surprised and forlorn at the way television had coped. In the news producers' desperation to illustrate what they thought was going on eight thousand miles away in the South Atlantic and in the absence of satellite pictures, there were strip cartoons on all channels showing air attacks, land assaults and sinking ships, lantern-jawed marines, slim moustachioed paratroopers, the bugler playing an heroic Last Post over San Carlos. It was *Boy's Own* without the POWs! and WHAMs! But it was not war. Not as I knew it.

Leafing through my diaries, noting the dates and details of

countries and capitals, air schedules and contact names, hotels and room numbers, all the scribblings of a sometimes lonely correspondent, I realise how little I saw of Blighty during those years. I was often away from home and family for eight months of the year, mostly abroad and usually a long, long way away. My singular usefulness to ITN was to endure dangerous places, that was what abroad usually meant. If I had something of a monopoly of war reporting then, I suspect it was because nobody else craved it in quite the same way.

It has been an odd occupation: death as a matter-of-fact reason for being there. And it has been difficult to catalogue the twenty and more years of it and not doubt the recall. Who would believe how many war hours the world has lived through in one generation? Those little wars.

Do you remember the starving face of Biafra? the Palestinian grenade rolling down the aisle of a PanAm jet? the pits full of corpses on the birthday of Bangladesh? the belly of a six-year-old blown open in Lebanon and the faceless napalm babies of Vietnam?

Who remembers Idi Amin's Uganda, the House of Death in the Congo, the cannibals of Cambodia, the headless missionaries in Rhodesia and the black bleeding red in Soweto? Cyprus and war, Israel and war, the Falklands and war. Afghanistan, Nicaragua, El Salvador, Sri Lanka. And war.

> Sound, sound the clarion, fill the fire,
> Throughout the sensual world proclaim,
> One crowded hour of glorious life
> Is worth an age without a name.

Neil Davis wrote those lines in the flyleaf of every work diary he kept during his years in South-east Asia. Their message was his motto and his philosophy until the day he died.

Neil was a kind and gentle man. He was Australia's finest combat cameraman, which put him among the world's best. He was more cunningly competitive than most; he had astonishing stamina; he was never afraid. He survived many wounds in Vietnam and Cambodia and lost many friends in both those wars. He was addicted to filming combat, and it never occurred to him that he would ever get hit.

He once told me, as he had told others, that if it were ever done, it was best it was done quickly.

'I'm not afraid of being killed but I don't want to be wounded and lie out there with a gut full of shrapnel. I've seen a lot of wounded die like that and I really don't care for it at all.'

At the end, Neil did die with a gut full of shrapnel – victim of high-tech and a tuppeny-ha'penny attempted coup.

In Vietnam as in other wars, cameramen in the sixties and early seventies could move on their own whenever they wished. They could simply disconnect the cable that attached them like an umbilical cord to their sound recordist and move unhampered in dangerous situations, running across a battlefield, jumping from foxhole to foxhole, from cover to cover. Some of Neil's best war coverage, like that of others with him, was done lying flat in a trench with one hand holding the small wind-up 16mm camera, on a wide-angle lens, over his head. You ran the risk of losing a camera – even a hand – but that was preferable to the other option.

Electronic news-gathering – the video camera, big and cumbersome, weighing fifteen pounds, and with a sound recordist lumbering behind carrying a recorder twice as heavy – has turned the clock back in terms of field mobility. It has made the camera crew twice as slow and doubly vulnerable. That was how it was in Bangkok that morning, the ninth of September 1985.

Caught in crossfire between pro- and anti-government troops, Neil ran with his soundman for cover. Both were hit by shrapnel, both fell, Neil's stomach torn open. By chance, the camera continued running and recorded the story of his dying.

It was a fitting postscript and Neil would have liked it.

CHAPTER ONE

Nigeria – Biafra,
1968–69

Africa's Land of the Rising Sun

IT WAS NOT, I suppose, the ideal way to begin a career as a foreign correspondent: to arrive in Nigeria the day Soviet tanks rolled into Prague. In August 1968 the world watched on television as the Czechs stood defiant at the start of their doomed revolution and I, stranded thousands of miles away, mourned what I thought was ambition stillborn.

The day before, the Nigerian civil war had seemed the only story that mattered. Its headlines spanned column inches, its gore and ghastliness was the staple diet of every newspaper and colour magazine. Television news and current affairs editors were loath to let a day pass without a reminder of the suffering in the tiny enclave we called Biafra and of the monster Nigeria starving it to death.

This was my first war, and it would, I thought, end my long years as a Home Desk reporter, randomly covering dock strikes and coal strikes and the never-ending and always-hostile pickets outside the nation's silent car factories. No more hours waiting in the cold rain outside Number Ten or Congress House for a glimpse of one of our illustrious. No more humble gratitude for the bland clichés thrown out in the name of an interview.

Now, with the luck that was to aid and plague me for the rest of my life, I was on the first step of the ladder to the jealously-guarded ranks of the Foreign Correspondents, that legendary band of globe-trotters with the trademarks that set them apart: the battered and stickered portable typewriter and the tattered and travelworn passport nestling in the pocket of a wash-'n'-wear suit – the ninety-four-page special edition, crammed with multi-coloured visas and exotic entries and exits from Peking, Phnom Penh, Peru . . . Laos, Lesotho, St Lucia, Senegal.

But as I sat in steamy Lagos, listening to events in Prague on the BBC World Service, I leafed through my passport, thin and virginal, convinced it would never again see the sun beyond Dieppe. A cable was surely on its way ordering me to abort and return home. It would take some time to decode, of course; editors in those days were obsessed with Waugh-like cable-ese. It would probably read:

> URGENTLY EFFORTING UPWIND NIGERIAWISE DUE
> EDSOCCUPATION PRAGUEWARDS STOP ADVISE DEPARTPLAN
> SOONEST BESTEST STOP

It was all to do with saving the company money, which was a nonsense because what would come later would read:

> SORRY OLD LAD STOP EDITOR SENDS HIS REGRETS AND
> PROMISES TO MAKE AMENDS STOP FAMILY WELL STOP
> REGARDS TO CREW STOP SEE YOU BACK AT BASE AND DONT
> FORGET THE AVOCADOS STOP

I had been so frenzied a few days before. Out of the blue, it had been decided I should go on the story and I was sick with anxiety that any one of half a dozen senior reporters would come barging into the newsroom smelling of after-lunch brandy and take the prize from me. The foreign editor had summoned me and together we waited for the editor-in-chief to give the final okay. He in turn was waiting for the accountants to complete their costings.

Some foreign editors were not desk men, that is, they found it exceedingly hard to sit behind one, which was unfortunate because, as more and more of the important everyday editorial decisions were taken from them, the longer they sat wondering why. The devolution was forced on them by younger, brighter men with university degrees and the ability to produce what occasionally passed for original thought. Many foreign editors then belonged to the age when journalists worked by the seat of their pants, guided only by hunches. Many were fond of saying, 'If you want a new idea in television, go back five years and you'll find it!'

There were those who sat alone in their rooms, sipping neat warm gin from a paper cup – the same paper cup – watching the bustle of the newsroom through an open door and wondering why, contrary to all expectations, they had become less and less in charge of affairs. I knew of one night editor who had seldom been abroad, and knew the world only from the ageing *Daily Telegraph* wall map in his room. Before he sent any of his reporters away, he measured their journey on it with the palm of his hand. His span, he reckoned, equalled exactly a thousand miles and he would frequently estimate, say, the flying time to Bombay by skimming the Alps, thumb to little finger like a crawling crab, across the Mediterranean and the Middle East to the Indian Ocean. London to Madagascar was apparently just over five and a half thousand palm miles. He considered himself lucky to have such a hand. A smaller one, say an 850-mile span, would have made the calculations much more complicated.

In those days a junior reporter only got a foreign story that took him beyond the Channel ports when none of the others wanted it. The veterans had an eye for when a running story was slowing down and could hop off it and join another that was gathering speed. To many seasoned hacks, in that autumn of 1968, the Nigerian civil war was already suffering over-exposure. They were better off in Prague. Or Saigon.

Nigeria had been reported most thoroughly by ITN reporters before me. I had envied their films and had watched them return home heaped in herograms to be taken to the editor's perfunctory lunch at the Reform Club. This was considered a great honour: to share a taxi and a meal with Him from the outer office, whom you might normally only see on your first day of employment or your last. It was a typically mean managerial manoeuvre, of course. There was not a reporter who would not have taken a cash bonus instead, or at least a visit to a decent restaurant. The Club's food was so regularly bad that the editor's favour was considered more of a punishment than a reward. It was referred to then as the Penal Reform Club!

Finally, that baptismal day, my telephone rang. The accountants had finished their sums and reluctantly admitted the trip was within the limits of their monthly budget. Accountants would make the most efficient censors, telling no one anything in case the telling involved spending!

But now at last I was on my way and the Pretty Thing on the Foreign Desk held out my air tickets and an envelope full of dollars. She looked at me without interest. Understandably, she felt no generosity towards me. She simply bit her lip and shouted something across to the Home Desk editor, whose mouth was always black at the corners because of his habit of chewing HB pencils. He waved a friendly nonchalant goodbye to me, leant back in his chair and with relief and a wet pencil drew a line through my name on the weekly home reporters' duty roster. Nicholson was off shift.

By some it was called the Nigerian civil war, by others, the Biafran war of independence. In the early sixties, in Nigeria's post-colonial infancy, it was generally believed that at least it would escape the wasting diseases of tribalism, nepotism and corruption that were already infecting other newly unshackled African nations. With its immense natural resources and potential wealth, Nigeria, one of Africa's largest and most populated nations, had all the qualifications to become the leader the dark continent so desperately needed.

But machine-gun fire in the early dawn of a Lagos January morning in 1966 ended all such optimism. The slaughter that day was followed by a similarly bloody coup and counter-coup, and in a series of appalling massacres Africa's giant tore itself apart.

It all had to do with tribalism, which is peculiarly African, and greed, over which it has no monopoly. Nigeria is split tribally three ways: the Moslem Hausas govern the north, the Christian Yorubas the west and mid-west, and the Christian Ibos the east. Outsiders thought it an oddball formula for unity, and expected the Hausas to be the disruptive force. Instead it was the Ibos. They were called the 'Jews of Nigeria' because they worked and schemed harder than the others and consequently, because they came to dominate, were resented and despised. The Ibo was fond of explaining the difference thus: there is a coconut at the top of a palm tree. The Hausa will sit and pray it will fall; the Yoruba will shake the tree in a fury; the Ibo will climb and pick it.

The Ibos, endowed with such a natural talent for enterprise, had been blessed with something even more marketable. There was abundant oil in the Eastern Province. Given the uncertainty of Nigeria remaining unified, some prominent and ambitious Ibos and their clandestine international backers decided it would be worthwhile going it alone. On April Fool's Day 1966, a young Ibo colonel, Emeka Ojukwu, the Oxford-educated son of a man who had made his millions in the transport business and who had been knighted by the Queen of England, announced that the Eastern Province was appropriating all Federal revenues and responsibilities, and would take over the running of all the East's railways, schools, courts and army. Soon, with white-hot separatist passion, Colonel Ojukwu was to declare himself master of a new Ibo nation. It was henceforth to be called Biafra.

Trumpets were sounded, oilmen and arms dealers rubbed their hands in glee and, confident of international support, Ojukwu crossed the River Niger and invaded the West. For a while it looked as if he might win, might indeed march on Lagos itself. But he was an unlucky man with a knack for making wrong decisions – or the right ones too late – and his fortunes and those of his new-born Biafra quickly turned around. His war for independence became a human tragedy on a massive scale.

On the last day in August I landed in Lagos with cameraman Chris Faulds and recordist Hugh Thomson. Above the airport building was a gigantic billboard: WELCOME TO NIGERIA . . . WHERE BABIES ARE HEALTHY AND HAPPY. The airport was not.

Lagos was and is a bad-tempered place, but exuberant and entertaining. On our first night the radio announcer solemnly reminded people that the Obas (the traditional rulers and the chiefs of Lagos State) had banned 'drumming and merrymaking' because there was a war going on.

One fellow-journalist recorded a conversation with a Lagos taxi-driver:

'You got a cold?' the driver asked.

'Yes,' said my friend.

'In this country you must protect yourself. I use codeine every night and Aspro in the morning. And always Nivaquin for malaria. But my big problem is smoking.'

'Try a little will-power,' my friend suggested.

'Thank you. I will. Does it come in liquid or tablet?'

After days of trooping up and down corridors in the Ministry of Information and being handed reams of deceitful propaganda, I saw a notice inviting entries for the 1968 beauty competition for the title 'Miss Information'!

On our third evening we met one of Nigeria's champions. Not President General Gowon, an uncharacteristically soft-spoken and gentle man, but one of his colonels who was neither of these things. He was called after one of Africa's deadliest creatures: the Black Scorpion. Benjamin Adesanya Maja Adekunle considered himself his nation's saviour and was known privately to prefer the title 'Black Napoleon'. His father was a Yoruba and his mother a Bachama from the north-east, one of the country's most belligerent tribes. There was no doubting he was his mother's son. He was already notorious in war, having razed the historic Calabar prison with three hundred soldiers inside simply because they had not surrendered quickly enough.

He completed his cadet training at genteel Sandhurst, like so many officers, Federal and Biafran. This was to prove a dreadful handicap. Throughout the war the officers on both sides clung to the British army's rules of war and to its rules of personal conduct. But they were out of place in Africa. An American reporter at the time observed that it was 'the code of Kipling that influenced the way the war was fought'. Until the very end the Nigerian and Biafran chiefs of staff aped the archetypal British general with their polished Sam Browne belts, ceremonial swords, and a khaki chauffeur-driven Humber for all occasions. Their officers followed suit, with clipped moustaches, swagger-sticks and batmen. The war was fought as if it were on Salisbury Plain and not in the jungles of West Africa.

But Colonel Adekunle appreciated something his colleagues could not or would not: that Sandhurst training was fine for officers who could count on a general level of competence among the ranks, but it gave few clues on how to handle illiterate, naive village boys who had never heard the sound of a gun in their lives. So he commanded respect and obedience by brutal bullying. He also promoted the myth that he was invincible and bullet-proof, which is why he was fond of the other nickname his men whispered under their breath . . . OGEDENGBE, the legendary Yoruba warrior whose magic could snap a spear in mid-flight, and whose body could blunt the cutting edge of a machete. Soldiers would swear they had seen him catch bullets in his teeth and believed, or said they believed, that no one standing in his shadow could be harmed in combat. Except, that is, by Adekunle himself.

It is commonly held in Africa that you cannot expect a man to respect you unless he fears you and whatever else he had learnt at his British finishing school, the Black Scorpion held that to be true. I saw him club boy conscripts with their own rifles and club them again if they failed to thank him for it. He whipped men about the face with his swagger-stick until they bled, and those who needed further punishment were attacked with his favourite weapon – an American baseball bat he called the 'Louisville Slogger'.

'Terror,' he said at our first and only dinner, 'is the short cut to discipline. To turn a peasant into a soldier takes time and patience. I haven't either. They may be afraid to fight the enemy, but I make them a damned sight more afraid of me!'

Colonel Benjamin Adekunle sat next to me at dinner that evening, immaculate in his crisp starched khakis, his colonel's tabs on his collar, his Sam Browne coiled like a cobra on the couch beside him. Above his rows of campaign ribbons, and stitched in black silk, was the shape of a scorpion, its tail curled over its back, raised in attack.

To him, all of Nigeria's evils – all of Africa's – were prefixed 'white'. The civil war was the white man's invention, an international conspiracy to steal Nigeria's oil. Biafra was a creature of the white CIA employed by America's oil emperors, a puppet state doing the white man's bidding: 'The white man has no conscience about the way he has crippled Nigeria. The planes they send into so-called Biafra are not full of flour and medicines; they carry machine-guns and mortars and white mercenaries to keep this war going. I have banned all aid in my sector. I have forbidden the Red Cross to come anywhere near me. None of you –' he dabbed his finger on my face as if to emphasise my whiteness – 'none of you want to end it. If you did, it would be over tomorrow.' All this was shouted at us between courses as his manservant, in a white jacket buttoned to the neck and wearing white linen gloves, changed dishes. Finally, Adekunle, the teetotaller, served us brandy.

In the middle of the table was a large bowl of flowers and throughout the tirade he had leant forward and pulled them apart, squashing the petals and sniffing the scent on his fingertips. Now, as he screechingly accused the British of destroying the Nigeria its own Lugard had created, he stopped in mid-sentence, reached for the flower bowl and pulled out a revolver. The steward gently took the brandy bottle off the table, very slowly walked backwards into the kitchen and stood there watching as the double-hinged door swung backwards and forwards. Adekunle pointed the revolver at each of us in turn, slowly around the table, level with our eyes . . . first Chris, next Hugh and finally at me, sitting next to him. Then he pressed the barrel into the skin of my temple and pulled the trigger. It went click.

I suppose the silence could have lasted only a few seconds but when he began laughing it did seem as if I had been waiting a very long time for it. He said I was whiter than any white man he had ever seen. His man in the white gloves was laughing too as he came back into the room, still with the brandy, and it occurred to me that he was not seeing his master's little jest for the first time. Nor, I supposed, with the war having such a long way to go and with so many more dinner guests to come, would it be the last.

'Security, security, always security,' Adekunle shouted, waving the gun. 'It's the password for a long life. Nigeria has enemies here and abroad and so do I.' He dropped the revolver neatly into the middle of the coiled Sam Browne on the sofa.

'I have a dozen guns hidden around the house and not even he knows,' he said, beckoning to his steward. 'He, especially, does not know where they are.'

He turned to me, pleased to see the sweat on my face. 'This war in Nigeria is between brothers,' he said, 'and without you it would have been settled by now. The British press has fuelled our war with its inventions and deceit and if I had my way I'd let none of you into the country. But my orders are to take you to the front, and I will. But tell a lie about me, about my country or my troops and next time I will certainly shoot you!'

I remember the finale to that dinner particularly well. It was such an absurd piece of melodrama that once we were back in our hotel, free of him, we wondered if the entire evening had not simply been a bit of pantomime to relax a war-weary officer.

Chris and Hugh left but I stayed to finish my brandy and agree the final arrangements for our flight the next day, east to Port Harcourt and the colonel's headquarters. There we would join his 3rd Marine Commandos. I shook hands and exchanged the usual after-dinner banalities which seemed so absolutely out of place in the circumstances. Attempting to make light of the revolver scene, I promised to behave myself at 'the front', adding that it wouldn't do to have a loaded gun in the flower bowl next time we came. The colonel turned abruptly, went back to the couch and picked up the revolver again. 'But,' he said, 'my guns are always loaded. See!'

He aimed at the ceiling and the blast took away a piece of plaster the size of my fist. One chamber only had been kept empty for me and his evening's entertainment.

It was all theatre, of course. So much of Africa is, though I was not to know it then. Nor did I know his other nickname until some time later. In their pidgin English, the Yorubas called him 'ne cinema'. It means 'a grand show'.

THEY SAY GOD'S ON OUR SIDE BUT HE'S NOT.
HE'S BEHIND THE BIG BATTALIONS AS USUAL.

That despairing graffito and a shattered mammy-waggon, its front axle blown apart and the multi-coloured slogan GOD'S WILL painted along its side, were the first things I saw in Port Harcourt.

Federal forces had taken it only a few months before and Biafra's leader General Ojukwu had lost his only access to the sea and seaborne supplies. The town had been thoroughly blitzed and the jungle was fast taking it back – the houses, shops and offices, all that had made it a busy port disappearing beneath elephant grass and creeper. Only the military barracks and Colonel Adekunle's head-quarters in the Shell-BP building stood free of the tangle of soaking, rotting vegetation.

In the storm ditches along the road towards the swamps was a trail of rusted fridges, rotting furniture, denuded cathode ray tubes, bedsteads, all the litter of the hasty evacuation of people fleeing to the hinterland of their newly-announced Biafra, an infant nation already on the run.

It was raining hard but although there were dry rooms in the military barracks Adekunle told us he preferred not to have us there. He 'received' us in his own cosy quarters dressed in a black kimono, listening to soul music – Sam Cook and Wilson Pickett. Then we were bundled into what was mockingly called an hotel, a derelict slum covered in creeper and shrapnel holes. The roof had been blown away and the ground floor was used as a lavatory by patrolling soldiers. The front door had not survived but, astonishingly, the hand-painted plastic sign above it had. So we booked into the 'Cedar Palace', paid the Lebanese owner fifty American dollars each in advance and camped on the first floor. He sold us Lagos beer and tins of corned beef which we discovered later were our rations, given to him free by the army.

Within an hour it was dark. We lit our candles, drank the warm beer and ate the corned beef, mashed with baked beans we had brought from London. Somewhere outside, a few miles away, we heard gunfire – too close to be the enemy, the Lebanese told us – probably Federal soldiers high on hash or palm gin settling a few scores. I listened to it, fascinated: a long low rumble which I presumed to be a machine-gun, then the chatter of rifle fire, staccato, then another long burst and a final few shots answering. I had never heard such sounds before. Whoever was out there in the rain, in the dark, in the jungle, and why ever they were firing, it was the sound of war, and for the first time in my life I felt the irrepressible surge that told me I was close to danger. I held my breath, turning my ear to the night outside, but there was nothing more to hear, only the rain and that tropical sound which kills all sleep. We searched frantically in a box marked SOS for our mosquito repellent.

I did not sleep. I sat huddled under my mosquito net savouring my first jungle night and read newspaper cuttings by torchlight. Newspaper diplomatic correspondents, echoing sources in Westminster and Whitehall, were mostly predicting a quick end to the war. Over by Christmas! But Nigeria's President Gowon had announced yet another of his final offensives against the Biafrans and they were just as confidently talking of launching their own counter-offensive. By Christmas, maybe, but not this year. But, I had not come to cover offensives, nor, necessarily, the fighting. The file of newspaper reports I had brought with me (stuffed inside my underpants as I had sweated my way past police control at Lagos airport) had been saying that Federal troops were committing atrocities against the Biafran civilian population on such a scale that it amounted to genocide. Eye-witnesses reported entire villages set on fire, with families still inside the huts, indiscriminate shelling of refugee camps and the murder of prisoners-of-war. But in the absence of photographic proof it was easy for the Federal government to deny it and blame it on the efficient Biafran propaganda machine.

When we left Port Harcourt early the next morning, the Lebanese did not appear to give us change for our fifty dollars. Perhaps the rain kept him in bed. It was blinding and we could see nothing out of the windows of our battered coach which trundled its way along the Ogwe road. How on earth could anyone see to fight a war? But they could and they did and within the hour we were in no doubt about it.

We had joined a column of the Black Scorpion's 3rd Marine Commandos, a preposterous title for such a rag-tag bunch. Some wore uniforms, some only their tunics, some only trousers, some only a helmet and shorts. But the weapons they carried, mostly British government supplied, were new, and we were thankful for that soon enough.

The road began to meander down towards a small river which was crossed by a ford. The night's rain had flooded it and the stepping-stones were submerged, so, being sensible, we stopped to take off our boots. Had I not been advised by old Africa hands of the safe and simple rule: dry boots, dry feet; wet boots, septic sores? The soldiers knew it too, because they stopped and unlaced theirs. Or perhaps it was simply an excuse to sit down.

It was then that the firing began. Suddenly the ford seemed an obvious place for an ambush. There were only single aimed targeted shots from the other side – the Biafrans could not afford to waste a bullet. But our side replied with automatic fire, finger on the trigger until the magazine was empty, then slap in another and press all the harder. The trees and undergrowth surrounding us

11

were so dense no one could see more than ten yards ahead, so they fired everywhere and anywhere, some with their boots on, some without. The officers and NCOs screamed at them and they screamed at each other. I saw one man fall headlong into a ditch and, lying on his back, continue firing into the trees above him. Chris and Hugh sat in there with him, filming. Empty shell-cases spun about and I could not see the road for brass. Firing continued for at least another five minutes, and the jungle disintegrated. Whoever had been hiding there, whoever had been brave and foolish enough to declare themselves, were certainly dead now.

When the last marine commando had stopped firing, the sergeant kicked and whipped a search party across the river and soon they were shouting and laughing back to us. The sergeant held up ten fingers and said cheerfully, 'Maybe more – maybe less. Too many pieces. But no more Biafrans!' With that, his men cheered and began singing and back-slapping as the bloody, torn and tattered corpses were pulled out of their hideaways for everyone to see.

I sat down. I was trembling. This had been my first encounter with war . . . hardly combat . . . a minor massacre. And I was elated, and curiously unashamed that I felt that way.

We left the bodies unburied for the ants and a thousand other scavengers of the forest and moved north. Chris and Hugh and I said little to each other but we all knew as we went from village to village that we were getting the story we had come for. Whether it was because of our camera, or in spite of it, whether it mattered that we were with them or not, the soldiers went about their business thoroughly. Every village was searched, every village was found empty, every village was set on fire. Behind us, looking a day's march back towards Port Harcourt, the road was a long avenue of spiralling smoke.

The soldiers poked around the edge of the forest but the villagers had gone deep and they were not prepared to follow. Not that it mattered. The jungle would not save them.

Late that afternoon, an hour or so before dusk, I saw something that made me realise we were not the first to come along the road that day. We entered a village and made camp for the night. The men broke into groups and lit their fires ready to cook their first and only meal of the day. Chris began unloading the film from the camera magazines and Hugh began reloading more, cataloguing each can. I wandered from the huts to a circle of animal pens about fifty yards away, to be alone with my notebook and describe all I had seen. It is important to write the words while the smell of the day is on them.

There were no animals but there were the swarms of flies that follow and settle wherever cattle have been. I wondered if it was a slaughterhouse – the stench was sickly and sweet, like nothing I had smelt before. In the half light, I could see sacks against the wall inside . Maize, perhaps, or even offal? They were seething with flies and the smell was unbearable. But they were not sacks. They were piles of bodies, bloated and grotesque, trussed up like chickens, their hands tied to their ankles behind their backs. Some had their stomachs slit, some had been shot in the head, others had their skulls crushed. Old men, old women and some children. Suddenly it was clear to me. Only a day ahead of us were the killers, murdering anyone who would not or could not run away fast enough. The troops we were with were following behind, ready to catch anyone who assumed that the death squads had passed and came back from the forest.

We filmed what we dared that evening before the light went and I decided that the next morning we would find some way to catch up with the killers ahead. Chris and Hugh cautioned, saying it would be wiser and safer to return to Lagos. They argued that we had what we had come for, more even than we had expected. We should ship the story to London, then decide what next to do.

But I suffer from an impulsive lack of foresight and I ignored the advice. The next morning we went forward to an encounter that ended in the violent deaths of two young men. In those early days I might have been foolish enough to call it a scoop.

Lieutenant Macaulay Lamurde, like his commanding officer Colonel Adekunle, came from the fighting Bachama tribe. His name meant 'a royal place' and when he left his village at the beginning of the war to begin the long trek to Lagos to enlist, his family reminded him he went as a Bachama warrior with a royal name. He travelled for nearly a fortnight along the Benue River, which his

tribe called the 'Mother of Waters', first by canoe and then aboard a
paddle steamer to the junction where the Benue meets the Niger.
After two weeks of walking he presented himself to the recruiting
sergeant at Lagos barracks.

In the Biafran retreat from Port Harcourt, Lamurde, then a
private, was wounded, but he had fought so well and set such an
example the Black Scorpion awarded him a field promotion. When
he returned to his unit, the new lieutenant did what his officers had
done to him, demanding obedience not through respect but
through the favourite method of his commanding officer: pain and
terror.

Adekunle used a baseball bat; Lieutenant Lamurde a horsewhip.
From stock to knotted tail it was nine feet long and that day I
watched him use it mercilessly on men who until a few months
before had been his suffering equals. He wore only trousers and
sandals and his left foot was bandaged from a recent bullet wound.
He was handsome, with his tribe's slanting eyes and high cheek-
bones. He smiled when he saw us, politely shook our hands and
introduced himself. He was fascinated by our equipment and Chris
spent some time showing him how to operate it. It must have
seemed quite incredible that we had come all the way from London
to film him and his commandos.

His interest over, he turned back to his soldiers and to the crack
of his whip they began their rampaging, firing wildly into the forest,
lobbing grenades and setting fire to the rows and circles of neat
little thatched huts, not looking or caring if anyone was hiding
inside. We followed and we filmed.

We had been with them only a few hours when they brought out
a young man, an Ibo, the tribe of the eastern province that had
renamed itself Biafra. They dragged him to the lieutenant with a
rope around his neck, punching and kicking him. Lamurde hit him
across the mouth with the stock of his whip and said something
in his own tongue. The man replied in English: 'I am not a Biafran
soldier. I am looking for my family. I am not a Biafran soldier.'

Lamurde smiled and prodded the man in the chest with his whip
stock. 'You are a Biafran soldier.' He said it again in an oddly
friendly way. The prisoner began to cry.

We were still filming. I said to him, 'You are a prisoner-of-war now and you've nothing to fear. It doesn't matter whether you're a soldier or not; you are protected.'

I remember saying something about the Geneva Convention. How absurd it all seems now, to be quoting the rules of war to a man who knew nothing about Geneva or its Convention. But I was naïve and I persevered. 'You will be taken away for interrogation but you will not be harmed. You are a prisoner-of-war.' I said it again, a third time, as much to reassure him as to remind Lamurde.

Somewhere in my notebook I had scribbled the line from a newspaper cutting that should have warned me, but in the hysteria of the moment I had forgotten it. Lamurde shouted an order and they pulled the young Ibo to the ground, tied his hands behind his back, looped the cord around his neck and pulled it tight. I remembered the village elders and the tiny children trussed up exactly the same way, their heads crushed, their stomachs gaping; and the newspaper headline reporting that neither side took prisoners.

In the casual way of a man who had killed many times, the smiling lieutenant took a rifle from a soldier and, resting the butt on his hip, fired with one hand into his prisoner's chest three yards away. Nine bullets. When it stopped, Chris was still filming and Hugh was recording. No one moved except the lieutenant, who turned very slowly to us, his gun still at his hip, the barrel pointing at my stomach. We waited, certain we knew what the smiling Lieutenant Lamurde would do next.

Knowing that our film could be seen throughout the world, he would pull the trigger again and victim and witnesses would be buried together. But he did not. It did not occur to him he had any reason to: he did not consider he had done anything wrong. Had he not been killing prisoners all the way from Port Harcourt? Everyone in his battalion did. And did not Biafrans shoot Nigerians when they were captured? That was how both sides fought this war; they knew no other way. So our smiling warrior with the royal name had no reason to hide what he had done; he had no reason to kill again. We were safe.

Many times since we three – Chris, Hugh and I – have been held responsible for the death of that young Biafran. But if we are to be indicted, it should not be because we contributed to that murder; rather because we helped to kill Lieutenant Macaulay Lamurde.

That evening we sat again in the stench of the Cedar Palace. Chris catalogued the remaining film cans and I wrote my commentary by the light of my one remaining candle.

Hugh is a perfectionist and nothing short of the perfect recording is acceptable, however impossible the conditions. That night the conditions were awful: rain hammered on the floor above us and soldiers high on hash and palm gin danced and hollered below. Hugh built a soundproof igloo of filthy, rotting, bug-infested mattresses and shoved me, my script and my candle inside.

Our concern now was to get our film to London before reports of the killing trickled back to Port Harcourt and the Black Scorpion. We decided I should leave secretly the next morning for Lagos and airfreight the film on the first London flight. Chris and Hugh would stay. There was no way they could smuggle themselves out with so much equipment.

I left the Cedar Palace as soon as the night's curfew ended and walked to the airfield. There was a heavy drizzling mist and I felt panic rising. No visibility meant no landings and no take-offs and therefore no way to Lagos before Adekunle was alerted and the search for me began. I sat in the wreckage of a collapsed Dakota enclosed in the mist, safe from the occasional patrolling guards, their faces hidden inside the hoods of their capes.

After an hour the mist began to lift and through the torn fuselage I saw a line of small, flickering yellow flames. They had lit the goosenecks, the parallel rows of paraffin lamps along the runway. A few minutes later I heard the sound of an aircraft engine and the squeal of its tyres on the tarmac. I watched it taxi and stop. Then I joined the hubbub around it, hoping the guards would assume I was a crew member. A long line of walking wounded were already queuing to go aboard. Some carried their own plasma drips, and each hugged a large brown envelope, the X-rays of his injuries, his passport out. They shuffled slowly forward, the rain rinsing the blood from their bandages.

The stretchers were dumped sloppily under the wings but there was no protection there and soon the blankets were sodden and the sharp bites of rain fell into the wounded men's unblinking eyes so that I thought they might already be dead. Then out came the full black plastic bags, floppy and cumbersome and slippery so that

Hugh Thomson, Mekong Delta, Vietnam 1969.

Neil Davis. Travelling light
and further than most.

Alan Downes and a wounded Don McCullin.

Execution of Lt. Lamurde by firing squad, Port Harcourt, September 1968.
(*page 18*)

orderlies simply dragged them across the tarmac and left them by the stretchers . . . the dead and soon-to-die side by side. I could hear howls of agony in the queue: an NCO was completing his final search for deserters, poking his stick into men's wounds to make certain they were what they appeared to be.

The plane had brought in new troops, fresh out of training, smart new boys, and I will always remember the look on their faces as they came down the steps and saw what was there. Only then did they realise what was waiting for them beyond Port Harcourt and the jungle hinterland we were calling Biafra.

As the last plastic bag was hoisted aboard I clambered aboard after it and sat for two hours among the dead and the wounded. The smell of old dressings, fuel oil and the sickly-sweet smell of blood was suffocating. I tried to move but there was no room so I vomited in the space between my legs.

By midday I was in Lagos and that same evening my three cans of film were on the flight to London. The story was transmitted throughout the world the following day.

When I returned to Port Harcourt, Chris and Hugh were waiting for me in the military compound and the three of us were marched between an armed escort to Colonel Adekunle. He threatened us with a public whipping, our heads were to be shaved and our skulls tattooed with his own personal emblem – the black scorpion. He hit me across my thighs with his baseball bat and pushed me out of his office on to a verandah. Waiting there, handcuffed between two guards, was Lieutenant Lamurde, stripped to the waist. His head had been shaved and there was a weal under his left eye. He held out his hands to touch me but Adekunle brought his bat down hard across his wrists.

'Is this the man? The man on your film?' I nodded. Adekunle hit him again with his bat, hard across his stomach, and the young man fell to his knees.

'Take him away and shoot him!' the Sandhurst-trained colonel screamed. They tied him to a *sheki-sheki* tree in front of the school buildings and read out the charge and the punishment: guilty of an offence against the army's code of conduct; death by firing squad. Fifteen paces away, four men loaded their rifles, one bullet per man.

Just before the provost sergeant tied the blindfold of white cloth over his eyes, the proud and brutal young Bachama warrior with the royal name saw something that must have confused him in the last moments of his life. Three white men – a television crew and reporter – were hurrying about their business recording his execution. Thankfully, not us. The Nigerian government had demanded that we attend – 'to finish what we had started' was the phrase, I remember. But we refused.

The camera crew belonged to the BBC and they had been summoned by the Federal government to witness justice being done. They were the only crew present and they were ready to film. The blindfold was tied. 'Take aim!' shouted the officer-in-charge and four rifles came up to the shoulders. But just before the order was given to fire, the reporter shouted out, 'Hold on!' and Lieutenant Lamurde waited unseeing, not knowing why. The cameraman changed a flat battery, then gave his nod and Lieutenant Lamurde was shot dead.

Nigeria's General Gowon, attempting to recover from a major propaganda disaster, quickly reaffirmed his government's code regarding the treatment of prisoners-of-war as laid down by the Geneva Convention. He also reprinted thousands of pamphlets restating his own code of conduct which had first been issued at the start of the war. It ended: 'You are not fighting a foreign enemy. Remember at all times, the world is looking at us.' He also announced that any soldier violating that code would follow Lamurde to a lime grave.

It would be comforting to think that Gowon's soldiers took note. Perhaps they did for a while. Or maybe none of them was foolish enough again to kill with the world as witness.

Biafra was just across the road, as it were, but I had to leave Africa and return to Europe in order to travel to that tiny enclave. You could go the long hard way from Lisbon by boarding a piston-engined second world war Super-Constellation, nicknamed the Grey Ghost. With the refuelling stop, the flight took about seventeen hours. One ITN crew, depressed at the prospect, took an extra-large dose of sleeping tablets with an extra-large helping of brandy once they had strapped themselves into their seats. Ten hours later they woke up on the floor of the airport terminal, still in Lisbon. An engine had failed just before take-off and they had had to be carried off on stretchers.

I made my way to Biafra via the island of São Tomé, a tiny Portuguese colony in the Bight of Biafra, also known as the armpit of Africa, a hundred and twenty miles off the Nigerian coast. It had once been a Portuguese penal colony, known as Death Island, and had remained closed to the outside world. Now it was the major transit and re-supply base for all of Biafra's food aid and military hardware and, at its peak, the busiest airport in Africa. Aircraft flew in from Europe and Scandinavia, sometimes with markings, often without, and their cargoes were rapidly transferred to other aircraft for the night-time hop across the sea to a strip of tarmac close to the town of Uli that was a road by day and an airfield by night. It became known to all who used it as 'Airstrip Annabelle'.

The crew (cameraman Alan Downes and sound recordist Micky Doyle) and I had waited a week on the island for permission from the Biafrans to fly in, and it looked as though we would have to wait at least another. But with the help of Father Byrne of Caritas, who was always seeking ways to promote the Vatican's charitable role in Biafra, we bluffed our way on to the flight-list and parked ourselves and our equipment at the airport.

Day or night, the airfield was never still. Arc lights flooded the loading bays, priests in dirty soutanes directed the loading and unloading, kicking and cursing black porters, dripping with sweat. Pilots sat drinking on the open café terrace, many with wives or girlfriends, flown in from London or Bonn, Stockholm or Paris. The air was always heavy with kerosene and the smell of hot engines but sometimes, when the breeze turned from the sea, there was the scent of frangipani and bougainvillea from the town. The terrace was so close to the parking aprons, a wingtip often passed overhead and a pilot, careless, drunk or simply mischievous, would open his throttles and the downdraught of his exhausts would turn over tables and waiters, vodka and vinho verde and briefcases full of dollar bills. It was the best-paying part of the mercenaries' war and those who survived retired very well off.

When the war began, both sides became quite hysterical about the other's 'dogs of war'. The Biafrans first accused the Nigerians of using battalions of British ex-national servicemen. The Federal government countered with charges that the Biafrans had 'Chinese-looking' soldiers in their army and even white soldiers painted black. Both sides desperately needed pilots, whatever their colour or nationality.

The first to offer his services to the Nigerians was the flamboyant Colonel Fauntleroy Julian, who preferred to be known as the 'Black Eagle of Harlem'. As a black American pilot he had flown for the Ethiopians against the Italians in 1935. That made him over seventy years old. The Nigerians declined his services.

Nigeria had MiG-17 jet fighters supplied by Moscow but the Russians refused to supply pilots or ground crews. Nor would they allow any Westerner to fly them, so the Federal government employed Egyptians. It also took on an English mercenary, John Peters, to train Nigerians to fly light spotter aircraft and troop transports. Peters extended his lucrative deal with the Nigerians so that he might, at a wonderfully high rate of commission, recruit Western pilots to fly converted DC-3s on bombing raids over Biafra. He offered his recruits a thousand pounds a month, and all the drinks and girls they could manage.

They quickly became known as the 'whisky pilots' and one of the most notorious, an ex-Royal Air Force flight lieutenant, signed his log book 'Boozy Bonzo Bond'. He flew wearing a Muslim praying cap and boasted that on his bombing raids he would drink a bottle of whisky before he reached his target. Another identified himself as the 'Intruder' and called up the relief pilots on their own frequencies, often by their Christian names, warning them to stay away. One of the night bomber pilots was less friendly: he was a South African who, before he released his bombload, repeated in his heavy accent: 'Good evening, Uli, this is "Genocide". Prepare for another night of terror!'

Closing Uli and putting Biafra's food suppliers and gunrunners out of business became the Nigerian government's first priority. By the end of 1968, forty flights a night were delivering something like five hundred tonnes of food and weapons to the Biafrans, with up to fourteen aircraft stacked, waiting for permission to land. Without Uli, Biafra would have collapsed in weeks. Not only was it the vital lifeline, it was also the symbol of a people's resistance. But it was not an easy target. At night it could be identified only by the avenue of lights switched on for a few seconds as the planes came in to land. By day it was a wide strip of tarmac road between Onitsha and Owerri close to the town of Oguta, with the lights, parking bays and warehouses cleverly camouflaged under spreads of palm fronds. When it was hit, the Biafrans simply moved the landing strip further along the road.

But another reason why Uli – Airstrip Annabelle – remained open was because the mercenaries had decided it made no business sense that it should close. If that happened, neither side got paid. This was confirmed later by the best-known pilot of all, the Swedish Count von Rosen, who flew supplies into Uli for the churches before attempting to launch his own Biafran air force. He said there was support from the pilots on both sides to keep Uli open and he told a story of the odd man out.

In June 1969, seven months before the war was to end, a forty-year-old ex-Royal Air Force pilot was signed on by the Nigerians. He was an excellent flyer, astonishingly keen and was immediately posted to the 'Genocide' squadron of night bombers based at Benin. He flew his first seven missions over Uli as a co-pilot but every time he returned he complained to his Nigerian de-briefing officer about the failure of the pilots to locate the target. He said they always had an excuse: bad weather, faulty navigation, technical failures, Biafran flak, all of which were untrue. So, flying his own first sortie, he insisted on an all-Nigerian crew. He had no difficulty at all in finding Uli by night. He simply followed the relief planes down and his crew manhandled the fifty-pound bombs out of the cargo hatch. Some of the planes on the ground were hit and Uli was out of action for nearly a week.

The Nigerians were delighted but fellow mercenaries were not, and for reasons that remained one of the war's best-kept secrets he never flew again and Uli stayed open. Had the Nigerians paid their mercenaries by results instead of monthly cheques to Zürich, Uli would have been bombed out of existence by mid-1968 and the war and the suffering ended a good deal sooner.

When the war was nearing its end and the pilots realised their bonanza was almost over, they tried to increase the number of flights into Uli to earn more . . . edging their first take-off at twilight, even in daylight . . . risking not only bombers' random searching but also being sighted by Federal MiGs. A Swedish Red Cross plane was caught this way as it was crossing the Nigerian coast. The jet fighter was piloted by an English mercenary who ordered the Swede to alter course and land in Port Harcourt or he would open fire. The Swede ignored him and flew on. The Englishman gave a second warning and then opened fire with his cannons. The relief plane exploded, killing all the crew.

The International Red Cross never flew into Biafra again and the Englishman apparently had a nervous breakdown. A few weeks later he crashed his MiG into the runway at Port Harcourt and killed himself.

I had planned to fly from São Tomé aboard one of the relief planes with a British pilot named Scott. I had met him at a tiny hotel at the far and very private end of the island which the pilots used as their club, some as their brothel. Scott told me he had flown for the Royal Air Force in the Berlin airlift. He was earning around ten thousand dollars a month cash, which was three times what he might have been paid had he flown for the Federals. He had no regrets and considered he earned every penny. He agreed we could film him preparing for the flight, the aircraft being loaded, the flight checks and so on. We could also film him during the flight and interview him on our return. He told us of the small cemetery at the side of Uli airstrip where pilots killed on mission were buried. He said there were about twenty there and the world ought to know that not all the pilots retired as millionaires.

But that evening we were ordered to change aircraft because apparently Scott's plane was overloaded. I wondered if it was more likely he was carrying military supplies and somebody considered it would not be wise for a television crew to see them. So we flew instead with a drunken Texan. It was a terrifying flight. He fell out of his seat shortly after take-off and cut his hand on the bottle of whisky that fell too. But we would not have survived that night had we not flown with him because Scott went in too low on his approach to Uli, hit the tops of the trees and blew up.

That was the first of many occasions when my wife Diana thought I was dead. Before we left São Tomé, I had telexed John Mahoney, my foreign editor, a single one-liner: GOING IN TONIGHT WITH BRITISH PILOT. John told Diana. The following morning BBC radio news reported that a relief plane had crashed in Biafra and that the British pilot and three others aboard had been killed. For some days my crew and I were assumed to have been aboard. Diana and I had been married for a year exactly and the date of Scott's crash and my safe landing at Uli was 16 December – our wedding anniversary.

From Uli we had a long black ride through the jungle night in the back of a ten-tonner, sitting on sacks of maize flour. At daybreak Alan, Micky and I arrived in the town of Umuahia and St Finbar's mission, greeted by Father John Ryan.

'Biafra is the funniest place on earth,' said the tall thin Irish missionary. 'And I'd laugh if it didn't hurt so much!'

We were sitting on the balcony, eating biscuits and drinking whisky: my biscuits, his whisky. Earlier, I had offered food to the crowd assembled below us – men, women and children squatting, silent, staring and quite obviously starving. But Father Ryan stopped me.

'You'd do best to keep the provisions to yourself,' he said. 'We're no help to them if we're hungry too,' and he shooed them away with the sign of the cross and a blessing. 'That's all they'll get from me today. That's all I have to give away.' And he poured me another whisky.

Umuahia was not a large town but it was crucially important simply because it was the only one the Biafrans had left, and despite the battalions of Federal troops surrounding them, cutting away more of Biafra every day, its people were anything but forlorn. The talk was not of survival but of victory. The Biafran flag flew from every window: a tricolour of green, black and red with the rising sun, the new dawn, in the middle of it. Everyone was supremely and infectiously confident even if it was mostly make-believe. Watching Umuahia go about the daily business of preparing itself for war was like watching a small English country town practising a Civil Defence exercise.

Posters were everywhere:

> IN CASE OF A BOMB
> DON'T SCREAM OR SHOUT.
> IF IN THE MARKET PLACE
> FALL ON THE FACE.
> DO WHAT YOU ARE TOLD
> AND LIVE TILL YOU'RE OLD.

Another was a comic strip showing Nigerian paratroopers landing.

> WHEN THEY COME,
> STAKE ALL OPEN FIELDS
> FIGHT WITH EVERY AVAILABLE WEAPON
> STAB THEM TO DEATH
> AND LEAVE THE SKULL BASHING
> TO THE WOMEN!

A third read simply:

> WATCH OUT FOR PEOPLE
> WHO SPEND MONEY
> THE WAY THEY SHOULD NOT

There remained a great enthusiasm for the war and it involved everyone. Electricians and chemists together made improvised rockets, bombs and claymores and the railway engineering shed turned out mortars of sorts. Garages teamed up to cannibalise the lorries and bulldozers and the Biafran army boasted several Umuahia-made tanks and armoured cars. We were told they made their own petrol by 'cooking' low sulphur oil and distilling it in huge watertanks by the rail terminal. Schools had become recruiting camps and schoolmasters, drill sergeants. Villagers manned lookout towers and road blocks: one barrier had the sign: EVERYONE MUST HALT HERE EXCEPT H.E. AND MRS H.E. – H.E. being His Excellency, the nation's leader, General Ojukwu.

Judges and counsel in crisply-pressed gowns boasted that all criminal cases were promptly heard. Bail was readily given because there was, after all, no way to skip it.

'Nearly two years into its violent creation and Biafra still has nine High Courts whose judges wear powdered wigs, five hundred lawyers, two hundred doctors, four football pools, a brewery, an oil refinery, a civil service devoted to bureaucracy in triplicate, a chain of banks that print their own notes, and a railway that runs on time.'

Whenever Biafra was written about it was invariably suffixed 'an infant African nation, struggling to survive against savage odds'. Such was the sympathy among journalists, who should have known better. Silks and wigs, football pools and, beyond the bush, countless little children sucking the nipples of grandmothers who had not given milk in thirty years. All of us desperately wanted to believe in Biafra, despite the odds, despite the facts.

'I have seen an African dream come true . . .' It was the standard opening cliché.

Richard West, writing about his visit to Umuahia, for the *Sunday Times*, reported:

> A people I respect and like are threatened with persecu-
> tion and death. I cannot therefore pretend to be impar-
> tial. But Biafra is more than a human tragedy . . . it is the
> first place I've been to in Africa where the Africans them-
> selves are truly in charge . . . where there is a sense of
> nationhood . . . free from the African vices of graft, super-
> stition and ignorance.

I suppose there were few journalists who went to Biafra and did not write similar fantasy. It turned normally responsible reporters' emotions and judgements upside down. The Biafra story was seductive.

It seduced Freddy Forsyth.

Some nights after our arrival in Umuahia, there was a knock on the door at St Finbar's and in came the model mercenary: military boots, pressed camouflaged combat fatigues, cravat, dark glasses, beret, all neatly tied up with an ammunition belt carrying a British army issue automatic. Then I remembered him as a BBC reporter who had come to Biafra some months before to report for radio and television news. But he too had quickly become emotionally attached and it showed in his reporting. So the BBC gave him a choice: he could return to neutral ground – professionally speaking – or return to London. To the Beeb's surprise and possible relief, he chose instead a third course and stayed in Biafra, becoming a media factotum to General Ojukwu and freelancing for British newspapers, among them the *Observer*.

Forsyth told me he was enjoying his job and the privileges that went with it. He said he lived in his own caravan, moved with his own bodyguard, had the ear of the most exalted Biafran of all and was privy to many of Ojukwu's wheelings and dealings. He was not in the slightest bit keen to share any of it with me but it did enable him to write his first book: *The Biafra Story*, hailed as partisan and unexceptional, and quite unlike anything he has written since.

But, as it later transpired, Forsyth's special relationship with Ojukwu was his undoing and almost cost him his life.

The MiGs attacked just after noon. We heard the children whistling first. They were excellent air-raid sirens and could hear the jets long before anyone else . . . children whistling as they ran and then, all around us, the panic and pandemonium of children dying. An anti-aircraft battery opened fire behind the mission and another beyond the church and then a dozen more until there was so much gunfire, we did not know bombs had been dropped until we saw black smoke erupting from the railway sheds. They had hit the fuel depot and thousands of gallons of burning oil cascaded from the towers on to the people below.

The MiGs followed one another in no great hurry, it seemed, strafing and bombing, casually turning and coming in again in line. I counted four though there might have been more. I sat crouched, microphone in hand, doing my first report into camera under fire. Alan zoomed in to the aircraft as they passed us only a few hundred feet high. I kept repeating the day and the date – even updating the time, as if the viewer could have thought that relevant, and I described the MiGs as mark 15s, 17s and 19s, all in the same breath.

It was not that I was afraid. I was simply excited. It was a sensational spectacle and I was the spectator. I remember feeling absolutely safe because I was under the impression it had nothing to do with me: I was on the sidelines. How easy it was to be brave.

The aircraft's cannons scythed the groves of banana trees and left them five feet high and people ran in and out of the lines of shells as they hit the ground. The railway sidings were hidden in flaming, exploding smoke and all we could hear was the screaming of the sirens, the ack-ack batteries and the cracking of cannons. I can recall a little boy standing on open ground peeing, not even looking at the sky, as if nothing important were happening. An old woman picked up a sandal and placed it carefully by the body of a man who had been ripped apart as he ran for cover. 'If in the market place, fall on your face . . . and live till you are old!'

When the MiGs had gone and it was quiet, they laid the dead in a row outside the Queen Elizabeth Hospital and covered them with palm leaves until the graves were dug. They told us there were over sixty bodies, but I didn't count. They said there were more where the railway sheds used to be but they never expected to find them. Only their names would be buried. So we filmed the dead and the dying and those who were so horribly burnt they must have prayed that they too would quickly die.

Somebody pulled us towards three little bodies lying side by side – two brothers and a sister, who had been suffocated in a bomb blast. The force of it had simply squeezed all the air out of them. They could not have been older than six or seven. Someone, anxious we should show their tragedy to the world, had joined the children's little hands together. The smaller boy had his eyes open. I closed them and we left.

That evening, Alan and Micky and I together drank two bottles of whisky and we threw our supper of biscuits and Spam out of the window without looking. We did not want to see who was waiting there.

The next morning a policeman came to arrest us. Solemnly, he told us we were in the country illegally. Father Ryan offered him a whisky. I offered him my passport. There had been a mistake, Father Ryan said. He filled the glass again and when the policeman had gulped it down, he formally charged us and we followed him between armed escorts, to what the Biafrans called their Ministry of Foreign Affairs.

Those who aspire to nationhood guard the trappings very jealously, so it was a formal affair. We were asked how we had crossed a national border illegally. We explained that there was only one known way into Biafra and we had taken it.

'You should not be here,' said the High Official.

'But we are!'

'You have come ahead of schedule. You should have waited for our invitation. We have no programme for you.'

Then, quite unexpectedly: 'You must leave and come back again.'

Africa, tragedy and farce! To be deported now would be both. I was quite unable to cope with the situation. I shouted abusively, then cajoled them, changed tack again and threatened the worst publicity and finally humbled myself. I blush at the memory. I collapsed in a heap and may even have been about to weep.

But then Alan, a stalwart five feet five in his stockinged feet, produced what remains perhaps the finest oratory of his career. I only wish I could remember it. He spoke of the Biafran struggle as if he were its only champion. He told them how determined he was to record its tragedy, not simply because he was a television cameraman paid to do a job, but as a matter of deep personal commitment. The world had to know, and for that he had been prepared to fly dangerously into Biafra.

'But,' he finished, 'I'm damned if I'll do it twice in a week if it makes my children fatherless on the way.'

It did the trick. We were friends, saviours; we were official. A filming programme was hastily agreed and our passports were duly stamped 'Enugu Immigration Control'. Enugu, Biafra's capital, had been in Federal hands for a good nine months.

With hindsight I doubt the Biafrans would have made us leave if they had had the slightest fear we would not return. Our camera was too important a weapon not to use. We already had dramatic footage for their propaganda cause and the best and worst pictures, depending on the point of view, were still to come.

Starvation, the imposed famine, did a power of good for the Biafran cause. Ironically, the infant nation could not have survived for so long without it. It galvanised world sympathy which was cunningly converted into cash and aid. It has been the model for charity campaigns ever since and honours go jointly to the Biafrans' public relations consultants, Markpress of Geneva, and to the many television camera crews from all nations.

In the twenty and more years since Biafra, we have all become aid-saturated, chock-full with televisual helpings of Third World suffering and the subsequent relentless singing, prancing, walking and running of the well-known, well-nourished First Worlders. But in 1968 how new it was. And how shocking that we television reporters delivered it so neatly into people's front parlours. Biafra's was the first famine made famous by television.

That was the time when we first began to talk about the politics of aid. The political lobbyists, the churches and the charities would have us believe the famine began with the war. It did not. The rate of starvation, malnutrition and infant mortality had always been exceptionally high throughout Nigeria and most especially in the eastern province renamed Biafra. The war simply made things worse.

Nor did the relief operation do much to stop it, even though there were sometimes forty flights a night into Uli, carrying five hundred tons of supplies. Yet how cleverly it was put about that the war was the cause of so many deaths by starvation and that only by increasing and accelerating relief aid would both war and suffering end. It was the line that I and so many reporters took as gospel.

That Christmas we were all particularly vulnerable, victim to the gentle persuasion of the most fervent of all white propagandists, the Catholic missionaries. They went far beyond their religious humanitarian brief and unashamedly sold the Biafran cause. They became political priests and when the war ended they paid the price. They were expelled from Nigeria and very few were ever allowed to return, which was a tragedy for those who had lived and worked in the region all their lives. Some we met had spent thirty years and more among the Ibos.

The Catholics did most and lost most, particularly those priests and nuns of the Irish Order of the Holy Ghost whom we got to know best. They were immensely brave, hard-working, often irreverent, generous and likeable. But they were dangerously passionate.

Father Kevin Doheny was all these things. He was built like a bull but was a very gentle man and best described as Spencer Tracy's *doppelganger*. For the weeks that we travelled in what was left of Biafra, he was our guide, interpreter and humorist. He took us to hospitals and clinics deep in the bush, to the refugee camps and the dying villages, to the war front and back again. My cynicism came much later, with the impeccable wisdom of hindsight, but in that fortnight with Father Kevin, in that desperate, marvellous little enclave, it was hard not to believe what he believed.

We were then at the height of the worst period of starvation, and Father Kevin took us to one of the worst-affected camps at Umburu, due west of Umuahia. It was only eight miles from the fighting on the Owerri front. Four thousand children were in the camp, every one a refugee orphan and all of them hungry. As we entered the camp, Alan and Micky filming as they walked, the children began singing. Naturally, I thought it had been prearranged, something they did for every visiting camera crew and journalist. But I later discovered that very few journalists had been there. Even fewer came after us.

This was the song they sang and this is the commentary I wrote to Alan's filmed story.

> We are Biafrans
> Fighting for our freedom
> In the name of Jesus,
> We will fight on.

As they wait for their food, they sing the Biafran fighting anthem as automatically as they once chanted the alphabet in the schools before the war began.

They have a little food today. They have a little for tomorrow. They hope there will be some spare for the day after that. But this is their crisis. The root of the cassava bush, grated and dried, and the root of the yam are the basic diet of these people. But because of the Federal blockade they've eaten not only all of this year's crop, but the seeds of next.

If there is not a cease-fire soon, or an agreement for a land or river corridor, or an immediate increase in the air-lift supplies, these children cannot expect to survive.

This child did not live the day out. We arrived at this camp at noon. When we left at two, six-year-old Abuke was dead. But hundreds more dead children are never found. They become too weak to walk and finally too weak to cry.

But the old suffer too. Every morning at first light, they queue outside the camp gates waiting for scraps. There are never scraps. This old man is seventy-four. When the Federal forces took Port Harcourt, he walked a hundred and forty miles here to find his family. His family is dead and he died shortly after this film was taken.

Starvation was the killer at Umburu and there were many ways of dying; the old, exhausted, huddled in corners, away from movement and life, not wanting to be disturbed ever again. The young went more slowly, fleshless skeletons who stood quite motionless, as if they knew the slightest movement would be their last, the pus of conjunctivitis oozing from their staring bulging eyes, their bellies empty and distended, flesh peeling off their feet. They were dying not just from lack of food but from a total protein deficiency which deformed the brain. We called it kwashiorkor. The Biafrans called it the Harold Wilson Disease, blaming him, as prime minister of Britain, for not supporting them in their war.

There have been many estimates of how many civilians died in those two-and-a-half years. The mean figure rests at around half a million. Most were killed not by bullet or by bomb but by kwashiorkor.

I interviewed two nuns who looked after the clinic at Umburu. They sat side by side on wooden boxes, immaculate in their white caps and robes, each with a wedding ring on the third finger of her left hand, signifying her marriage to Christ.

'What will you do if the Federals come any closer?'

'We'll move out a little further away from here to try and find shelter deeper in the bush.'

'You must leave the camp?'

'We must – the children wouldn't stay and we should have to go with them. It does worry them – the guns in the distance, hearing the shells coming closer and closer.'

'How will you survive in the bush?'

'We have our little packs ready. And we'll take some water. We shall last.'

'Is there any question of your getting out?'

'No. Not of our own choice. We'd never dream of leaving the people. We must stay with them. Even to the bitter end.'

On our last night in Umuahia, Freddy Forsyth sent an urgent message saying he had to see me before I left for Uli.

It was very late when he eventually climbed the stairs to my room. It had been raining all evening and he was wet. He was not in uniform. He looked ill. He said he was tired. He carried a bulky brown-paper package under his arm.

He told me in little more than a whisper that there was a plot to get rid of him; he said he assumed I knew what that meant. I assumed I did. His 'special' relationship with General Ojukwu had created intense jealousies, rivalries and hatreds. He had made some rather dangerous enemies. He said they had taken his caravan away and refused to allow him to see the general and without Ojukwu's protection they could kill him and nobody would know how or why or where. But he had kept the gun. He was not going to part with that. It was lying in his lap.

In the semi-light of that candlelit room, on a warm, wet, black African night, with the prospect of a long night's drive to the most dangerous airfield in the world, Forsyth and his gun had persuaded me that he did not expect to live out the week. I asked him if there was anything I could do, knowing there was nothing. In an hour I would be on my way to Uli and the night flight out to São Tomé. But he nodded and gave me the brown-paper parcel which I promised to deliver to an address in England. We shook hands and he went out into the black, warm rain. I didn't see Freddy Forsyth again until the moment many, many years later when he autographed my copy of his *Day of the Jackal*.

I reminded him of that goodbye in Umuahia and asked him something that had plagued me all the years since. Did the brown-paper parcel contain the original *Jackal* manuscript? Had I that night carried out of beleaguered Biafra the book that made him his first million? He said no. Simply no. Which is a shame. It would have made a good ending to a most unlikely story.

A month later, in January 1970, Federal troops overran Biafran positions. When they reached Umburu they found the camp empty.

On the night of 11 January, a little after midnight, two relief planes crossed each other in the darkness over Uli. One was taking out General Ojukwu and his entourage, the other was landing with eighteen tons of food aboard. The pilot did not realise it was all over until he had landed. This is his narrative:

'I shouted over the radio, "Turn your lights on and leave them on. Don't worry about the bombs. I'm coming in now."

'I was just turning downwind when I saw the lights go on, just a few on the right-hand side and all the way down I was repeating over and over again, "Keep them on – for Christ's sake keep them on." And they did. We came in short, a heavy landing, maximum brakes. We were skidding, everything was burning, you could smell it. When we turned around there was no one about. We taxied between the bomb-craters towards the unloading bays but the Biafrans had gone.

'Then out of nowhere white people came running towards us: priests, nuns, relief workers, and Christ! they were frightened wrecks. They tried to get aboard but I screamed at them, "I've got to unload this bloody stuff or none of us leaves." And they did it, all of them, eighteen tons out of the back door in ten minutes. I didn't know it then but the Federals were on the rampage only two miles down the road.

'We got off with them and just as I pulled my gear up a voice came on my radio. I couldn't believe it. "This is Biafran Control. I advise all incoming aircraft that the airport is closed until further notice."'

The following day, Monday, at four-thirty in the afternoon, the radio announced the surrender, then played Beethoven's Fifth Symphony until it finally went off air. The fantasy we had called Biafra was over. Africa's land of the rising sun was no more.

When the foreign desks of the world heard it, they sent their reporters scampering to Nigeria and I was among them. It was too late, of course. With the relief flights finished, there was no way in. Many of us ended up again on São Tomé, the island where we had first begun our confused Biafran love affair. Among the latecomers was Ian Mather of the *Daily Mail*. He had spent thirteen extraordinary days and nights travelling down the West African coast trying to thumb an airlift into Nigeria and being bounced out of one hostile country after another – ten in all. He was very bruised and close to a physical collapse, and spent most of his days and nights at the cable office, eating aspirin with his vinho verde.

When most of us had given up all hope of anything but going home, Mather received a cable marked 'Urgent' from his foreign desk. It might have broken a lesser man. It read: MAKE LIKE HELL BIAFRA BOY BEFORE SUNDAYS UPMOP WITH EMOTIONAL FRONTLINER.

CHAPTER TWO

Civil War, Jordan, 1970

Twenty-seven days of Black September

IT WAS A HAUNTING EQUATION and I shared it with many. The more I flew, the nearer I thought I was to dying. I had a shameless sense of relief whenever there was news of an aircrash because it seemed to make my own odds of survival that much more accept-able. At every take-off and landing there was sweat in the palms of my hands, and rather than find ways to stop worrying I created my own anxieties. I dwelt on all the things that could go wrong – ice on the wings, an unlocked cargo hatch, flaps withdrawn too soon, engine failure, pilot error.

And the altitude bomb. This had become very popular with the various terrorist armies who had declared their separate little wars on the world. They found it effective because it precluded the pos-sibility of an aircraft being delayed and the mechanical timing device blowing up a plane while the passengers were still safely in the departure lounge.

A Swissair Coronada exploding in the air south of Geneva in February 1970 was my first experience of reporting altitude bombs and of the Palestinians whose speciality they were then. Many of the passengers had been Jews on their way to Tel Aviv and with the satisfaction of someone discovering gold, a Swiss investigator dressed in a protective rubber apron and gloves pulled a circum-cised penis out of a plastic bag for us all to see. In at least three air crashes I reported on, the altitude bomb had been set to explode at ten thousand feet. I calculated that it took about fifteen minutes for an airliner to get there; so on take-off, strapped in my seat and whispering goodbye to the ground, I counted those minutes. Then I had my first drink. It was an odd way to go to work!

It was Monday, 11 June 1970. I heard my name clearly on the loudspeaker above the din of the international departure hall at London Heathrow and made my way to the information desk, certain I knew what it meant. They had decided to send someone else. But I was wrong. It was the melancholy voice of foreign editor John Parker and he read out a Reuter lead: the Palestinians in Jordan had set up roadblocks between the airport and the capital Amman and were hijacking vehicles and kidnapping people. To which I expected John to add, as any reasonable man might, 'We've decided it's too risky for you, so come on back.' But he simply added, 'Play it safe and keep your head down.' He could have been sending me off to a game of rugby.

I caught my flight to Jordan and, sure enough, on the road from the airport to King Hussein's capital, my taxi was stopped, and the end of a sub-machine-gun beckoned me into another car. Blindfolded, I was driven to one of the seven hills overlooking Amman.

My kidnappers belonged to the Popular Front for the Liberation of Palestine – the PFLP. This was the decade of ubiquitous terrorist initials. Its leader was the murderous Marxist intellectual, Dr George Habash, who had split from Al Fatah, the military wing of the PLO. Habash had two immediate objectives; to seize the initiative and gain control of the PLO and to torpedo any Middle East peace plan that did not honour the Palestinian demand for nationhood. A plan excluding the Palestinians was on the drawing-board in Washington.

Some months before, in an interview with the Italian journalist Oriana Fallaci for *Life* magazine, he had said, 'This is a thinking man's game. We are too small to wage war – imperialism is too powerful. The only way to destroy our enemies is to give a little blow here, a little blow there and advance step by step.' He ended the interview with the best advice he could possibly have given Fallaci: in future, he told her, it would not be wise to travel El Al.

Had his ambitions for the months ahead been generally known then, few people would have thought it wise to have travelled on any airline. But this was June and Black September was still three months off. Taking foreigners hostage in Amman was the most outrageous thing Dr Habash and his gangsters would ever attempt – it was thought!

My kidnappers held and questioned me for two days in a house overlooking Amman. My interrogator was a fat man – not unlike a young Sidney Greenstreet – who found the heat unbearable and whose mouth seemed always full of phlegm. He told me he had graduated from the London School of Economics and this probably explained why he thought he recognised me. The LSE is at the back of the former Rediffusion House in Kingsway, central London, where ITN once lived. I suggested to him that we might well have shared a table at the Kardomah coffee house which was squashed in between, or queued for the same number eleven bus.

Certainly it was nothing more sinister, and yet he was convinced it was. He repeated over and over again, with brief intervals for coughing and spitting and wiping the top of his head with a filthy rag, that he had met me in King Charles Square, the habitat of the British Foreign Office. I said even that was not unlikely. It was common for reporters to spend hours there, rain and shine, in the hope of snatching a morsel of news from our own or somebody else's foreign minister. But the fat Palestinian was certain of something more disingenuous, though I never did discover what, and he had my passport and presscard checked with the PFLP in London. On the evening of the second day he came into my tiny room and with obvious regret told me I could leave the next morning.

That evening he allowed me out of my room to perform the necessary and painfully-overdue ablutions in the street. Two armed guards watched every detail, which took away a lot of my pleasure, though I was to learn later that Arabs are very nonchalant about such things.

We were higher up than I had guessed and there was such a view of Amman that I thought I could see the hotel I was booked into – the Philadelphia – and the larger, newer and considerably whiter Intercontinental. In the Philadelphia, I was to have my first intimate experience of Palestinian terrorism, and in the Intercontinental some months later, my last!

How sweet are the uses of adversity. Here I stood, my first time in the Middle East, on a hill overlooking Jordan in the cradle of Christianity, the desert stretching in a blue haze away north to Galilee, Golan, Tiberias, Damascus; and west, under the shadow of the setting sun, the River Jordan, Bethlehem, Jerusalem and the land that was once called Palestine. All there, below and beyond me.

As the light died, Amman became an outline of flat roofs and pinnacles of minarets with dark purple spaces between and, rising like a siren above it all, a sound I had never heard before – the wailing of the *muezzins*, calling Allah's servants to prayer. I stood there a little longer, marvelling, until the air chilled, then I turned back to the house, expecting my guards to turn with me. But I was no longer their concern; they were on their knees and elbows, their rifles on the ground, facing Mecca.

In my room, on the floor by the dirty mattress, were my passport and presscard. Also my diary, and that night I filled a few of its pages with jumbled nonsense, unconnected words which might easily have been mistaken for code; words I scrawled quickly to catch any one of the day's thousand images. I also doodled across an empty page, drawing a succession of grotesque faces, one growing out of the other, the last clearly some comic devil. Perhaps by premonition I was aware that something demonic was about to be born.

My guards walked me down from my mountain prison to the Philadelphia, and I was not prepared for what I saw. The hotel was ringed by a hundred or more Palestinians carrying Kalashnikovs and grenade-launchers, their belts and pouches heavy with ammunition. I counted seven machine-gun posts in the carpark and men were laying what I thought were sandbags under windows and around the doors. They were nothing so innocent; they were explosives. The PFLP had hijacked the hotel and everyone inside it and we would be held hostage while the Palestinians negotiated with King Hussein. Deadly ultimatums were being exchanged and in case of an attack by the king's army on the Palestinian camps, Dr Habash had us and another fifty people in the Intercontinental as insurance.

We chatted to our captors and possible executioners, young men and women – teenagers mostly – who, with strange charm, apologised for what they were doing and for what they might yet be obliged to do the next morning. It was macabre and unreal and I still remember their excitement, their expectation, the smell of their dirt and sweat, how, as we picked at our salads at dinner that evening, they emptied their rifle magazines on to our tables and polished the brass bullet casings, spitting and rubbing until they shone, then thumbing them back in again, carefully, one by one, nodding and smiling to us all the while. I remember the little black detonators wired to the sandbags only a few feet away, neatly stacked, five yards apart on the floor along the walls.

Our hijackers were like students rehearsing an undergraduate drama. Sometimes they stood apart shouting statements which drew their inspiration from recent Habash policy documents: 'Our blows are directed at the weak parts of our enemy's body . . . he who gives blessing to the prevailing order shall suffer . . .' Another pair, facing each other, exchanged political diatribes, solemnly parroting the dots and commas of the latest PFLP communiqué issued from Damascus, like two Jesuits mouthing litanies, convincing each other of their devotion. Some took the trouble to sit with us, moving from one table to another, preaching the sermon of the Popular Front. They encouraged me to write some of it down. How original I thought it all, then.

'You cannot condemn us for exposing innocent people to danger because of our cause. In today's world no one is innocent, no one is neutral. A man is with either the oppressor or the oppressed. Your lives and the lives of thousands more mean nothing in our struggle to recover our homeland.'

We were not told when the ultimatum would expire, though everyone seemed to believe it was nine o'clock – the time, some wag pointed out, when last orders were taken for breakfast. But as it got light, a little after five, those of us who would not sleep and those who could not got up stiffly from the armchairs and couches and went to the windows. Then we sighed and nodded to each other in the cheery silent way the British do when a crisis has passed. The carpark was empty. The sandbag explosives had gone. We went back to the women and children and woke them up and sat saying nothing.

The PFLP's ultimatum had been met or at least promises had

been made. King Hussein – the target of Palestinian fury – had, it seemed, come to an arrangement and the show was over, at least at this venue. Hotel staff suddenly appeared, smiling and courteous, beginning their morning shift as if nothing had happened in their absence. Waiters cleared the tables, swirled away the plates, the filthy ashtrays, the empty, crushed beer cans and dirty tablecloths and placed small vases of flowers on the green baize tops. There was the smell of coffee and I heard a vacuum cleaner. The receptionist brought me a neat white card and asked me to register. He even said, 'Welcome!'

I stood there, tired, dirty and unshaven and, to my regret, trembling. The young Palestinian terrorists, men and women, boys and girls, their red-and-white and black-and-white checked *kaffiyehs* covering their heads, rifles over their shoulders, came to us and shook our hands and said how pleased they were to know us . . . how they hoped we had enjoyed our stay and that we would have a pleasant journey home, how they wished we might all meet again one day. Some were cheering. Some wept. Some danced a jig and some prayed. Those who had been friendly became suddenly offensive and those who had kept aloof from us became strangely intimate. It was all quite absurd, but I do not remember feeling at all depressed; I felt quite jovial and detached, as if I were privileged to attend some madcap method school of acting. They were able, at the snap of a finger, to behave as though they had been our guardians and not our assassins-in-waiting during those horrible night hours, ready and willing, had Hussein dithered, to blow us to bits.

There must be many who spent that night in the Philadelphia who wonder how much of it they remember correctly, how much has been embellished in the re-telling, what was real and what has since been imagined. Memory is seldom certain testimony. In writing this story and what follows, my testimony is a fat black diary which, as a young reporter, anxious and astonished, I filled with scribblings.

Sunday, 6 September 1970.
Three months on, in the same fat black diary, another date is heavily underlined: the most eventful day in the history of air piracy. It began aboard El Al flight LY219 en route from Amsterdam to New

York. A dark and attractive ex-schoolteacher, hiding hand-grenades in her brassière, one in each cup, together with a male accomplice armed with a pistol, hijacked the plane and its 144 passengers. The young man has long been forgotten but her name is written into Palestinian legend. Holding a grenade in each hand, she introduced herself to pilot and passengers that day as Shadia, of the PFLP's Abdel Jaber Commando unit. Her real name was Leila Khaled.

We were still new to aerial piracy and our governments had yet to realise that hijacking was a self-perpetuating drama: the capture and imprisonment of one terrorist group led inevitably to another hijack to gain their release. So it was then.

The PFLP's plan to take on Israel and its backers that summer was given greater urgency by the news that King Hussein, in whose kingdom the Palestinians had established their bases, was meeting President Nasser to agree to Washington's Middle East settlement. The Palestinians saw the future being decided without them. Certainly if there was to be a pact with Israel, King Hussein would not jeopardise that peace by condoning Palestinian raids across the River Jordan. He might even order them out of Jordan. On Radio Damascus, Habash issued a prophetic warning to Nasser and Hussein: 'Settle with Israel and we will turn the Middle East into hell!' It was then that Habash and his top lieutenant, Dr Wadi Haddad, decided on something spectacular, something to show Hussein, Nasser, Israel and the world that the Palestinians would not, could not, be tamed.

Spectacular it was! Leila Khaled's was the first of five PFLP hijacks. Hers failed; she was overpowered, her accomplice shot dead and the plane landed safely at Heathrow airport. A grenade was found under a seat, the pin out. A faulty spring had saved flight 219.

That same day Habash's commandos took another three aircraft: a TWA Boeing 707 over Belgium, a Swissair DC-8 over France and a PanAm 747 out of Amsterdam. The jumbo was directed to Cairo and, with the passengers and crew running for their lives across the tarmac, was blown up on the runway – twenty million pounds' worth. It was said that Nasser saw the flames lighting the night sky from the balcony of his presidential palace.

The two other jets, each with 155 passengers and crew aboard, were diverted to Jordan, to a long-forgotten wartime Royal Air Force desert strip forty-five miles north-east of Amman. The Arabs knew it as Ga Khanna. The RAF, to honour an air vice-marshal, had called it Dawson's Field.

I arrived in Amman on Tuesday, 8 September, and checked into my hotel, the Intercontinental. Next morning, having done the rounds of press agencies and Palestinian offices, I hitched a lift to the British Embassy for the normal courtesy call. The timing was impeccable. A few minutes before, Bill Pink, the embassy's communications officer, had received a radio message from Whitehall. A BOAC VC-10 had been hijacked on its way from Bahrein to London and was at that moment refuelling at Beirut airport. That was less than an hour's flying away. 'I think we know,' said Pink, 'where it's going to end up.'

The hijacking of VC-10 flight BA775 was the Palestinians' fifth jet in four days. It had 105 passengers on board, including thirty British schoolchildren. With a revolver at his neck, the pilot, Captain Cyril Goulborn, was persuaded to fly his plane from Beirut to join the two waiting in the sand outside Amman. As he was making his final approach, and with a stunning sense of theatre, the Palestinian hijackers handed out landing cards. The destination was marked Revolution Airport. The drama of Dawson's Field was about to reach its climax.

Captain Goulborn touched down without difficulty and he remembers the hijackers whooping and screaming and hugging each other when the doors were opened. They even brought bottles of whisky aboard, so that the hostages might celebrate, though as Captain Goulborn said later, 'I found some warm Vichy water and stuck to it. The Arabs seemed to think it all hilarious but I must admit I didn't find it all that thrilling!'

That Wednesday evening King Hussein sent a small armoured convoy of the Royal Jordanian Army to keep sentry over the Palestinians guarding the three aircraft as he brooded in his palace at Hummar, himself hostage to events. Throughout the summer, the Palestinians in Jordan had become increasingly confident and cocky. Entire areas of Amman, which had been refugee camps since the Six-Day War with Israel three years before, were now training camps for young guerrillas dedicated to the destruction of Israel. Very quickly they had created a state within a state and neither the king nor his government seemed able to prevent it. Jordanian soldiers who lived in suburbs controlled and policed by the Palestinians found it necessary to travel to and from their homes in civilian clothes; otherwise they were insulted, disarmed and frequently 'dis-uniformed'. Palestinians organised protection and extortion rackets on local businessmen and shopkeepers. They strutted arrogantly into the hotels, rattling their rifles and moneyboxes under the noses of tourists. Jordanians were obliged to walk in the road if the pavements were full of Palestinian men and their Kalashnikovs. The Palestinian leadership encouraged it and their daily statements, issued to world news agencies and regularly broadcast over Radio Damascus, abused the king and his prime minister, and became more and more threatening. It was as if they were challenging Hussein for the leadership of his country.

That September it looked as though they might succeed by default. Rumours of an army coup were rife. One extravagant story going the rounds was that the king had lain down in the road to stop his tanks from leaving their base for a pre-emptive attack on the Palestinian camps. If the story was true he soon had cause to regret it. He had lost face and as the hijackers continued to flout his sovereignty, he ran the risk of losing his crown. His army and government were split, the generals determined to destroy the Palestinians and chase them out of Jordan, the politicians fearful of what the rest of Arabia would do, especially Syria, should that happen. I had heard a story which, true or not, summed up the royal dilemma. As he was inspecting a tank squadron, Hussein saw brassières hanging from a turret. He joked: 'You have women aboard?'

The tank commander answered, 'We are all women now, sir.' And the young king wept.

With a Palestinian escort, Ghassan Dallal, who was working indirectly for ITN as a freelance cameraman, I drove out to the strip that evening, following the tail-lights of an army convoy. The journey was slow; it seemed to us the Jordanians were not sure where Dawson's Field was. But a little before 1 a.m. we came to it, and less than a mile away my escort-cum-cameraman braked and turned off the engine. It would not be wise, he said, to go any closer. Not that it mattered. There was almost nothing I could not see and nothing I would ever forget!

It was cold and the Palestinians had lit fires between their tents. The moon was large and low and the three airliners, like the desert around them, shone white and silver. The moonlight magnified them and they looked enormous.

'This is a good airport,' said Ghassan. 'We could fill it with air-planes.'

I said, 'You'll start a war.'

He pulled a blanket over his shoulders and wrapped it tight. 'This war started long ago,' he said bitterly, 'when you gave Palestine to the Jews.' He tucked the folds of the blanket over his head and disappeared. He did not speak again, so I sat silent and shivering and watched the thin yellow fires around the shining prisons filled with people and waited for the night's vigil to end and the sun to rise so that my part in the story could begin.

Ghassan was up and filming with his small hand-held camera long before there was enough light for an exposure, but film was cheap. When the sun was high enough, it blazed into his lens and still he got nothing. So we moved a half-mile to our right, just in time to see a Red Cross convoy bringing in the first of the emergency supplies, including one thousand cardboard-boxed meals. At the tail of the convoy was a camouflaged water bowser sent by the Palestinians, an Arabic slogan painted on its side which Dallal translated as 'The Popular Front at your service'. Later that day, we learnt that an order had been urgently radioed to Geneva for baby food and powdered milk. Among the passengers were pregnant women and two three-month-old babies.

By mid-morning, the desert had turned from an icebox to a stove and with the light between us and the aircraft distorted in the shimmering heat, the jets might have been a mirage. Through my binoculars I saw that the front door of each aircraft was open but nothing appeared to be moving inside. Palestinian guards squatted under the wings for shade, others sat obediently behind heavy-calibre machine-guns and anti-aircraft guns mounted on

Landrovers and trucks. Beyond them were King Hussein's Centurion tanks and his Ferret and Saracen armoured cars parked in a circle, their noses pointed towards the planes. Between the Swissair and TWA jets was a large low tent, the red, green, white and black Palestinian flag limp above it. A little after midday a message was sent from it to the senior Jordanian officer and a few minutes later we heard the engines of the tanks and armoured cars start up. They turned on their tracks, juddering violently and spewing up columns of sand a hundred feet high, as they charged off to new positions further away from the planes. They had new orders but not from their king, not even from their commanding officer, but from the Palestinians in their tent, the young commanders of Dawson's Field who knew they were holding not only Jordan but half the western world to ransom.

Mercifully, even then, on that second Thursday of Black September, the desert hostages did not know of the Palestinians' ultimatum that had shocked and startled the world. They had demanded the immediate release of Leila Khaled in London and dozens more of their terrorists imprisoned in West Germany, Switzerland and Israel. Refusal by one or all of the governments involved, and the three planes would be blown up with the passengers and crew strapped to their seats. The deadline was set for Sunday morning – three days away.

The multiple kidnappings produced the most humiliating week in international diplomacy in recent years. For the next six days the chancelleries of major nations were forced to haggle with a tiny band of terrorists; three heads of state – Richard Nixon, Edward Heath and Willy Brandt – virtually abandoned day-to-day government to attend to this most outrageous international blackmail ever, political extortion on an unprecedented scale. It was to lead to a civil war in one country and the eventual near-destruction of another. It almost toppled a king and certainly hastened the end of a president. And it brought the third Arab-Israeli war one step closer.

Even if the hostages did not know of the ultimatum, they knew what they were risking inside the planes from heat and infection. The lavatories were overflowing and the cabin crews were demanding disinfectant and air sprays. The stench was intolerable.

Eventually the Palestinians agreed to dig pits under the planes and the stewards opened valves and let the sewage fall into them.

The International Red Cross in Geneva had now received the desperate list of urgent necessities and they would fill an aircraft. Tents, ladders, insect and deodorant sprays, three hundred blankets, three hundred torches, sanitary towels in large quantities, babies' nappies, five thousand paper cups and plates, butane stoves and saucepans for boiling water, talcum powder, a kilo of anti-diarrhoea pills, a kilo of aspirin and five litres of eau de cologne. There was even a request for advice on how to cope with mynah birds. There were forty in the hold of the VC-10, on their way to London pet shops. Frantic in the heat and dying from thirst, they added to the general pandemonium.

The children aboard the British Airways jet had been returning to their boarding schools in England and appeared to relish the interlude. They sang songs like 'My old man's a dustman' and 'One man went to mow', with occasional lapses into naughty variations. Their favourite was their own adaptation of the Beatles' 'Yellow Submarine' which began, 'We all live in a blue and white machine'. They even chanted the PFLP's political tirades back to them, infuriating one fanatic they nicknamed 'Bombshell Bessie' by repeating, like an advertising jingle, her own: 'Our heroic struggle has just begun. The worst, the worst, has yet to come.' They even learnt the PFLP's anthem in Arabic – possibly because the tune sounded very much like 'Good King Wenceslas'.

Food was still scarce and the Jewish hostages were having the worst of it because their kosher dietary laws allowed them to eat only the little fruit that was available. Then a rabbi on the Swissair jet issued a dispensation permitting them to eat the food the Arabs brought aboard.

The Palestinians decided it was time for the hostages' ordeal to be appreciated worldwide, for their stories to be told and their suffering to be seen on television in America, Britain, West Germany and Israel. What was needed was another turn of the screw, something to encourage those countries to think more urgently about their ultimatum. So they called a press conference at Dawson's Field.

It was bizarre and true to form. There were fifty or more journalists, photographers and television crews, all fighting one another for pole position. Cameramen used their lenses as battering rams to move the heads in front of them and the sharpest elbows in Fleet Street clove their way to the front for the best view of the twenty-five passengers and crew selected to meet us. We were kept twenty yards away but, little by little, with a resolute push from behind, we inched forward shouting our questions, the photographers demanding that heads should turn this way or that – all of us at once, screeching and bawling at the dazed and dirty people who stood so helplessly there in front of us, blistering in the sun and the hundred-degree heat. There was such a bombardment of questions from so many strangers and from so many directions, no one could hear the answers and so we all began shouting at one another, calling for order. How distressing it was for those poor people who had already endured so much and had looked to us for help and encouragement on that wretched day.

Things were getting violently out of hand when two Palestinians came running along the wing of the VC-10 pointing their automatic rifles and screaming in Arabic. A man called Bassam, who had organised the conference, began shouting through a loudhailer: 'Get back. . . be civilised . . . we will shoot if you do not behave . . . you are animals.' Which, in the parlance of my trade, was fair comment. We quietened down and when we finally got our stories and pictures it was agreed the hostages had possibly more to fear from the press than from the Palestinians!

Hour by hour, the PFLP guerrillas guarding the aircraft were getting more and more edgy. We knew why and, soon, so would the hostages. One reason was that the guerrillas at the airstrip were becoming suspicious of their leaders, negotiating from Amman. There were other reasons, too.

The BBC World Service, which I listened to in the comfort of my room in the Amman Intercontinental that evening, reported that the US Sixth Fleet, with aircraft carriers and assault ships, was sailing close to the Lebanese coast. There were also reports that the United States Air Force had flown twenty-five Phantoms and four troop transporters to Adana on the Turkish coast, less than thirty minutes' flying time away. I telephoned London. My foreign editor confirmed the American stories and added more. The Royal Air

Force were making secret preparations at their base at Lyneham in Wiltshire for a possible troop airlift to Dawson's Field, and news agencies were filing stories out of Beirut that the Israelis were getting ready for a paratroop drop. In a final contribution to the unlikely scenario, Damascus Radio was reporting sightings of Iraqi armoured units moving to new positions inside Jordan and nobody quite knew whose side they were on.

I thought of the Palestinians, sitting around their fires on that desert strip forty miles away, huddled around their transistors, expecting to hear from London that Leila Khaled had been released and that Geneva, Bonn and Israel had freed their Arab prisoners. Instead, they heard world news reports which amounted to preparations for war against them. To cap it all that night, the airstrip was enveloped in a *shimowa* – a sandstorm – so that should the attackers come – American, British, Iraqi or Israeli, singly or together – they would have the best possible cover.

The Palestinians were now desperate and confused. Abu Fadi, one of the leaders on the airstrip, ordered the hostages to write telegrams addressed to their own governments, appealing to them to meet the demands. One of the passengers aboard the VC-10, Major Fawkes Potts, wrote to Downing Street: ESSENTIAL YOU APPRECIATE THESE PEOPLE ARE NOT KIDDING. THEY WILL BLOW US UP. Major Fawkes Potts knew something about blowing people up. An ancestor, in 1603, had tried it on the Westminster parliament.

There was now no doubting the Palestinians' intentions. Parcels of high explosive were wedged into the nose and wing wheel-housings of each jet and black wires trailed from them to a generator inside the headquarters tent. If anyone were to attack, whoever they were and however they came, they would find no one left to rescue. Dawson's Field was on full alert; the fires were put out and there was radio silence. Nobody slept; not the captors squatting by their guns, waiting for the *shimowa* to blow itself out, nor their captives in the hot and stinking aircraft cabins, waiting for the alarm to sound.

Saturday, the twelfth day of Black September, and the hijackers' ultimatum now had less than twenty-four hours to run. At eight o'clock that morning a Middle East Airways jet banked over

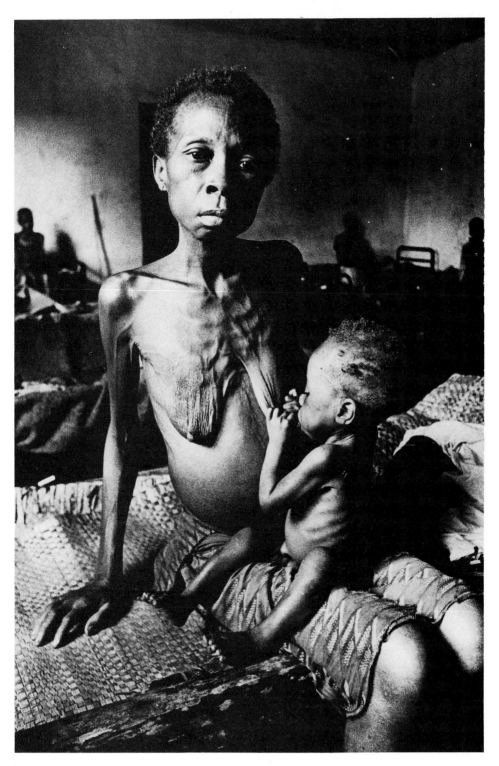

Mother and child, Biafra, Christmas 1969. (*page 31*)

Moment of explosion, Dawson's Field, 1971 – taken from ITN's 16mm news film. (*page 50*)

'Welcome to Cyprus', Michael Nicholson to Turkish paratroopers, 1975 – taken from ITN's 16mm news film. (*page 129*).

Dawson's Field and began its descent to Amman. The pilot made an announcement and passengers peered eagerly at the scene ten thousand feet below them, among them David Phillips, ITN's senior producer. Since Sunday, he had been producing news bulletins with a dateline that was now below him: a broad gash of sand which ran straight between a range of light brown hills and, at the edge of it, three objects, like dots on a domino. From that height there seemed no movement and Phillips wondered if the hostages had already been freed and the three aircraft abandoned. But his timing was, as always, impeccable and his assumption almost correct. The PFLP had just announced it was releasing all the passengers and they were being taken to Amman. A deal had been done with Washington, London and Bonn. The fate of the aircraft had still to be decided.

We heard the convoy a long way off – guns being discharged into the air, bursts of machine-gun fire, bursts of song. Then we saw them, turning into the forecourt of the Intercontinental Hotel, led by a jeep and on it young Palestinians, men and women in their camouflage and *kaffiyehs*, singing their Wenceslas anthem above the rifle shots. It was like the arrival of a triumphant army. Behind them were the coaches and out of them came a little girl named Susan, in school uniform and straw boater, followed by a boy named Michael, carrying his pet turtle. There never was a more unlikely scene.

The hotel foyer suddenly became a centre for refugees. Mothers with arms full of babies, nappies and powdered milk, embassy officials weaving in and around the mass of bodies, shouting out names and passport numbers, identifying their nationals and pinning labels to them; families split up in the transfer searching and yelling, children running wild in and out of lifts, up and down stairs – and everything further confused by us, the world's press, who were trying to do what we had been waiting six days for – to get our stories, our pictures, our television interviews and meet our deadlines worldwide.

With my interviews done, and leaving my camera crew to film everything that moved and much that did not, I crept away to find a corner to write my commentary, suddenly conscious of my own deadline. Soon the hostages would leave on the first available flights out of Amman and my story, my cans of film and my recorded commentary, had to be on one of those planes.

I was sitting on a lavatory seat writing when Ghassan found me. I flushed the pan for the sake of appearances. He was excited.

'You must come with me now – back to the planes. I must take pictures.'

'Ghassan, we've got more film of them than we could ever use,' I said. 'You go if you want to.'

I thought perhaps he simply wanted to shoot a little more film to earn a little more cash. But he insisted I should go, said he would not be allowed through the Jordanian roadblocks if I were not with him, that it was absolutely vital he should be at Dawson's Field quickly. So we went.

We got to the strip just as the last of the men hostages were leaving, but they were not Ghassan's concern. He did not bother filming them, which made me angry; after all, we had it to ourselves and every little bit of exclusivity would help at the end of the day. The coaches stopped about half a mile away and Ghassan seemed to take that as a signal. He ran forward and I ran after him. We stopped about six hundred yards from the planes and I waited as he turned the turret on his camera to take the long lens. I could see men jumping from the plane and others under the wings and nose. But I still had no inkling why.

Then they ran from the planes and drove off in a jeep towards the waiting coaches. As Ghassan braced himself, with his camera wedged hard against his neck, I realised what they were about to do. I heard the camera running and I counted. At five the VC-10 exploded – first the nose, then the tail. The TWA Boeing went up in a flash of flame seconds later. Then a pause, and the Swissair DC-8, twelve million pounds' worth of aircraft, suddenly disintegrated in front of us, a mass of black and grey and orange. I sat down in the sand and watched.

The captain of the VC-10, Cyril Goulborn, was watching it too from inside his coach, and said later: 'I thought I'd be shocked but I wasn't. Not after what we'd been through. I simply thought it better the planes were blown up empty than blown up full!'

I drove back to Amman as Ghassan unloaded his precious roll of film, a scoop of scoops, an astonishing world exclusive. I knew what it was worth. I congratulated him.

'But how on earth did you know?'

'They told me. I am their brother.'

'Brother?'

'I am a cameraman sometimes,' he said. 'But I am always a Palestinian.'

Ghassan was a comrade and active member of the PFLP. He refused to hand the film to me and took it directly to his head-quarters in the slums of Amman for the central committee to decide how best to use it. David Phillips followed and, not an unpersuasive man, he argued that it was ITN property. Ghassan argued just as persuasively (he was also a student lawyer) that, as he had not been commissioned by ITN to shoot the explosions, the film was his. It was another five hours before the film was in David's safe hands.

He rushed to the airport. It was empty. The final flight carrying the last of the hostages to Beirut had left an hour before. But on the parking apron was a Jordanian Airlines Caravelle scheduled to fly the following morning. Negotiations began all over again and, in what was probably the best deal of his life, David counted out ten thousand dollars, borrowed from Bert Quint of CBS, hired the airliner to fly him to Cyprus, and was in London by midday the following day.

While David was wrangling with the PFLP, I had caught the last hostage plane out of Amman to Beirut with my own footage of the day's extraordinary events, including the pictures of Susan's boater and Michael's turtle.

Soon after landing I was invited to give them away. As I was queuing at immigration, two Americans came bouncing towards me.

'You Nicholson?' asked the louder and fatter.

I nodded.

'Gimme!'

I wondered if they were drunk. It did seem an astonishing thing to expect me to do, considering what I had been through that day. I did not even know them.

'We're from CBS,' the other said. 'We've got a Lear Jet and we're birding you outa Rome,' as if that was all the introduction needed. I ignored them. Then in the style of American broadcasters, especially CBS at the time, they grabbed at the film cans, but, remembering early rugby training, I quickly turned my back and went into the position of what I think is called 'a maul presentation'. It threw them. It also rather upset the immigration officials. Inside their glass cubicles they shouted and blew whistles and as I stood there feigning total innocence the two transatlantics were bustled away at the point of a policeman's revolver, cursing me with obscenities I had never heard before and have seldom heard since.

It was a clumsy try-on. Some local deal had obviously been struck between CBS New York and UPITN, the syndication service of ITN, to satellite my story in time for their national evening news. Maybe it was all tied in with Quint's ten-thousand-dollar loan. But I had no way of knowing whether my London desk had okayed the deal or even knew of it and assumed that ITN might prefer our own viewers to see the world exclusive first. And they did. Cameraman Roly Carter, on assignment in Beirut, waited while I recorded my commentary on a tiny Sony tape recorder, sitting (as usual, you might say) on a lavatory seat, pausing between door-slams and Lebanese coughs and farts.

Then, with my rolls of film under one arm and a large airline timetable guide in the other, Roly caught the midnight Air France flight to Teheran (going east and in the wrong direction) where he was certain he could catch the overnight British Airways flight (going west and the right way) for London.

The next day, Sunday the thirteenth, ITN transmitted the entire coverage, including the exclusive of the blowing-up of the planes, by the Eurovision link and by satellite to the world, six hours ahead of all opposition. They called the programme *Deadline at Dawson's Field*.

It is tempting to leave a story when you are riding high on it and return home clutching the herograms of congratulation before interest wanes. But many stories considered finished explode and expand again, rewarding those who stay, punishing those who leave. It has little to do with judgement. As always, it is mostly to do with luck.

I remember Reggie Bosanquet waiting months in 1965 in what was then Southern Rhodesia, for the declaration of UDI that everyone was convinced was coming. But with his and ITN's patience and budget exhausted, he flew out of Salisbury on the morning BOAC flight for London. The plane was over Zambia, less than half an hour out, when the captain announced that Mr Ian Smith had declared his illegal independence.

That evening, in Beirut, in the splendidly-ostentatious Phoenicia Hotel, I sipped Bollinger and picked at langoustes on the verandah overlooking the harbour and the Mediterranean, wondering if I ought to catch the morning flight home to a slap on the back and lunch at the Penal Reform Club. To go back to Amman now, I reckoned, was to return to a long and possibly unproductive wait. King Hussein's war with the Palestinians was inevitable but was it imminent?

Decisions! More lobster or smoked salmon? Chablis or the Sauvignon? To stay or not to stay? My head had scarcely touched the pillow when a familiar voice from London told me to catch the early morning flight back to Amman. An ITN crew were already packing their bags to join me.

My foreign editor reeled off the agency tape. The PFLP had kept back forty male hostages and hidden them as insurance against any last-minute double-dealing until Leila Khaled and seven named Palestinian prisoners were released from European jails. The fighting between the Jordanian army and the guerrillas had suddenly resumed and Syria was now making threatening noises on the Palestinians' behalf. If Syrian tanks crossed the Jordanian border, the Israelis might well cross the River Jordan over the Allenby Bridge to help Hussein – whether he wanted them to or not. If Israel did that, would Moscow step in to help the Arabs? And the Americans to help Israel? With such a massive military build-up in the eastern Mediterranean, how much of a shove would Washington need to commit itself further to Tel Aviv?

The answer came on Wednesday the sixteenth when King Hussein announced: 'Every day Jordan sinks a little further. Things cannot go on as they are. Our unity is at stake.' Broadcasting live on Amman radio from his palace at Hummar, he declared that his civilian cabinet, which had tried so hard to come to terms with the guerrillas, had been dismissed and he had appointed a government of seven generals and brigadiers, two colonels and three majors.

The Palestinians, quite rightly, took it to be a declaration of war. Six thousand miles away, President Nixon, in his own ingenuous way, hinted that by keeping his warships close to the Israeli-Lebanese coast and his fighter-bombers on the alert in Turkey, he was giving himself the option of intervening if and when he wanted to.

That Wednesday the gunfire spread slowly across the city. There was no other sound. The streets and the souks were empty, the long queues outside the grocers were gone and the busy criss-crossing lines of people, old and young, pushing handcarts filled with food and water-churns, had already hurried home. Shops were now boarded up and at petrol stations mounds of sand were heaped over the inlet covers of the fuel tanks. Where there had been a picture of King Hussein or the PLO's Yasser Arafat hanging on a wall there were now darker unbleached squares. War was about and Amman had shut up and gone to ground. The only cars on the move belonged to the foreign embassies, each adorned with its own large flag and the white flag of neutrality. I walked and thumbed but nobody stopped. I went to the PFLP offices but they were abandoned, the furniture and filing cabinets had been taken away and somebody had made a fire in the middle of the floor of all the official papers they did not carry away. It was still smouldering: flecks of ash swirled in the hot air and settled on me like black snow. Over the side door someone had scrawled in chalk, KEEP YOUR FINGERS ON THE TRIGGER.

On the steps underneath and alone was a girl with a *kaffiyeh* shawl over the shoulders of a brand-new army shirt. She was wearing dark glasses but I knew her. She was Muna Abid El-Sajid, the girl who had helped hijack the BOAC VC-10. She did not speak. She hummed quietly to herself as if nothing had changed or was ever likely to. She offered me sheafs of Palestinian propaganda broadsheets but it would not have been wise to carry them in the streets of Amman that evening, the political geography was likely to change so fast, street by street, hill by hill. So I gave her an American dollar and walked away, leaving her busily rearranging the heap of pamphlets at her feet, like a corner-stand newspaper seller getting ready for the commuter rush-hour. I wondered if she was mad.

Then I heard the tanks and ran as fast as I could through the narrow, dipping, winding streets until I saw them – King Hussein's Centurions, his banner flying from their radio aerials, turrets open, his Bedouin crews perched on top, their white headdresses turned inside-out, as Arabia's fiercest warriors traditionally do when they mean to fight to the death. They stopped at the junction where the road splits north to Al Husseini and south to Wahdat. Both were Palestinian camps and within easy shelling distance of the Centurions' guns.

At the hotel, a man was waiting for me. His name was Ibrahim and he had always been helpful as a guide and translator. Now he was anxious. He said he had heard there was a plan for the Palestinians to take over the hotel and hold us all hostage too and he urged me to leave. He gave me the key to his brother's house, less than four hundred yards away on the road to the British Embassy. I knew it. We had eaten a meal there once with his brother and family. He said there was water and I would be safe, so I took the key and thanked him and when he had gone I packed a bag. A move to a quieter place, if only for a couple of nights, seemed a sensible precaution. Then the telephone rang. My replacement crew had arrived at the airport and were on their way to the hotel. I quickly forgot about Ibrahim and his warning, which was just as well. It almost certainly saved my life.

The noise outside overwhelmed me. I crawled to the window, looked out and then crawled back on all fours across the room and opened the door into the corridor. It was just as I remembered a public air-raid shelter in the London blitz. Families, including small children, were sitting in their pyjamas, silent and terrified. I dressed and found cameraman Paul Carleton and together we climbed the service staircase to the top of the building. We could see the tanks and the smoke from their targets, the Palestinian camps right and left of us. But much closer, less than a mile across a shallow valley, shells and mortars were exploding at Jebel Hussein, the Palestinians' headquarters. It was clear the king was not committing his infantry; there would be no fire-fight, house by house.

This was going to be an armoured duel fought at a distance with shells and mortars, rocket grenades and heavy machine-guns. The battle for Amman had just begun but the devastation promised to be total. I looked left towards the British Embassy, beyond the roundabout known as the Third Circle, to the house of Ibrahim's brother. I thought I would identify it by the tamarisk tree in the front yard. Strangely, despite the blast, the treetrunk was still there but the house was gutted and smoking: the roof had gone and so had the back wall. I still had the key to the front door in my pocket.

At ten-thirty that morning, all telephone and telex lines to the hotel were cut. One hundred and five journalists, press photographers and television crews were stranded with everything to report but no way of reporting it. At midday a major came into the hotel and told us that anyone attempting to leave would be arrested and anyone taking pictures ran the risk of worse. If any of us doubted him, we were quickly persuaded that afternoon. A Swedish television cameraman, Ole Ohlson, three rooms along from me, eased his lens between the curtains to film the Bedouin below. I heard the bullets hit the stucco and the windows shatter but it was another five minutes before Ohlson came crawling into the corridor, his leg ripped open and pouring blood. Somebody gave him whisky or maybe it was brandy and poured more over his wounds, which made him scream. We tore up a sheet and used a pyjama cord as a tourniquet, and together we carried him down into the basement kitchen and washed him clean. Later an army doctor came and took him off to hospital.

Arnoud de Borchgrave of *Newsweek* got a message from the Spanish Embassy that Geneviève, the photographer wife of François Chauvel of *Figaro*, had been wounded filming a Palestinian attack on the American Embassy. Then Wilborn Hampton of UPI was hit in the back by a bullet that ricocheted off the lobby wall. We all began to speak of 'brand new holes' – bullet and shrapnel holes that had not been there five minutes earlier.

What happened next morning was not easy to explain, unless of course the correspondent had not heard of Ohlson – which was unlikely – or thought it could not happen to him, which was more probable. A Soviet reporter-cum-cameraman, confident he could not be seen by the Bedouin, began photographing them on a long lens. Later that afternoon he was found shot through the left eye.

The Jordanians had six mortars in the carpark, as many 106mm recoilless rifles, bolted on the back of Landrovers, about a dozen armoured cars – British-built Ferrets and Saracens – and the tanks, which were being used as artillery pieces. The Intercontinental Hotel was on a hill called Jebel Amman between the Bedouin and their targets across the *wahdis*. It was largely built of glass, as most in the chain are, designed with a view in mind. They are not meant to be fortresses in the middle of a battle zone. Most of the injuries were from glass splinters and the wounds were very bloody. As people passed I saw tiny splinters of glass stuck to their faces; in the dark unlit corridors they sparkled in the light of torches and candles. People would have been safer in the basement but they were more afraid of the darkness there than of the amplified terror in the corridors.

Bandages were made from towels and bedsheets. I saw a boy, perhaps twelve years old, holding a sopping red towel to his right eye. When he saw me he took the towel away; the eyeball was loose from its socket and only the pressure of the towel was keeping it in place. Mattresses were up-ended along the walls to absorb the sounds outside and the blasts. I was advised by one American newsman to place my mattress against the wall in the corridor next to my bathroom, to have the maximum number of walls between me and the incoming shells. Some people wandered from corridor to corridor, floor to floor, all day and night, searching for their families.

Only at arranged times did the press congregate, normally in the foyer. This made us especially vulnerable to fire from both sides, but it was the only place where the radio signal was strong enough for us to hear the strains of 'Lillibullero', the wonderful morale-booster which introduces the BBC's World Service news. Usually we had to lie prostrate on our bellies or backs to listen to what the outside world thought was happening to us, or – more to the point – what it considered *might* happen to us! Bodies and cameras were strewn across the floor as bullets hit the walls above and incoming mortars took out another floor of glass.

It was an enormous advantage to know with some certainty the difference in the sound of incoming and outgoing fire. Those who did could appear fairly relaxed and dip for cover only when it was needed. Novices, and that included me, ducked at everything. It was a mental as much as a physical strain; not knowing what was coming or going gave the impression that nobody was on one's side. I was doing my 'piece to camera' when the twelve-foot glass doors behind us exploded, showering me and cameraman Carleton with splinters. 'Let's get the bloody hell out of here!' I shouted with the camera still running, and this was later transmitted in full.

Danger can be a wonderful tonic, but by the third day and with the hotel under total siege, with no light or power, little food and little water, it began to hurt. That afternoon, Paul's recordist left his sound gear in the foyer, walked to the front door and, in a quiet, matter-of-fact way, announced that he was going to drive to Damascus. He had never been to war before. Nor to Damascus. Perhaps, until that moment, he thought he could cope.

No two people cope with fear in the same way and some cannot cope at all. I have always been wary of those who profess not to be worried. Hugh Thomson, my early mentor, summed it up neatly, as he did most things. 'The fellow who doesn't look worried doesn't know what's going on.' Our recordist had become affected by the growing hysteria around us: 'to the man who is afraid, everything rustles'. We did not let him out of the front door; instead we gave him a bottle of water and some chocolate and he went passively into the black and stinking cellar and stayed there until the war was over.

Water was the problem. In the hotel we felt sorry for ourselves with a ration of about two bottles a day, forgetting that thousands in the city and in the refugee camps had none. Twice, in the lulls, we had seen army tankers distributing water to people in the streets, people living in the 'safe' Jordanian-held territory. But we had heard Al Fatah Radio, representing the biggest guerrilla organisation, talk of the thousands of 'innocents' dying of thirst. Thousands did not die, but the suffering must have been real enough. The Red Crescent (the Arab Red Cross) broadcast an appeal: 'Your children are dying of thirst; we cannot help you except by telling you that you may be able to save their lives by letting them drink their own urine. It will do them no harm.'

Four journalists, including myself, were returning from Amman airport in an armed escort (having just seen more journalists leave in the Red Cross planes). The army driver stopped the truck by a closed and barricaded shop and asked us if we would like a bottle of lemonade. We thought he was joking. He wasn't. Inside the shop an old man and his wife were squatting by a crate of two dozen Pepsi-Colas. They had no water supply yet they were not willing to break open the bottles, because they were all they had left, all that remained of their shop, the difference between having stock and having none: being on the right side of starvation.

Those of us who had seen our war movies had filled our baths on the first day, which, as it turned out, was the day supplies ran out. Not everyone had been so prepared and there began an internecine war between the various nationals of the international press corps. The French especially seemed expert in stealing everything, including water. Worse, one English reporter found a French photographer standing naked in his bath, washing in the precious stuff. The British photographer Don McCullin, then into his fifth war, banished the Australian writer Murray Sayle from his room when he found him peeing into his washbasin. Sayle, indignant, pointed to the overfull lavatory and said, 'But you don't expect me to pee in there?'

Finally, it was decided the press corps should form a committee to take over the running of the hotel and organise water and food supplies. We even arranged for working parties to clean up the filth because it was agreed that sewage, flies and rats were now more likely to kill us than Bedouin or Palestinian bullets. We had a meeting. We felt like POWs and there was a touch of play-acting by the Brits. Michael Adams, from the British-Arab Council, had been an RAF prisoner-of-war in Germany, so he was made chairman of our self-help committee which included *Newsweek*'s elegant Arnoud de Borchgrave, the far less elegant Murray Sayle, Eric Rouleau of *Le Monde* and a Swede, Herman Lündquist. BBC cameraman Bernard Hesketh, who was some years later to work with me in the Falklands War, represented the British. His sound recordist became our quartermaster and also dug latrines, and Bill Tuohy of the *Los Angeles Times* was in charge of refuse collection. This was dumped into the empty swimming-pool, mornings and afternoons.

One pair of French photographers lived in such filth that Tuohy and Borchgrave gave them an ultimatum: their room was to be cleaned within the hour or they would be thrown out of the hotel and left to the mercy of the Bedouin. They met the deadline with a welter of French obscenities.

Bill Pink, communications officer at the British Embassy, volunteered to bring a sheaf of radio messages received over the embassy radio from newsdesks all over the world and to take back messages for transmission. It was a four-hundred-yard walk from the embassy to the hotel along Fahran Street from Parliament Circle through open ground and a dozen gunsights. The embassy's Bedouin guard was his escort and Pink told us he held his hand all the way. As we cheered them into the hotel, Pink was shaking: 'Just as we left the embassy, a soldier was shot dead by a sniper only fifteen yards ahead of us. Then everything went berserk. Two Saladins opened up with their guns at a house fifty yards off and the whole bloody thing disappeared.'

That afternoon there was an explosion in de Borchgrave's room. Two 50mm-calibre shells came in through the window – one slamming into the wall, the other straight through the side of his wardrobe and several suits. Later Arnoud insisted that he stayed on in Amman when the rest of us had left only because he had to get a signed affidavit from the British Embassy confirming the loss of his suits so that he could claim them back on expenses.

In Damascus, a hundred miles away, the Syrians were examining the possibilities of joining in the war. Their sympathies were well known. A Jordan ruled by the Palestinians would suit them very well. Secretly the Syrians had asked Iraq to join them in an invasion of Jordan, but the Iraqis chose another and more cunning way to help. They had a brigade of one hundred and fifty tanks along the Syrian border with Jordan, close to the Golan Heights, there as part of the contribution to Jordan's defence against possible Israeli attack. It had long been agreed that whenever they wanted to move their positions they would do so only at night and they would fire green Very lights so that the Jordanians should not be alarmed. The Iraqis now decided to double-cross those they had pledged to protect and to do Syria's bidding. Soon after dark on the night of 19

September, a bright green flare lit the sky over the brigade's headquarters. Shortly afterwards the Iraqi tanks pulled out of their
positions and allowed Syria's Russian T55s to take their place. The
Syrian armoured invasion had begun.

We crouched over our transistors listening not only to BBC
World Service reports but also to English broadcasts over Amman
Radio and Damascus Radio, and it seemed that King Hussein,
desperate and without allies, might do something no Arab would
dream of in his blackest fantasy. To prevent a combined Syrian-
Palestinian takeover, he might let Israel cross the River Jordan to
intervene. Syria's response over Damascus Radio was almost bibli-
cal: 'The crimes of Jordan cannot be diverted by fictitious battles
with Syria. Let them know that if they want this battle to be decisive
and final, so be it and all their interests in Arabia will be destroyed.'

But twenty-four hours later, the BBC was reporting quite differ-
ently. Jordanian troops, entrenched to the north around Irbid, had
counter-attacked and had the Syrians on the run. Their Russian-
supplied T55 tanks were no match for Hussein's British-built
Centurions. The handful of ex-RAF Hunter jets that made up the
king's tiny air force had also hit the Syrians hard.

Reports from Washington and Tel Aviv confirmed that America
and Israel were poised to intervene and from Cairo that President
Nasser was dispatching a pan-Arab delegation to Amman to try to
negotiate a peace. In Hussein's capital the war was still desperate.
Despite six days of fighting and destruction, much of the city was
still flying the Palestinian flag.

Diary entries, Amman:
Artillery fire non-stop. Sound from carpark unbelievable.
Hotel shudders. Great columns of black smoke all around us.

Another six tanks pass the front door. Huge posters of the king
stuck to turrets. King's soldiers jog behind, wearing British second world war helmets and khaki greatcoats. Why greatcoats?
It's sweltering.

Lunch of cold stewed goat. Glass of water each. Some of us
took plates on to terrace, alfresco despite stench from rubbish
in pool. Explosion at far end. Glass and concrete splinters.

Plates smash and everyone's on the ground. Somebody shouts, 'Incoming mortar!' Tuohy shouts back, 'Quick thinking, Charlie. You saved our arses!'

I hitched a lift with the Red Cross back from Amman airport. We stopped at the Maasher Hospital where there was a direct radio link with the Red Cross in Geneva. Sitting on the lawn among the rose bushes was Dr Saad. He was dressed in green operating clothes and sat with his elbows resting on the newly-made coffin of a European who'd been killed in the fighting. He told me:

'I had no idea the army would do this. About fifteen of them arrived in their jeeps; two armoured cars positioned themselves on the road outside with the barrels of their guns pointing straight at us. One of the soldiers – he seemed no different from the rest, he had no stripes and he wasn't an officer – came to me and demanded to search the hospital. I asked him why. He said we were sheltering Palestinians, he said he would find them and take them off. I told him as a doctor I treated anyone, I said we asked no one how they came to be wounded or what side they were fighting on. The soldier pushed me down in my chair. The fifteen then went into every room and every ward, searching. I didn't know who we were treating, I didn't want to know. When the soldiers found a door they couldn't unlock they fired bullets at it and forced it open. At the base of the lift shaft a steel door housing the machinery could not be forced so they threw a hand-grenade into the shaft and blew it up. On the second floor they found some young men with bullet and shrapnel wounds, one was severely burnt in the face and neck. The soldiers carried them down and loaded them into their jeeps, saying the wounded were Palestinians. The wounded cried in pain as the jeeps jolted away from me, but I could do nothing. An hour later the hospital was shelled and machine-gunned, bullets spraying the front of the building and what I think must have been a rocket blew in the side of a room in the nurses' hostel. Our generator was damaged and we're having to work by candlelight.'

Dr Saad went inside and I waited by the Red Cross car for the Red Cross doctor and driver to reappear. The hospital was running short of candles and someone had remembered a stock was kept in a schoolroom a hundred yards down the road. Volunteers were needed to walk to the school to get them. Throughout the day and previous night Palestinian snipers had been firing at everyone moving outside the hospital gate. No one volunteered. The risk seemed too great. Then the front door of the hospital opened and a large middle-aged nursing sister marched through, dragging behind her a young male orderly. He couldn't have been more than twenty and was obviously determined not to accompany her those hundred yards and back. As they passed the Red Cross car she took out the white flag from the back seat and carrying it high in the air the two passed out of the gate and began their walk down the road – holding each other's hand. We watched them. So did the snipers. They did not fire.

I saw the Centurions moving in single file towards Jebel Hussein, the source of much of the Palestinian rocket and mortar fire. The day before, I had watched men laying mines on the roads. Now Palestinian commandos ran out from the foxholes and braced themselves a hundred yards from their slow-moving targets, rocket-launchers on their shoulders. The third tank in line took a direct hit, burst into flames and accelerated out of control into a house. The other tank's machine-guns then opened fire and also bombarded the road in front of it with shells. One by one the anti-tank mines exploded until there was only grey and brown smoke and tanks moving through it. Later that day, shortly before dusk, higher up in the hills I saw the first white flags – not more than a dozen or so – but white flags they certainly were, and flying in a Palestinian area.

By the light of a candle that evening, I wrote in my diary: 'This is not the end yet. But I reckon it's the beginning of it.' I ringed the date. Wednesday, the twenty-third day of Black September.

By nightfall not a single Syrian tank was left in Jordan. They had withdrawn completely, taking their dead and towing a hundred wrecks behind them. By daybreak the desert at the foot of the Golan Heights was empty, and the wind had swept it clean of shell craters and tank tracks. It was as if there had never been a battle.

In Amman, the pounding of the guns increased on Thursday and for most of it I sat on the floor behind the reception desk trying hard not to listen. At dusk, after the dinner ritual of warm tea and cold boiled rice, I climbed the stairs to the roof. The sky was orange with the fires. Someone came and stood by me: a lieutenant in the Jordanian army; he introduced himself as Ahmet Shali. He had been in the army twenty-five years and had received his commission only a few months before. He said his wife and children were very proud of him. 'I haven't seen them for ten days now,' he said. 'I've tried to get near my house but it's impossible with the fighting. I tried again yesterday but I lost my way. There's been so much destruction, I can't recognise one street from another.' He took my arm and shook it hard as if I had not understood. 'All my life I have lived in my mother's house but yesterday I could not find it.'

He led me to the edge of the roof to show me where it ought to be, continuing to talk about the war and what he planned to do when it was over. We watched the red tracers criss-crossing high above our heads, then ducked as an explosion lit up the round shell of a vivid green minaret a hundred yards away. Another quickly hid it in bright smoke. We stood straight again.

'Where is the house?' I asked. 'Where do your family live?' But he did not answer. He was looking towards the minaret and the new fires and in their light I saw he was crying.

Next morning we heard an aircraft circling. Some brave pilot and crew were risking their lives to bring something or someone in and within the hour we knew it was both: a consignment of relief supplies and International Red Cross doctors. One of them was a Dr Sweigi and he arrived from the airport bloodied and trembling and near to tears.

'We painted big clumsy red crosses on the sides of the trucks and nurses sat by the drivers, holding white flags out of the windows. We wanted to get through to the Al Husseini camp where we were told most of the Palestinian casualties had been taken. We came to the post office . . . bodies were strewn everywhere, bloated in the sun, but still no one fired at us. Then as we turned left to go up the hill towards the camp, there were explosions on the road only about thirty yards ahead and suddenly, without any warning to us, the Palestinians were firing from everywhere. Behind me an ambulance caught fire, I saw the driver jump out but the nurse was trapped inside and screaming at us through the windscreen. She was on fire, she was incinerated. I shouted to everyone to swing into a petrol station . . . there was room enough for us to turn around but as we did, a bullet ricocheted off the wall and hit my driver in the stomach and another driver behind was hit in the head. I don't know how I got away. We cannot try again. It would be suicide. And we came to help them. We came to save them.'

Dr Sweigi sat on the bonnet of the van, dazed and shaking. Opposite us a mother and a boy – he was about ten – came out of the ruins of a house. The little boy walked in front carrying a piece of cardboard and written on it was PLEASE HELP US. The doctor was talking to himself: 'We did our best; we couldn't do more.'

The plane that brought Dr Sweigi into Amman took evacuees out – some British, some Americans and a few Swiss – mostly from the embassies. I went with Paul to the airport to film them leaving. Bill Pink from the British Embassy was among them. Bill had done sixteen months' tour in Amman and that morning he had decided it was enough. So, as he told it to us, he packed his bag, walked into Ambassador John Phillips's office and said: 'I just thought I'd say cheerio. I'm off!' I never did discover whether Bill received a medal for his brave service but no one deserved it more.

We took the back way to the airport because the Palestinians still controlled the main road through the centre. There were more white flags flying now but our army driver was not certain whether they were signs of surrender or neutrality. He did not think anyone showing themselves in a Palestinian area would live long. As we climbed the last hill we were blocked by three Jordanian Saracen armoured cars. Snipers were hidden in a house higher up. Paul left the jeep and filmed the Saracens' guns blasting an area two hundred yards up the hill and two hundred yards across it – stick and clay houses crumpling and tiny white flags spinning in the air. One, two or three snipers to be killed and a hundred and more houses destroyed, and who was there to care how many people, how many families, had been hiding inside.

We got to the airport in time to see the last evacuees step into the jet. The steps were just about to be pulled away when a mortar bomb landed. Then came a second about a hundred yards ahead of the plane and people came piling out again, running down the steps, men and women, many of them elderly, across the tarmac towards the main building, some vomiting and covering themselves in bile as the third, fourth and fifth mortars exploded in a wide circle around them.

A handful of young Palestinians, sitting in a foxhole somewhere out there in the sand, were playfully reminding us they had yet to make up their own minds whether the war was over or not.

All this time, the men hostages, hidden in a small room of a small house built of clay in the Wahdat Palestinian camp, were waiting too. For nine days and nights they had listened to the war going on around them, not knowing who was winning or losing, or whether they would survive long enough to see the victor.

On the Friday morning, Major Fawkes Potts was up early. 'I looked out of the tiny opening in our cell that passed as a window and saw that some of the Palestinian commandos were giving themselves up. Others were running away over the hill. So we decided we shouldn't try to break out but wait and see who came for us next. We were praying it would be the Jordanians. The Swissair captain asked me if I knew any suitable expressions and I gave him a few four-letter words but that's not what he had in mind. He thought we ought to have something ready if the army turned up. So I told them to shout out "INGLEEZ" – it didn't matter whether they were Swiss – we couldn't go through that rigmarole. Then all of a sudden one of the Swiss chaps started shouting "INGLEEZ . . . INGLEEZ . . ." and he stuck a grotty white handkerchief out of the window. Somebody threw a grenade. I don't know whether it was meant for us or not but it went off close enough. Then the door opened and we were up and out. There was a tough little Bedouin soldier and when he saw me he flung his arm around me and kissed me. We started running down the alleyways, the soldier in front shouting, "Stop . . . Go . . . Stop . . . Go . . .", until we came to a command post with a Jordanian major. He told us he hadn't known we were there – the little Bedouin had found us by accident. I just couldn't believe it.'

In the Intercontinental, I could hear the strains of 'Lillibullero' from the cellar to the roof. And the cheering! Yasser Arafat had agreed to stop fighting. The radio reported his announcement word for word: 'As supreme commander of the Palestinian revolutionary forces . . . to save further bloodshed and for the wounded to be cared for . . . I ask my brothers to observe the cease-fire.'

We did not know it then and the mass of Palestinian commandos – filthy, bleeding and exhausted in their dugouts at the end of their failed revolution – could not have known it either, but Arafat had broadcast his message of defeat from Damascus, a hundred miles away. At the beginning of the fighting he had taken shelter in the Algerian Embassy and had escaped from Amman dressed as a woman.

I slept in my room that night for the first time in eight days. It was cold and I woke early, shivering and hungover from the evening of canned beers that had suddenly appeared for sale in the bar at an astonishing price from a smiling barman. The sweat was damp and sticky on me and my legs and back ached. All at once I felt a casualty.

The fighting outside had stopped. The occasional sniper's bullet whined across the waste ground towards the carpark but none of the Bedouin moved. I could see from the glow in the sky that parts of the city were still burning though they were probably old fires that no one dared to put out.

I edged my way to the window and looked over the sill. The cold air coming in through the broken panes smelt of cordite and charcoal and, oddly enough, tobacco. Then, as the first rays of the sun hit the rooftops one of the king's men ran to the side of the carpark, shouting, as if he wanted to be the first to announce the peace. He was young and bearded and when he got to the gates he pulled himself up on to one of the pillars and waved his rifle, still shouting loudly. Then he was cut in two. Many times since I have wondered if I imagined it but it always reappears in my mind's eye, unchanging. The soldier was suspended in mid-air, jumping two feet off the pillar, when heavy machine-gun bullets split him apart. And I saw daylight in between.

I expected an immediate bombardment and lowered my head, but nothing happened and when I looked again I saw why. The machine-gunner, a lone Palestinian far away from the main fighters, was walking slowly towards the carpark, his hands spread across his chest. He was young and bearded too and might easily have been the other's brother. Near the gates he stopped, not more than twenty yards from the man he had just killed, and went down on his knees to face the sun and pray. As his head touched the tarmac it exploded to pulp. We were just into the first daylight hour of the cease-fire but I knew he would not be the last to die in Amman that day. Nor the last to die praying.

At eleven forty-five that Saturday morning we watched and filmed as a military convoy came slowly up the hill towards Amman airport: four Ferret armoured cars, two Saracen personnel carriers and bringing up the rear two jeeps carrying 50mm machine-guns. It crossed the tarmac and stopped, guns pointing outwards, close to a Middle Eastern Airlines Comet. The Saracens reversed slowly to the front steps leading up to the first-class cabin and the hostages ran up without looking back. It was over within seconds. At eleven-fifty, the Comet was climbing on its way to Cyprus. Twenty days after Leila Khaled had hijacked the first plane, the last hostages of Dawson's Field were on their way home.

The next morning, the twenty-seventh day of Black September, so was I. Before I left I was asked to pay my bill in full at the Intercontinental Hotel. Service was charged at the usual ten per cent.

CHAPTER THREE

India – Pakistan,
March–December 1971

'Shoot Indians from Paradise'

PAKISTAN MEANS The Land of the Pure, Dr Mohammed Jinnah's sanctuary for Asia's Muslims, safe and separate from India's Hindus. In 1971 it split in two and the atrocities committed by one part on the other can be compared to Hitler's Holocaust, Stalin's Great Purge, and Pol Pot's Year Zero. What the West Pakistanis under the direction of Generals Yahya Khan and Tikka Khan did then to the Bengalis in the East was recorded in detail at the time. Yet unlike their greater masters in genocide, the Khans' atrocities, so callously and casually arranged, have been forgotten, and even condoned by some.

October 1970: A chilled beer, a hot damp perfumed face-towel monogrammed PIA, a handful of cashew nuts and India thirty-five thousand feet below me, a vast brown and tan landscape, one thousand miles of it from Islamabad to Dacca, dividing the two Pakistans, East from West. Pakistan International Airways was about the only thing the two halves had in common.

I was on my way to East Pakistan. For more than three hours I watched India pass below me, an endless arid desert where no one lived. Ahead, a cyclone had hit the Ganges delta and the news agencies were reporting enormous casualties. My foreign desk had dithered about whether I should go or not. Perhaps the death toll was simply not believable. Perhaps noughts had mistakenly been added somewhere along the six-thousand-mile telex journey from

Dacca to Europe; perhaps it was just another charity organisation's hyperbole to get the aid chain into motion again.

The final count of the dead was never officially agreed. Possibly it was never compiled. Who knew how many people lived in the Bay of Bengal? But it was said that the winds that brought the swollen waters of the Ganges and the Brahmaputra to the sea drowned upwards of two hundred thousand people. They were to kill all over again, because once the waters subsided, out of the silt and debris, like a sodden phoenix, rose the Bengali nation. Maybe it would have happened another way sooner or later and maybe even peacefully, but the year after those October winds, a new flag was flying over Dacca and people who had once only dared whisper it would be shouting at the tops of their voices, JOI BANGLA, JOI BANGLA - LONG LIVE BANGLADESH.

That cyclone might have healed the rift between East and West Pakistan had the Westerners shown the slightest interest in their other half's suffering. But their indifference was monumental. President General Yahya Khan could not afford the time to fly east to witness it, the Pakistan navy did not send ships to search for survivors and tons of grain sat in warehouses as Pakistani Air Force helicopters which could have delivered it remained on their pads. The response of international charities and governments and the delivery of their aid was rapid, but once it arrived in Dacca its distribution was casual. We, who were there, reported that much of it was purloined and sold on the black market by senior government officials and generals who were already millionaires.

Corruption, incompetence – and worse, indifference – was how the West Pakistani government reacted to the catastrophe. Yahya Khan, one thousand miles away in his splendid palace in Islamabad, later rebuked me in a critical interview. To my question, 'How will you deal with the theft of international aid to the flood victims?' he snapped back, 'My government is not made of angels.'

General Agha Mohammed Yahya Khan was an impatient, contemptuous and resentful man with the typical military attitude that the only people you could trust were your fellow-officers. He was a former army chief of staff who was pushed into the presidency two years before by another dictator, Field-Marshal Ayub Khan, grown weary of ruling a discontented people. When he handed over power to Yahya it seemed that parliamentary democracy might be about to be installed, but Yahya decided not. After all, a return to civilian rule would threaten the military's power and perks and the Punjabis have a saying, 'A general galloping is slow to dismount.' So Yahya continued Ayub's iron fist regime. In my interview with him he said cockily, 'I owe the people nothing. They did not bring me to power. I brought myself.'

Because of the cyclone, a general election due to have been held in November was postponed until December. It was the first national election East and West Pakistan had had since the country's independence twenty-three years before and the results shocked the West because the Easterners voted for one man. His name was Sheikh Mujib Rahman, leader of the Awami League. It was not what President Khan and his coterie had anticipated. It surprised even Mujib, and he overplayed his hand. The election was not a mandate to rule – it was simply the beginning of a plan to set up a constitutional assembly. But Mujib insisted instead that there should be a new constitution to give East Pakistan a degree of autonomy which would have led to the disintegration of Pakistan. It was an outlandish plan and Mujib lost the support of the only civilian politician whose help was needed to make the national assembly work – Zulfiqar Ali Bhutto. Bhutto, as dismayed as Khan by the election result and playing his own politics, withdrew his support for the national assembly and sulked. The process of democratisation was in tatters. Mujib feared a double-cross. In a speech in Dacca he said, 'A million of our people have died and suffered in the cyclone. Another million may need to make the supreme sacrifice so that we should be free.'

Suddenly, Mujib was the prophet, the catalyst. He was not in any sense a revolutionary, but Bengali nationalism, simmering for so long, crystallised around him. That December he declared a national strike in East Pakistan and it was total. The country was paralysed. To Mujib in Dacca it was simply a token of civil disobedience, Gandhi-fashion, to protest at what he considered political promises broken. To General Yahya Khan in Islamabad, it was a declaration of war.

*

71

In the spring of 1971 Mujib was preparing a new campaign of civil disobedience. I flew a second time to Karachi, expecting to connect again with the PIA flight to Dacca. I waited ten days in Karachi. Every morning and every afternoon I went to the PIA office to ask for three tickets on the Dacca flight. The answer was always the same: flights were fully booked. But why, when there was a flight scheduled every day, virtually a long-distance shuttle, were the Boeings full? I went to the airport to see who were filling the planes, who were suddenly flocking to that Eastern city few in the West would ever dream of visiting. From the terminal building I could see the Boeing 707s with the PIA insignia, parked on the aprons. I counted seven; their engine cowls were off, steps were at the open doors and military guards stood under each wing and at the nose and tail. There were no passengers, yet the check-in desk confirmed that all flights to Dacca were fully booked.

I should have dallied a half-hour longer at Karachi airport that day; I should have been just a little more inquisitive, a little more suspicious.

My taxi left the airport road just as the first lorry of a military convoy passed. That in itself was not unusual; there were barracks at both ends of the city. But, unknown to me, those trucks were full of clean-shaven, spruce young men in neat civilian suits and highly-polished boots, two divisions of soldiers, the 9th and 16th, on the move. They had been brought by train from their camps at Kharian and Multan, carrying only their battle-packs and light rations. Their weapons and ammunition were being flown separately by military air transport C-130s. They were the passengers in PIA's commandeered Boeings, the first of General Yahya Khan's shock-troops, about to invade East Bengal to cower and colonise by slaughter. It was, in Yahya's own words, spoken publicly, 'The Final Solution'!

General Tikka Khan – no relation to the president – was the military commander in the East. He was known as 'Red Hot' Khan, also as the 'Bomber of Baw Chistaw', because in 1965 in that town he had cold-bloodedly ordered the massacre of over a thousand people. His own favourite name for the eighty million Bengalis, whose safety and well-being were his official concern, was *'macchar'*, the Urdu for 'mosquito'. At one diplomatic reception he was heard to say, loudly and laughingly, 'The *macchar* whine, they irritate, and when you squash them they bleed.' That then was Tikka Khan's brief: to squash the Bengalis until they bled.

In March 1971 he ordered his tanks to destroy the so-called hot-beds of Bengali nationalism. They crashed through the narrow streets of Dacca, blasting houses, schools and hospitals. Men, women and their children were shot by troops who set up machine-guns on the pavements, and flame-throwers set fire to the square miles of wooden shack slums. Students at Dacca University were herded on to the football field and a single machine-gun sprayed bullets, killing line after line of them. Their heads were later found rotting on the roof of their hostel, Iqbal Hall, but the torsos were never found. Weeks later there was still a foul, sickening smell everywhere, even though the floors were covered in DDT powder. The walls were pitted with bullet holes and streaked with blood, despite hasty attempts to wash them clean.

Senior officers carried lists of those to be killed; individual Hindus and Muslims, Awami Leaguers, students, doctors, lawyers, any who had been or could be supporters of Mujib. Men were stripped of their *lungis* and if they were circumcised, they survived; if they were not, they died.

We assumed that Sheikh Mujib was among the first to be killed, but he was taken prisoner to Mianwali, a Western garrison, until he could be tried by a military court for treason. General Yahya had already delivered the verdict. 'The Beast of Bengal', he said, 'will be hung by the neck'. Of the Bengalis he said, emulating his devoted Tikka Khan, 'The mosquitoes are being taught a lesson. If some of them are dying, put it down to national unity!' A British diplomat stationed in Islamabad sent a letter to London that day. He wrote, 'There is only one man who can save Pakistan now and that is Sheikh Mujib. Yahya says he will hang him. The day he does, this entire bloody country hangs with him.'

The terror and slaughter spread well beyond Dacca. It was relent-less and it was methodical. Soldiers were not on a rampage out of control, crazed with blood, roaming at will; they were disciplined units killing to order, who were allowed to rape and sodomise as a daily reward for their thoroughness. Much was recorded in his

notebook by a Bengali journalist, and found with his rotting body
and his belongings many months later.

A young mother was hiding with fifty other villagers in
the cover of a jute field as an army patrol passed close by
to them. Her six-month-old baby son began to cry in her
arms. To save herself and the others, she strangled him.

An old man had hidden his two teenage daughters deep
in the jungle and smuggled food and water to them daily.
Soldiers heard of it and of how beautiful the girls were, so
they tricked the man into believing that there was an
amnesty to all families who returned to their homes and
to their land. Trusting, the man brought his daughters
from their hideouts and when he got to his village the
soldiers were waiting. A dozen and more raped the girls,
forcing the man to watch; then they ripped the girls'
breasts off with a specially-fashioned knife.

Assembling the young men at the village of Haluaghat in
East Pakistan, the West Pakistani army major told them
that his wounded soldiers urgently needed blood. Would
they be donors? The young men lay down in makeshift
straw cots, needles were inserted into their veins and
blood was pumped out of them until they were empty
and died.

Little by little, one by one, the stories filtered back to those of us
who could relay them to the world – but to a world already so jaded
by a diet of death and calamity that at first it received them with a
curious disbelief. We filmed so much of it: Chittagong's busy, buzzing Hizari Lane reduced to rubble, shopkeepers and shoppers
buried beneath; the vast central bazaar in Jessore blasted by tanks
to a bloody mess of mangled bodies and twisted metal; Kushtia, a
town of forty thousand people, looking like the morning after a
nuclear attack.

Others with greater clout contributed evidence. Senator Edward
Kennedy disclosed the contents of a confidential cable sent by a US
diplomat in Pakistan describing the extent of terror and slaughter.
The World Bank, which was helping to pay for the weapons,

received its own secret report which spoke of the devastation in the East as reminiscent of the second world war.

Yet America, like Britain and the rest of Europe, remained serenely oblivious. Governments so publicly and self-righteously concerned with *single* human rights violations could not focus on violation on such a massive scale, just as our fathers could not believe Belsen. The lack of world interest encouraged West Pakistan to believe that it could get away with murder as long as it was kept domestic.

A West Pakistan journalist on a Karachi newspaper was taken by the West Pakistani army to the region of operations. Later, haunted and disgusted by what he had seen, he fled Pakistan and in June 1971 he reported in the London *Sunday Times*:

'We got an old man,' the officer said. 'The bastard had grown a beard and was posing as a devout Muslim. He even called himself Abdul. But we gave him a "medical inspection" and the game was up. I wanted to finish him there and then but my men told me such a bastard deserved three shots. So I gave him one in the balls, one in the stomach and after a while finished him off with one in the head.'

How could we who were there conceive so much brutality amid so much beauty? The yellow-coloured jute fields and the dark, lush, dripping jungle at their edges, the soil so fertile that vegetation sprouted at the drop of a seed. There were great green carpets of rice paddies from horizon to horizon and, between, splashes of bright red *gol moher*, the 'flame of the forest', in full bloom; there were mango, banana and coconut trees heavy with fruit and festooned with flocks of multicoloured birds. There was everything except man. I was in the most crowded part of the world and suddenly it was empty; the Bengalis had left and those who had not got away in time remained. But where? Look at the slight mounds of earth where nothing grew and, if you had the nerve and the irreverence, kick away the topsoil. Look into the ditches and part the weeds and creepers with a stick and peer at the white things showing through the dirt. Follow your nose to the crumpled mass of houses and wonder why there was everywhere such a sweet and sickly stench and why the dogs lay panting in the heat, their stomachs swollen.

Even those who had escaped were now dying elsewhere, in rivers and on countless jungle paths as East Bengal haemorrhaged into India. Fifty thousand refugees a day were leaving from Bihal North, all the way down the border to Calcutta, endless wretched despairing columns of women carrying their children, men carrying their crippled fathers or mothers, families hauling their cardboard-box and plastic-sheet homes, kettles and cooking pots, trudging barefoot through the monsoon rain, the yellow mud sucking at their feet, their eyes unblinking, seeing only a yard ahead of them.

The monsoon did not bring relief from the heat and dust. It brought instead cholera, pneumonia, dysentery, diphtheria. The sick sat down when they could no longer walk, and died when they no longer wanted to live. Many had been walking for a month or more, leaving their families dead behind them. I was told that whenever they could the Hindus placed a hot cinder into the mouths of their dead, or singed the body in lieu of cremation. We filmed them until there was no point in filming more, the same unending shuffling queue coming from terror to nothing, looking for shelter, looking for food – and finding none. I wrote that they were so exhausted and so despairing that no one, not even the children, bothered to cry any more.

The little boy was about three years old, his mother no more than sixteen or so. They sat in the mud in a drainage ditch below the road level, he in her lap. The skin on his face was stretched, with a yellow tinge, his stomach was distended, his feet swollen, his arms no thicker than my thumb. She held his tiny chin with one hand and in the palm of the other was a tiny mound of boiled rice. She tried to put it into his mouth, turning his chin with her fingers to make him chew. He stared at her wide-eyed, puzzled. Finally, he swallowed, convulsed, and then died. For a little while longer she held him. Then she dropped him beneath her knees and buried him in the yellow mud between her feet.

By the middle of that summer of 1971 the pogrom was complete. The East had been tamed, and President Yahya Khan was pleased. It had all been so neat and final in the best military tradition and he sent his congratulations to his brother-in-arms, Tikka Khan, with the rider: 'We must be absolutely sure that, having undertaken such a job, we have finished it. We can't keep going back every few years. Let's be certain that now this is done we shall never need to return again.' This is how I reported it to ITN:

Dacca, East Pakistan, 3 July 1971:
There is a great deal of tension and fear still in Dacca. The city where a million and a half people once lived is half-empty. Normally at this time of day the pavements and roads would be crowded and choked with traffic. More than half of the city's shops stay closed and even now obey a strict self-imposed curfew; open at nine, close two hours before dusk. It is generally thought not to be safe at any other time. What is extraordinary is that unless I had been here before, in pre-civil war times, that is, it would be difficult to appreciate the total damage. The authorities have applied cosmetics. Shell-holes have been plastered over, partly damaged buildings screened off with corrugated sheets. Other buildings, long demolished, are now overgrown with grass. They might not have existed at all. The army has totally destroyed areas where Hindus and Awami League supporters were known to live. What was once the largest and oldest Hindu temple, the Rmana temple, was being finally demolished by the bulldozers as we filmed. Nothing remains of the four-storey offices of *Iteafaq*, the popular Bengali newspaper. The machines and the men who worked them were hit first by army mortars, then they and their offices were set alight. Wide areas have been flattened and only the hard mud foundations remain to remind you of the hundreds of houses that once stood, and the thousands of families who once lived here. The green-and-white flag of Pakistan is everywhere. Every house flies one; it is pinned on almost everyone's breast and flutters from almost every means of transport. It is a mark of loyalty first, I was told, and the badge of safe conduct. No one believes either. The Pakistan government says things are returning to normal. It is my impression things are not.

Quickly Yahya Khan began to 'cleanse' the East. Bengalis were to be re-educated, there was to be strict Islamisation of the masses and confiscated Hindu property would be used as a bait to win over the

Bengali poor middle class, the box-wallahs. There was to be no further recruitment of Bengalis into the armed forces or police. Bengali pilots in the air force and PIA were grounded; banks, businesses and industries were to be cleared of Bengalis. Hundreds of West Pakistanis were to be sent to the East: doctors, nurses, teachers, technicians and propagandists for radio and television. A new law made it possible for civil servants in the West to be transferred quickly to the East without their families for an indefinite period. The colonisation of the East was to be absolute. And that, said Yahya Khan, was that.

He was wrong. It was only the beginning. But, sitting in his splendid palace in Islamabad, how could he have known? Who was to tell him that in the dense Madhupur jungles, in the swamps and riverways of the Ganges and the Brahmaputra, a new name was being whispered? How could he have gauged the potential of the men and boys who were moving silently across East Bengal in the night, recruiting, assembling, training, dispersing, sabotaging and killing, a guerrilla army of liberation, the Mukti Bahini?

The cities and surrounding countryside had become a network of its willing collaborators. A piece of paper would sometimes be slipped under the door of my hotel room or placed beneath the covers of my bed, or on the tray of the early-morning cup of tea: closely-mimeographed information sheets, obviously written by a Bengali journalist in hiding, telling us of guerrilla successes, the number of West Pakistanis killed, the number of sabotaged railway lines, the weapons seized. The street boys of Dacca who came running up to sell the government-controlled daily newspaper would slip the same war reports between the pages and wink as they took my coins. On ferryboats, strangers manoeuvred close and, with an eye on the watchful soldiers in the wheelhouse, indicated with a nudge and a nod what village or part of the jungle on the riverbank belonged to the 'liberators'. Before they moved away they would whisper the same plea: 'Please tell the people outside what's happening: please let them know.' In my diary I wrote, 'Is this what it was like travelling in Nazi Germany among the Jews?'

Soon we no longer had to depend on the hotel room boys and the newspaper sellers or the chance traveller to find out what was happening. Soon the guerrilla successes were known to everyone. They sabotaged the bridges and ferries to stop the movement of West Pakistani troops. They blew up the main rail artery between the capital and the port of Chittagong and ambushed the parallel roads. Nowhere was safe for Yahya's men. At first the Mukti Bahini moved only by night. Then, more confidently, they attacked by day, with direct lines of information through informants in the government offices, the post office, the military headquarters. More and more of the countryside became theirs, a countryside ideal for such an army – so like Vietnam's Mekong Delta governed by the Vietcong – a labyrinth of secret hidden waterways, sunken rice paddies, forest and banana groves. Like the Vietcong, the Mukti Bahini had the support of the people, who fed them and hid them, provided intelligence, carried their messages and their weapons: people willing at last to risk their lives and play their part. Back in June the villagers in Moakhali province had pleaded with the guerrillas not to blow up a bridge nearby, for fear of military reprisal. Now, in July, they were asking to be taught how to blow the bridge themselves.

There is that moment when conflict moves into limbo, sideways into a timewarp. Like a children's game of statues, the music stops and everyone stands perfectly still. So it was in East Pakistan, and so it continued for some months, an emotional and political vacuum, a country half-emptied of its people, drained. The spring and summer of slaughter had exhausted themselves and now, in early autumn, there was a pause as life marked time. Come the winter, the killings would begin all over again.

I left Dacca and, except for a short visit to Calcutta to report on the refugees and their hateful camps, did not return to Asia until November. Throughout that autumn of 1971, only fragments of information trickled out of Pakistan: four-line stories on the foreign pages, an article in an obscure Asian digest, snatched comment from the BBC World Service.

What had happened to a country which had seemed ready to explode? Where was Sheikh Mujib? Why had he not been tried and hanged, as General Yahya had promised? What had happened to the army of liberation? Where was liberated Bangladesh?

A television news story has a curve of diminishing utility that can be very sheer indeed, and Pakistan's tragedy had slid right off the graph. But now it was on my mind again because I was in South-east Asia reporting Cambodia and, having finished my tour, I suggested to London that I come home via Pakistan to see what was going on. However, it is generally held by correspondents of their editors, that they cannot contemplate more than one story at a time and then only if it is no further than the end of their nose. So it was, and I left Phnom Penh, capital of Cambodia, for London. Within a fortnight I was back in Dacca. I recorded:

Dacca, East Pakistan, 21 November 1971:
The Army has moved out of Dacca to areas close to the border with India. Every house still flies the green-and-white flag of Pakistan. Many are torn by the wind, many more are bleached by the sun and rain, but nobody seems anxious to hoist replacements. They are digging trenches in and around the city's boundary, to save people – they tell me – from possible Indian air attacks. The Indian threat is a reality. Indian soldiers captured this week were shown to us and we were told they belong to the Nagar Regiment and had been caught two miles inside Pakistan.

The two neighbours were preparing for war. Indira Gandhi, India's prime minister, was ready to grasp the moment and exploit it to her nation's advantage. My 21 November report was screened on the night that Mrs Gandhi arrived back in Delhi after her tour of Europe and the United States. She had gone to the separate heads of government to appeal for aid to support the millions of Bengali refugees now in India, and to seek promises that the West would impose its own political solution on Pakistan. She returned to Delhi empty-handed, but with her mind made up. If the world would not bring peace to Pakistan, she would. Unknown to those she had been pleading with in London, Paris, Bonn and Washington, her guns were already in place and her forward infantry poised.

Hilli, East Pakistan, 27 November:
The exchange of fire at Hilli started on Thursday and in the three days since, an estimated two hundred to three hundred men have died on both sides. According to Pakistani Intelli-

gence reports there are between ten and fourteen thousand Indian regulars strung along the twenty-mile border each side of Hilli and there cannot be more than two or three thousand Pakistanis to defend it. It is generally agreed that in the event of a major prolonged offensive the Pakistani troops could not expect to hold out for more than a week or so.

The war had barely begun and already I was in trouble. A few days before, after whispered conversations, followed by a meeting in the hotel lobby with a mystery man whose face was hidden behind a newspaper, a night rendezvous was arranged for my cameraman and me with a unit of the Mukti Bahini. Suddenly my Norwegian cameraman developed pains in his stomach so acute that he left the next day on, as it happened, the last flight out of Dacca for a fortnight.

My freelance Punjabi helper, Daud Subhani, ever anxious, ever keen, ever friendly, never consistent, said he knew of a local cameraman and we hired him. But in filming the story from Hilli under mortar fire, our freelance, who was called Hassim, ran one way, we the other; the camera was tugged off his shoulder and the lens was snapped. From that day on Jacques Chaudensen, my Paris sound recordist, became cameraman and Daud the occasional recordist. My working association with Hassim had lasted only one day but it was to save his life.

Jessore, 1 December:
In the twilight land between Jessore and India the Pakistanis have begun digging in. They seem happy at the prospect of a fight and not put out in the least by the fact that they have no adequate back-up. I saw no Pakistani tanks and no one pretended there were any here. If the Indians make a push for Jessore, they could do it in less than a day. It is all very pastoral and tranquil and everyone seems rather nonchalant.

On the other side of the border, less than thirty miles away from me, British journalists were writing much the same. Henry Stanhope of *The Times* reported:

Thin cucumber sandwiches and tea from matching teacups greeted journalists on their first visit to the front. A unit of engineers from Bombay are guarding this frontier post with two wrought-iron gates that would do justice to any stockbroker's home in Surrey. They stand flung open on the dirty, dusty road to Jessore. Yet, while Indian soldiers stalk through the trenches, eyes flashing above bristling moustaches, a small girl with a coolie hat is picking flowers in the field.

Ed Behr, reporting for *Newsweek*, wrote:

All was quiet until suddenly a hail of shells sent us scampering to the bunkers, rudely interrupting the 'As I stand on the banks of the Tawi river' piece to camera by a CBS reporter. Indian shelling continued for some time and it was only later that I discovered that it had been caused, not as I suspected by the iridescent baby-blue outfit of a dashing Italian cameraman on our side, but by another CBS crew on the other side of the river. Intent on shooting war scenes, they had charmed the local Indian artillery commander into having a go.

But the farce was not to last. On 3 December Jacques and I were flown by helicopter to Comilla on the eastern border. This was the day the real war broke out.

We were shown Indian prisoners who had been captured the previous day along the main Chittagong to Comilla railway. Their senior officer was carrying secret documents, one a map codenamed 'Nutcracker', the other a plan for a concerted Indian attack, called 'Quicksilver'. We were shown the prisoners but we were not allowed to film them and I understood why. They had been interrogated and obviously tortured. Their faces were cut and bleeding and many could not stand because of what the interrogators had done either to their toenails or to their genitals.

That afternoon we went forward with the tanks, walking behind one of them like infantrymen, Jacques and I enjoying every second of it. It was all we had hoped for in filming terms and we knew that when the time came all that was needed was a request on the field telephone for a helicopter to whisk us away to safety. Then came the awesome dreadful whistle, seconds later the explosion, the zing of shrapnel and the searing panic as a man in khaki reeled back, red and bloody, not knowing which way to go and then falling dead, his eyes and his wounds wide open. Still new to war, it never occurred to me that it was possible to be shot and not see the enemy, to see his shells exploding but not see his guns. These shells were coming from nowhere and from a gun battery that could not even see us. We were simply a co-ordinate on a gunsight. Yet their shrapnel was tearing men apart.

Jacques and I spread ourselves flat in a shallow ditch and crawled slowly towards a culvert made from corrugated iron. We pushed our way in against the crouching bodies of Bengali families already squatting there, terrified, and we pushed hard – they would not give us room. They were hostile, blaming us, afraid that we would bring the shrapnel in after us. We waited, hoping to hear our tanks fire back, but they did not. What we heard instead was their engines revving as they turned about. They were pulling out. We got up and ran after them in panic and when we touched the tanks we felt safer as the shelling fell away behind us.

By nightfall we were back in Dacca, feeling very brave. Safely in my room, showered and shaved, with the filthy clothes shoved into a cupboard, drinking my first beer, I could not remember being afraid at all. I had been in danger and now that I was out of it I forgot my fear, as I would forget my promises never to do it again. It had all been washed away with the adrenalin, leaving only the filtered recollection of others' fear and others' deaths.

Déjà vu! A cackle of journalists, photographers and cameramen in a city under siege, the airport closed, power and water supplies cut, telephone and telex out of action, and sitting in the middle of a battle-to-be, in the Dacca Intercontinental Hotel. I was, as ever, in substantial company, eminent among them Donald Wise of the *Daily Mirror*, the doyen of British foreign correspondents, based in Hong Kong, Gavin Young of the *Observer*, Stephen Harper of the *Express*, John Humphrys of the BBC, on his first major foreign assignment, and Claire Hollingsworth of the *Daily Telegraph*, a cross between Margaret Rutherford and Miss Marple, always bustling, often bullying, exceptionally precise, a superb writer, and with more war experience and gung-ho than the rest of us put together.

The war was moving slowly towards us by land. Soon it would arrive dramatically and lethally by air. We had no choice but to stay put and wait for it and, given a bit of luck, we would sit it out until the Indians came and proclaimed their Bangladesh.

Every evening at about eight, after we had finished our meagre ration of curried chicken and rice, we congregated in the darkened ballroom, lit by five bulbs in a huge crystal chandelier where there should have been fifty. Tables around the dance floor had been laid for dinner a week ago and there was a grand piano on the parquet dance floor with sheet music open at 'Night and Day'. Here we waited for the military briefer to tell us what he imagined had happened that day. Like all propagandists, like all directors of corporate image, he believed his own inventions as he stood reporting West Pakistan's fictitious victories. Such briefings were followed by question-and-answer sessions remembered by us all thus:

Question: You say you killed five hundred Indians today. How is it you have no dead?
Answer: In our army we believe no one ever dies in battle. He goes straight to Paradise, so he is not dead.
Question: Can he still shoot Indians from Paradise?
Question: Is the Indian claim that they have a bridgehead at the Ganges true?
Answer: There is no bridge there so how can there be a bridgehead?

We called them the 'eight o'clock follies'. The writing press experienced a breakthrough in word manipulation, and they called it 'write-in' censorship. Instead of editing journalists' stories with blue pencil or scissors, the Pakistani censors were writing their own interpretation of the war and sending it with the reporters' copy, so that when it arrived in London or elsewhere the news desk assumed it was coming from their own man. One reporter wrote: 'Sheikh Mujib Rahman is imprisoned in West Pakistan.' But the story arrived to a puzzled news editor as 'The traitor Mujib, who is actually an Indian agent . . .' A *Washington Post* reporter received from his concerned editor: 'Assume your reference to *the so-called Bangla-desh, which is actually an Indian stunt* does not indicate that you are losing your objectivity!'

Television crews suffered in other ways. When we showed our camera out on the road there was inevitably a rifle shot and troops came running, prodding us, pushing us, demanding identification, authorisation. They always wanted a piece of paper with an official stamp. Sometimes we showed our British press cards or our passports or even a driving licence – anything official was enough to console them. Often the soldiers would demand to see our film. Knowing the drill well enough, Jacques would open the front of the magazine and offer them the unexposed roll which they then unrolled, carefully examined and gave back to us. Another cameraman, Roly Carter, covering the fighting in the west, was filming a railway when a major accused him of spying. He asked the sergeant for a revolver to shoot Carter, but the sergeant could not find a revolver and the major considered it beneath him to use a sergeant's rifle. Carter survived to film another day.

Telex and telephone communication was now impossible, so it was decided that the twenty or so correspondents should send a pooled despatch every day via the British Consulate's own radio links. We sat in a circle after supper, contributing our experiences, which were then condensed to two hundred words, and sent in convoluted cable-ese, unrecognisable as English and possibly therefore censor-free, to the Foreign Office in London. There it was duplicated and sent to each correspondent's office where it was deciphered and added to from press agency wires to make a fuller story.

Gavin Young of the *Observer*, a man of many elegant words, wrote:

> God knows what editors in London are making of the news they are getting from us in Dacca. Correspondents here are still receiving much-delayed cables from their offices asking where the stories are. One idiot editor even suggested that his correspondent sent copy out by plane. Doesn't he know the airport has been closed a week?

And the equally elegant *Daily Mirror* man, Don Wise, wrote: 'For the past ten days now I feel I have been shovelling fog into a bucket.'

There was a full moon. Jacques and I and the others stood on the roof of the hotel, high above the darkened city, silent and more than half-empty. We sipped bottles of warm beer in the warm night and somebody was smoking a cigar, giving the moment some sense of luxury.

It was an exceptionally brilliant night, the moon white and enormous, so that the houses and streets below us shone sharp and clear. Someone said, 'It's what they used to call, thirty years ago, a bomber's moon.' Ten minutes later we heard them, invisible, high above, piston-engined and coming slowly towards us. I remember putting my beer bottle very carefully on the roof as if someone might hear and I saw the tip of the cigar go over the parapet, glowing brightly as it fell.

Jacques whispered, 'Are they Indian bombers?' No one answered. They circled Dacca for fifteen minutes or more but we did not see them. Then their drone became fainter as they went westwards towards Calcutta. Again Jacques asked, out loud, 'Are they Indian bombers?' and someone answered, 'No, old lad, not tonight. They'll be coming tomorrow.' And they did.

Dacca, Saturday, 4 December:
The Indians made a number of high-level sorties during the night, presumably using the full moon to stake out their targets. In their first morning attacks it was clear that they were only interested in the civil airfield where the Pakistan Air Force had parked its Sabre Jet fighters. They came in low to avoid Dacca radar control and they used the early-morning sun to hide their approach. With few exceptions they didn't fire their cannons. There was little strafing. They concentrated instead on dive-bombing and firing rockets.

On that first day we counted nine separate runs in five hours of the attack and nine Indian aircraft went down. We saw two Pakistani aircraft destroyed. Early next morning Jacques and I were ready on the roof of the hotel, waiting for the jets to arrive. At 8.20 the first did: below us! The Pakistani jets engaged in dogfights with the

Indian Hunters and Gnats, only a few hundred yards away and a hundred feet below us. One strafed us and the blast took the air-conditioning unit away; the enormous fan spun off the roof and floated down like a sycamore seed to the road below.

It was as if we were at some exclusive air show where the aerobatics and the spectacular climbs and turns were meant for us alone . . . jets closing on each other, racing below, climbing, wheeling and soaring above. The sound of their cannon obliterated the ground's ack-ack fire but we saw puffs of brown smoke as the shells exploded around the aircraft. Then the first Indian plane was hit and careered out of the sky, spectacular, revolving slowly as if the pilot was displaying his aerobatic skills. But he was dead, or perhaps he was trapped, because no one ejected and there was no parachute in the sky as the machine crashed on the far side of the airfield. We filmed the ball of orange and the squat mushroom of black smoke and, all of three seconds later, there came the sound of the explosion. Then the sky was empty and the anti-aircraft batteries were silent. Except for the columns of smoke rising from the wrecks of three crashed aircraft, there was nothing. Jacques smiled and shook his wrist the way the French do.

The Indians came back that afternoon, and this time there was no one to stop them, in the air or on the ground. The Sukoy fighter bombers came so fast, they were over Dacca before the Pakistani pilots could scramble, and so low the ack-ack gunners did not even see them as they strafed and fired their rockets. Jacques and I stood in the carpark and filmed them coming directly at us, the tiny spurts of flame as their cannons fired, puffs of grey smoke as their rockets left the undersides of their wings, and the cracking explosions; then as they climbed into the sky we ran out on to the streets to film the burning targets and dash back before the next sortie. They came in waves of four aircraft every thirty minutes or so all afternoon, so regular and so unopposed that towards the end we stopped filming. It had become so much of the same.

That evening, black and oily with the soot of the fires, and smelling of dirty sweat, I stripped and sat naked in the few feet of dank water left in the swimming-pool. There was an empty wine bottle floating near me and at the far end a notice a week old offered the day's special of crayfish mayonnaise. There was a strict blackout and the curtains of every window on every floor were drawn. On the ground floor, by the flickering yellow light of paraffin lamps, I could see hotel boys shuffling by, carrying candles behind cupped hands. The water was warm and a sooty film moved away from my body like an oil slick. Something – water fleas or leeches – bit my ankle and then my bottom. Soon it would be suppertime – boiled rice and the same yellow chicken gristle. Gavin Young said he might even prefer, for a change, some boiled rat. Someone said he would arrange it. No more crayfish mayonnaise for a while. No more East Pakistan, ever. The war was now only two days old but none of us doubted how it would end. Only how long it would take to finish and how many of us would be among the casualties.

I had no supper that night. I even gave the military briefer a miss. To the question, 'How many Indian planes attacked Dacca today, and what were the casualties?' he would almost certainly have answered, 'What bombers? What casualties?'

I crossed the foyer to climb the stairs. Gavin Young was drooping at the piano, others were playing poker on its shiny black top. The press corps sprawled everywhere – tuning transistors, scribbling stories, smoking, snoozing. Gavin stopped playing and we listened. Outside, a long, long way off, we thought we heard just the faintest boom of artillery. That night, remembering Amman, I slept in the corridor with my mattress next to the bathroom wall.

The Indians were now reporting the capture of about a hundred and eighty square miles of East Pakistan territory and eight border towns. Their navy had completed its blockade of sea-routes to both East and West Pakistan and their air force had bombed the port of Cox's Bazaar, set the oil refinery at Chittagong on fire and raided eight airports in West Pakistan and four in the East, destroying thirty-three Pakistani aircraft. There were no tactical air strikes by the Pakistani air force.

The Indians continued their air attacks on Dacca throughout Sunday, Monday and Tuesday. On Wednesday we were taken to Maryanganj, a sprawling, dingy port eleven miles away. The Indians had bombed it the night before though no one could understand why: no Pakistan jets were there, no military camp, no police. The real target, we suspected, was the power station well over half a mile away, but their bombs had hit the sleeping centre of the town and beneath the bricks and mud and hot embers, four hundred people had died.

Across the roof of the hotel our press committee stretched a huge red cross and put another on the lawn. We were now an international zone and West Pakistanis, believing there was more chance of being hacked to death on the streets than being bombed by the Indians, asked for asylum. Directed by our committee, we maintained our own sentries at the gate, insisted on passports and searched each person and their luggage as they came through. We did not want guns inside. If, come the day, the Bengalis wanted the Pakistanis, we would not defend them nor would we allow them to defend themselves with rifles and revolvers. Or, as we discovered in one suitcase, half a dozen hand-grenades.

Bombing at night is a deadly, random thing and the Indian bombers did not have the sophisticated equipment to direct their high explosives with any accuracy. At four o'clock on the Thursday morning the droning of a plane woke us up. It was much lower than any we had heard before; perhaps the pilot was trying to find his target by moonlight. Some believed he was after the railway terminal, others that he was going for the airport. He hit neither. We heard the explosions but it was too dark to see the smoke, and because of the dusk-to-dawn curfew there was no way of leaving the hotel. So we went to the roof and sat it out, waiting for first light.

The bombs had hit a boys' orphanage at Farmgate along the airport road and had killed more then three hundred of them as they slept in their dormitories. By the time we got there, only eleven bodies had been found and they were laid out under a thatched lean-to. Members of staff squatted in a circle around them weeping, rocking backwards and forwards on their heels in silent mourning. The other children, or what remained of them as human forms, were enveloped in a hideous mudcake. The craters were twenty yards across and at least twenty feet deep. Jacques did not film much of it; there was not much he could film that could ever be shown and there were no acceptable communicable words I could use to describe the scattered carnage in those ghastly pits already filling with water. I wondered what the pilot felt when the news of his bombing was broadcast to the world. Was he a father? Did he have sons? Did he ever see the photographs, and, if he did, did they haunt him? It is said that the B-52 pilots and bombardiers who dropped their millions of tons of high-explosive over North Vietnam did not suffer remorse or guilt when the enormous casualty figures were eventually disclosed. They had simply dropped their bombs into the unknown from fifty thousand feet: not on towns with families, but on maps with co-ordinates. Maybe there is an inverse equation: the higher the casualties, the less the individual guilt. Does the bombardier sleep nights while the wretched sniper counts his kills in nightmares?

Diary. 7 December 1971:
We have had our own bomb alert. One has been found in the ladies' lavatory and none of us knows how to defuse it. It is problem enough, but more worrying is who put it there, and why. Is it meant for us, the press, or the Pakistanis here? Our committee of elders cannot decide whether we should order them to leave. We all voted on it and it's a close-run thing. I reckon if we find a second bomb the Paks will be out on their necks, though God knows how we'd shift them!

A scribble is added: 'We have had search parties all day looking for more bombs. It seems that we are stuck with one. Quite astonishing! Hotel manager has declared ladies' lavatory out of bounds because "it is unsafe".'

Diary. 8 December:
Bombing attacks incessant but the red crosses on the roof and lawn are working. We feel much safer in our Fortress Intercontinental. Odd but the city empties and then suddenly fills again. Families who live here have moved out to the safety of the villages but people are still coming in. Presumably they live in the areas of fiercest fighting around Comilla, Jessore, Kulna and Faridpur. Some are in rags, others well-dressed, carrying smart suitcases in garden wheelbarrows. One man with everything in a pram told me he was a railway booking clerk from Chittagong, said his wife and three children had walked all the way. Fourteen days but he was quite immaculate. His hair was brilliantined flat, his white shirt had a stiff clean starched collar, quite unmarked. How do they do it? We

interviewed him, shook hands and watched him, with his family trailing respectfully five yards behind, manoeuvre his pram gingerly around the unexploded 500-pounders that litter the airport road.

Diary. Saturday afternoon, 11 December:
We can plainly hear the distant sound of artillery in the southeast. The BBC World Service tells us that Indian units have completely encircled the city and have arrived in strength on the east bank of the Meghna river at Daudakhani, twenty miles away. We have no way of knowing. Don Wise's 'shovelling fog' is wonderful. It perfectly describes how we all feel. I want to jump off the roof. Bitterly disappointed. By some miracle London came through by telephone when everybody had thought the lines were down. It was John Mahoney [foreign editor]. So typical of him to get the only telephone call through this week. I could hear him perfectly but he couldn't hear a word of mine and I had so much to say, so much to tell him, I could have spoken for an hour and ITN would have used the lot. Imagine – exclusive report from beleaguered city!

Almost every day the writing journalists were still somehow managing to get their two-hundred-word pooled despatch out by radio from the British Consulate. It was little enough compensation for all the risks. But John Humphrys and I and the other international TV crews had spectacular war footage destined to remain in our hotel bedrooms until the war was over.

I visited the headquarters of the Pakistan air force. I had made a friend there, who told me the pilots were flying a few planes out every night into Rangoon in Burma, a few hundred miles across the border. That evening I asked a pilot if he would take a suitcase of film out on the next flight, and we would somehow arrange with our various offices to pick it up. It seemed to me a clever little plan, and though not everyone agreed to it, some who were prepared to take the risk put their precious film cans into my suitcase.

But Murphy's Law, otherwise known as the Rule of Accelerating Cussedness, was operating massively that evening. The Indians sent their jet fighter-bombers in on an extra mission unexpectedly late and they made direct hits on the air force headquarters building, demolishing most of it. The planes for Rangoon did not take off. Many planes would never take off again and neither would many of the pilots.

Next morning I was on my hands and knees, searching through the rubble for my suitcase, never expecting to find it and certainly not in one piece. But I did, and it was intact. No one in the hotel was prepared to risk it again, but I was, and I did – and that night my pilot flew out, taking my film with him to what I thought was a world exclusive. With the next pooled dispatch I was allowed to add a service message to ITN, who immediately sent David Phillips (of Dawson's Field fame) to Burma to collect. He never did. My film was impounded by Burmese customs and they would not release it without government approval. It even went to cabinet for a decision but the Burmese government, sensitive to pressure from both India and Pakistan and keen not to offend either, decided the film should be kept under lock and key until the war was over. ITN even appealed to Lord Mountbatten, who it was thought still had some influence in the region, and he did make a request. But it was politely refused, and my film was not to be broadcast until a month after the war ended.

Diary. Dacca, 13 December:
We hear over BBC World Service – thank God for 'Lillibullero' – that the Royal Air Force is trying to bring in planes to evacuate foreigners, including about two hundred Brits here, families of embassy and companies. Someone should tell them that the airport is kaput. The Indians have been hammering it all week. It can't be there any more.

But it was – just! For some days the Foreign Office had been pressing the Indians to agree to a temporary cease-fire, long enough at least to stop the air attacks and give RAF aircraft time to pick up the evacuees, about five hundred civilians in all. Mrs Gandhi eventually agreed but only on condition that the Royal Air Force flew its planes to India first and returned again to India after they had left Dacca. She did not want prominent Pakistanis escaping. The Brits agreed. They would fly their planes first and last into Calcutta's Dum Dun airport. But the Pakistanis said no. They would not allow any aircraft that had landed in India to land in Pakistan. It was all seen as a cruel charade, disguising Pakistan's real intention to keep foreigners in Dacca as a negotiating chip for the final showdown when it came. But the Indians and Pakistanis were finally persuaded to allow the evacuation and that morning, Monday, the gangly British Embassy second secretary, looking every bit the British actor Richard Wattis, came to the hotel and asked us if we would help repair the airstrip. He reckoned the craters could be filled in and the tarmac generally 'tidied up', so that the Hercules transport planes could land.

With shovels and bare hands and stripped to our underpants, we laboured all that morning, putting the concrete back in place as best we could, while Pakistani officers watched us, enjoying our labours and frustrations, pointing with their swagger-sticks or shouting with their affected Sandhurst accents at any stone we had missed. We finished with less than thirty minutes to go before the cease-fire was due to begin at one o'clock. The Hercules had been given half an hour to land, load and take off. At one-thirty the sky would be at war again. As the evacuees came off the buses which brought them from their various assembly points an American strode up to the British Embassy secretary, bawling. The conversation went something like this:

American to bespectacled Brit, encircled by evacuees: 'Are you responsible for this ass-brained kamikaze crap?'

Brit: 'If you mean am I looking after the evacuation, yes.'

American: 'Mass murder, you mean.'

Brit: 'Our aircraft will be landing shortly and will take off again. I am confident of that.'

The American doesn't identify himself but he gives the impression he knows something of bombed airfields and C-130s. 'We built the goddammed aircraft. We should know. There's no way you'll get them in here.'

The Brit lifts his nose to the sky, perhaps sniffing for the first scent of the planes: 'I am sure that's something we should leave to those who know best.'

American: 'If you get them down you'll not get them up again.'

Brit nods and inclines almost sympathetically. 'I'm sure you mean well. But I think we should leave the decision to our pilots. They're very good, you know. I am told they're the world's best.'

American (quite beside himself): 'You'll not get me on!'

Brit: 'I'm delighted to hear it.'

With that, our bespectacled hero strode off towards the edge of the battered runway, with hundreds of people in a column – men, women and their children – following behind. He was Dacca's own Pied Piper.

We all stood there solemnly in a square about a hundred yards back from the runway. No one said a word. Even the children were quiet. Everyone was listening. Faces looked at the sky on all points of the compass, eyes and ears searching. It was ten minutes to one o'clock, ten minutes to see the specks, wait for them to grow larger, wait for them to circle, wait for them to decide: yes or no. At five minutes past one – I know because I have a nervous habit of looking at my watch at critical times – three Hercules dropped out of the blue. No one saw them first, we all seemed to spot them together and the cheer was deafening. They came towards us very slowly, so slowly that they seemed almost hovering and very low, so low we could see the pilots' faces peering out looking at the runway, deciding in those few seconds whether they could or could not come down. I remember every detail of that moment. Five hundred anxious people, surrounded by war, not expecting it, not prepared for it, more and more frightened as it closed in every day around them, fearing the prospect that, victory or defeat, the orgy of bloodletting might involve them all.

'I saw him waggle his wings!' Michel Laurent, the Associated Press photographer, said to me.

'I didn't see a thing,' I said.

'Yes,' Michel said. 'The middle plane, he waggled. That means victory.'

'Not a bloody thing,' I said again. But Michel was right.

When sun heats the air distant images become distorted. So it was then. They came towards us, mirage-like, thin and black and shimmering as if they were not entirely whole, and so slowly they appeared to be hesitating. Then, seconds later, they were vast and roaring and landing, their wheels on the runway and not an inch wasted. They shuddered as their propellers went into reverse pitch, blue smoke spewed from their wheels as their tyres skidded to a stop. Then they reversed, their back doors opened, their big empty bellies were exposed and down the ramps came the loading masters beckoning, shouting, but people needed no encouragement and they ran as fast as they could, dragging their wives, children and hand luggage behind them. One child broke free from her mother and went back to pick up her own tiny suitcase.

One person could not run. She could hardly walk. She was the fiancée of the American ABC reporter. He was sending film out with her and, panicked by reports that the Indians would confiscate any film in the planes once they had landed in Calcutta, he had taped his cans of film to the body of his girlfriend with thick adhesive; six cans, three strapped to the inside of each thigh. He reckoned the Indians would not dare place a hand there. Like a robot, painfully and stiff-legged, she walked slowly to the plane and her freedom.

Within ten minutes everyone was aboard and safely strapped in. The Hercules reversed farther, back to the very edge of the concrete. The twenty or so of us who remained crossed our fingers and those who thought it would help said their prayers. The aircraft shook violently again as their engines went to full power, then the brakes were released, and they jumped down the runway, lumbering, bouncing and dipping as they ran over our repairs, and far, far too slow it seemed, as they got closer to the bomb craters, still not airborne, and everyone willing them up. Then, in a blink, they were climbing, suddenly silhouetted against the blue, and I remember we clapped – ragged, half-naked, dirty journalists and cameramen looking at the sky, applauding with our blistered hands a wonderful moment of courage in a small paragraph of history.

We stood there a few minutes more until we lost them. It was twenty-five minutes past one and they had got away with five minutes of the cease-fire to spare! A siren sounded from the control tower, a signal for us to get out. As we reached the grass, we passed the pile of suitcases they hadn't been allowed to take, some with their contents strewn in a last-minute panic to retrieve something, others still neatly strapped and labelled. How incongruous the addresses seemed, written so neatly and expectantly: a house in suburban Surrey, another in Middlesex, like the luggage of a holiday package tour waiting for porters. Some yards away, piled in a very expensive heap, we saw two abandoned film cameras and recording equipment. The German television crews who like us had come to film the evacuation, had suddenly panicked and, with the doors of the Hercules closing, had dropped everything and run for it.

There was a slip of paper between the bedcover and pillow, a note written by Hassim, the local cameraman I had employed on that one day only, at Hilli. I had used him a few times since as an interpreter and guide and had asked him to make contact with the Mukti Bahini, any one of the dozen units that we understood now surrounded the city. The message from him was purposely ambiguous, inviting me to 'celebrate the birthday of a friend' he had not seen for some time and whom he knew I would be most interested to meet. He gave a rendezvous and a time. I should come with Jacques and bring a present. The next evening, once the air-raids were over and two hours before curfew, we waited, close to the Ramna racecourse, Jacques carrying his 'present' – the camera in a holdall. We sat in the shadow of a banyan tree, quite alone; the streets were empty, even this long before curfew. Occasionally we heard rifle fire, single shots some distance away, probably warning would-be curfew-breakers off the streets. The rendezvous time passed. Despite all his other failings, Hassim had always been punctual. We waited another hour. There was another burst of automatic rifle fire; it persuaded us to return to the hotel.

I quite expected Hassim to be there, full of apologies and excuses. Instead, his wife was waiting. Hassim, she said, had been arrested. That afternoon soldiers had dragged him out of the house and into a lorry. She said it was full of other people, many of whom she recognised: journalists, a doctor, another cameraman and somebody who had worked for the government propaganda department. She did not know where they had been taken, or why. She had gone to the police station but they had said they knew nothing. I made telephone calls to the police stations and to army headquarters but Hassim had disappeared.

The story might easily have ended there and so might Hassim's life, but I had arranged an interview for the following afternoon with General Farman Ali, military adviser to the governor of East Pakistan, and once it was over and we were drinking green tea from

Doulton china, I told him of Hassim's mysterious removal – I emphasised that he was a cameraman working for me and demanded to know what he had done and what I must do to get his release. Farman Ali promised he would do his best to find out, and he did.

The next evening Hassim's wife came to the hotel. He, and only he, had been released. He knew nothing of the others. She was crying and trembling. Hassim was sick and could not come to see me, would not come, dare not, she said. He had left for the countryside to hide and she did not expect to see him again until the war was over. She was extremely nervous, looking around the hotel foyer as she spoke and at everyone who came in and out of the door. She held my arm. 'My husband has seen terrible things,' she whispered, 'I cannot believe what he says he's seen.' Then she added, 'And what he says you will see one day.'

She left and I never saw or heard from her again. But a week later I did see what Hassim had seen, and it was indeed terrible.

Diary. Dacca, 14 December 1971:
We are near to the end now. We had all been thinking it would take weeks. Suddenly it is days. The hotel room boys, the rickshaw men and the newspapers are now speaking it out loud without fear. JOI BANGLA!

There are times, when the breeze is right, when we think we can even hear the tanks. The Indians are advancing on three sides with their ships still blocking the Bay of Bengal. Upwards of twenty thousand troops are now within striking distance of the city, and five thousand paratroopers are reported to have dropped near Tangail, forty miles north-west of us. The Indians are now shelling from the three directions and every hour or so the shells are landing a little closer.

General Farman Ali sent a message to the United Nations appealing for help to end the war on terms that amounted to a Pakistani surrender. It included the repatriation of Pakistani troops and the establishment of an East Bengal government. When he heard of it, President Yahya Khan cabled the UN to disregard it.

The Indian chief of staff, General Manekshaw, over Radio India, urged General Ali to surrender. 'Resistance is useless and will mean the death of many poor soldiers under your command, quite needlessly.' He ended, 'I have been extremely considerate so far in the amount of force I am using to reduce your garrison. I cannot allow any further delay.'

We marvelled at the language, so precisely and so delicately put – an exchange between gentlemen! God knows what was happening out in the killing fields where so many thousands were still being maimed and slaughtered, not only combatants but forlorn families crouching beneath air-raid shelters of bamboo and palm leaves, watching the Indian bombers come and go, day after day, looking at the skies and praying. And one gentleman-general was reminding another gentleman-general how considerate he had been.

Where were the West Pakistan troops? Where was the fight to the death their commander, General Niazi, had promised? That morning he had come to the gates of our hotel to give an impromptu and impassioned press conference. He was a tall man, a typical Punjabi in pressed starched khaki, carrying an ornate swagger-stick and with the arrogance of one who had never known defeat.

'There has been so much nonsense pushed out by some of you chappies ["chappies" was the word he used] saying I would run away to save my skin. Well, I have come to show you that I haven't. Dacca will fall over my dead body first. Indian tanks will have to drive over me before they take this city.' West Pakistanis safely on our side of the gates cheered and shouted, PAKISTAN ZINDABAD – LONG LIVE PAKISTAN, and the general strode off as if he had just won the war he was just about to lose. His last-ditch bravado was made easy by the fantasies that were appearing daily – hourly – in military communiqués and the newspapers.

With Indian tanks a half a day's drive away, the *Dacca Morning News* of Tuesday, 14 December, headlined: INDIA HUMILIATED. 'Pakistan has brought humiliation to India on all war fronts . . . our valiant armed forces have successfully beaten back the aggression and are holding on firmly to their positions.' In the next column was 'Thought for the Day', a quotation from the Koran: 'Allah's is the direction of the way and some roads go not straight. Had he willed, he would have led you right.'

But Allah had not willed and that afternoon, during one of the most concentrated air attacks we had seen, the government of East Pakistan resigned, publicly declaring that it fully dissociated itself from President Khan in Islamabad. As Indian MiGs dive-bombed his official residence, A. M. Malik, governor of East Pakistan, in a bunker below, wrote the draft of his and his cabinet's resignation with a shaking ballpoint pen. All morning Malik had dithered but the MiGs overhead, rocketing and strafing at will, had finally decided him. In the dirt and half-light of the makeshift bunker, surrounded by his ministers, Malik showed the draft to John Kelly, a United Nations worker, and to Gavin Young. Young had gone there for an interview and had been trapped by the air raid; he came out with one of the best stories of his stay. Malik put his surname to the dirty, crumpled piece of paper, then the elderly and religious man removed his socks and shoes, meticulously washed his feet, put a clean handkerchief on his head and, kneeling down in a dark, dank corner, prayed. With the air raid over, he followed Young and Kelly to the Intercontinental Hotel where he asked the four of us guarding the gate for asylum.

Diary. Dacca, 15 December 1971:
Twelve days of intensive war. Now the last hours of it. This evening, as we came out of our bunkers and trenches, the jets soared away. It could be their last attack. Rumours of one more attempt at a cease-fire. Rumours on rumours. With so little information we live by rumours. If the hotel phones were working we could dial 7 for Rumour Service.

That evening, inside our besieged hotel, we sat huddled around the radio and waited for the strains of 'Lillibullero' and the BBC World Service news – the only voice you feel inclined to depend on away from home. The Indians had offered terms, an ultimatum which expired the following morning at 0930 hours. Unless General Niazi gave a positive response the Indians promised that they would attack 'with the utmost vigour'.

ITN report, Dacca, 16 December:
This morning, we heard that General Niazi had accepted the terms after contact with President Yahya Khan. At twenty minutes past nine, with only ten minutes to go until the ulti-

matum expired, John Kelly transmitted Niazi's acceptance to Delhi through the UN radio network. Just after ten-thirty we heard in the streets the first public cry, JOI BANGLA - LONG LIVE BANGLADESH, and we knew that the Indians had received the acceptance. The war is over. A new nation has begun its first day. At first it was apprehensive but the chanting and the singing rapidly gathered momentum and by noon the Pakistani flag, which had been the symbol of so much horror and terror, was torn up and the red, yellow and green flag of Bangladesh was hoisted in its place on top of the Radio Pakistan building. On the roads leading into Dacca, soldiers of the defeated Pakistani army began their retreat from Tungi in the north, Comilla in the east, Faridpur in the west and Narungang in the south. They carried their rifles and their bedding. Everything else had been left behind. Their only concern now was to get to Dacca, to their barracks, and to await the promised safe return home to West Pakistan.

At one-forty-five that afternoon the first of the Indian paratroopers drove into Dacca to a welcome that probably surprised even them. They said they had come, not as conquerors but as liberators and that afternoon they were welcomed as such. Sadly, it did not last. The peaceful takeover became suddenly very bloody. As a contingent of Pakistani soldiers passed on their way to their barracks, shots were fired – maybe accidentally – and a street battle began. For nearly an hour Pakistanis and Indians fired at each other in the streets around us. No one could say it was deliberate, but in the crossfire civilians and Indian and Pakistani soldiers were killed. Then just as abruptly it was over. At four-thirty the first Indian tanks rumbled into the city, cheered on by the thousands who now lined the streets, and half an hour later Indian paratroopers formed a guard of honour in the centre of Dacca racecourse and the two generals, one Pakistani and one Indian, arrived to complete the surrender. Just as the sun began to set on the first day of Bangladesh, General Niazi finally signed the document that ended the war.

Few of us had thought it would come so quickly. When it did, we waited for the civil bloodletting to begin. We knew the Indians would not wait long to act as the peace-makers. 'For ten days,' one commander told me, 'we will be an army of liberation. On the eleventh day we will become a Hindu army of occupation.' The Indians knew it; the Bengalis knew it.

The Mukti Bahini announced a list of people who would stand trial once a civil government had been formed. Many on that list were living in our hotel and were expecting at any moment to be dragged into the streets and shot. One West Pakistani doctor in the hotel attempted suicide. We had already heard that Mukti Bahini kangaroo courts were condemning people to be strangled, garrotted or hanged, and we came across bodies of people who had been dragged into side alleys, gagged and then beaten or stoned to death so that wandering Indian patrols should not see or hear. In one back street close to the British Embassy we counted twenty-four bodies.

Daud Subhani, our tall, garrulous Punjabi assistant, was now subdued. He appeared to have accepted that he too was about to die. He was a kind and gentle man and I believed him when he told me that after all he had seen, after all his own people had done in the name of Pakistan, there had to be punishment. He was prepared for his.

He gave me a letter to his wife in Karachi and stayed in my room. The Bengali room boys knew he was there but no one came for him – at least not until the Indian army officially demanded that all the Pakistanis in the hotel were to be handed over as declared prisoners-of-war. Unlike the rest of us, Daud did not have that return ticket. He was sent to an Indian prison and, despite repeated appeals by ITN directly to Mrs Indira Gandhi, he stayed there for another eighteen months.

The morning after the surrender, Hassim came to the hotel. I had not seen him since the night of our failed rendezvous. He was considerably thinner and at first he would not tell me what had happened or why, simply that I must go with him to the dykes; all journalists and cameramen, he said, were going; the Indian army had arranged transport. The dykes were about five miles outside the city boundary and at the end of our lorry journey we walked the last few hundred yards along the walls. There was a warm, light breeze from the sea and we smelt them first. Only then did I know what to expect.

Below the walls hundreds of rotting corpses were laid out in a line. Someone counted two hundred and ten, though how it was possible to count accurately I shall never know, because bodies had been torn apart by packs of dogs. An Indian soldier scattered the dogs with rifle shots but they soon came skulking back like hyenas. Jacques filmed, but it was not likely that anyone would ever show this evidence of West Pakistan's final outrage in the closing days of the war. Determined to bankrupt the newborn Bangladesh of its remaining intellectuals and professionals, the army had rounded them up and brought them here to be shot and left in the swamps to rot. Hassim pointed to one faceless body, identified by its green jacket as a fellow-journalist who had been arrested with him. A new word in the vocabulary of war was invented: élitocide.

News of the massacre spread quickly throughout Dacca and that afternoon, with the Indians obliged to turn a blind eye, it was announced that public executions would be held in the football stadium. Prisoners of the Mukti Bahini were to be bayoneted to death in front of a crowd of twenty thousand. The press were invited to watch, photograph and film.

That morning cameraman Chris Faulds and reporter Richard Lindley had arrived to replace us. I said I would not cover the stadium executions and Richard and Chris agreed. That afternoon we counted the roars in the stadium as each prisoner was executed. It was like listening to a home team scoring its winning goals. All but two men refused to cover it. Horst Faas and Michel Laurent of Associated Press did go and they shared the 1972 Pulitzer Prize for the photographs they took.

With Richard and Chris now in charge, I looked for ways to get out. It was December the twentieth, telephone lines were down, the airfield looked like a gravel pit and it seemed likely that Jacques and I were condemned to the Dacca Intercontinental for a Christmas with party games in the ballroom and Gavin Young on the piano. But that afternoon I saw four Indian helicopters land at the airfield. I packed my bag with what little there was to be packed and paid twenty dollars to an Indian sergeant to drive me out there. Halfway along the airport road, I saw three of the helicopters lift off and fly overhead, going west. Luckily the fourth was still on the ground and when I got there the crew were repairing an oil leak. They said they were en route from Comilla to Calcutta and very soon I was in the air with them. In half an hour we landed in Calcutta and a few hours later I was wiping away the sweat and grime with a hot, scented Lufthansa face-towel, sipping chilled champagne and balancing tiny black fish-eggs on a sliver of toast. India was thirty-five thousand feet below me. Soon we would cross the Afghanistan border and leave India behind.

Ahead was an English Christmas of cold sleet and hot turkey, rum punch by a log fire, a fir tree and presents, plum pudding, Diana's mince-pies and a ten-shilling note in the carol singers' tin. What better reasons to hurry home? One. Diana was large that Christmas, and three weeks later Tom, our first child, was born.

CHAPTER FOUR

The Holy War of Yom Kippur
– and after,
October 1973–June 1975

YOM KIPPUR WAS MY FIFTH WAR and by all accounts that morning it ought to have been my last. What I remember, before I lost consciousness, was the roaring black shadow of a Syrian MiG, the car somersaulting into the air to meet it, the sharp prickle of glass splinters and what I thought was blood trickling down my neck. It was petrol. But to start from the beginning.

Human will alone propelled the yacht into Portsmouth harbour that breezeless October Saturday afternoon some days earlier. Throughout the tortuously slow jibe back, I imagined the telephone ringing in my London flat, and I could visualise an impatient foreign editor about to ring somebody else. There was not a breath of air in the sails. Southampton Water was like a millpond and only my own lack of breath stopped me from jumping overboard and dragging the boat into harbour by my teeth.

That afternoon, on the BBC one o'clock news, I had heard that the Arabs had invaded Israel. The Egyptian army had suddenly and cleverly crossed the Suez Canal into the Sinai Desert, the Syrians had crossed the northern border into the Golan Heights and the Iraqis and Jordanians were also about to join in. I, it seemed, might not.

I need not have worried. The first thing protagonists do in war is close their airports and there were no flights to Tel Aviv that day. But when I arrived at Heathrow Airport later that afternoon it was obvious the Israeli airline El Al was intending to resume just as soon as it was reasonably safe. The airport was crammed with thousands of young Israelis of dual nationality, young men and women of military age queuing up to join their brothers and sisters of the faith in their motherland.

It was a war that was two years in the planning. Egypt's President Sadat had called 1971 the year of decision, a year in which he was convinced his own diplomacy would yield results in the seemingly irreconcilable conflict in the Middle East. He was pro-West by sentiment and he thought that, given time, he could persuade the Americans to commit themselves to bringing about an Arab-Israeli peace. The Americans would not.

Sadat despaired. If there was no prospect of a peace, there was also no chance of settling it with a once-and-for-all war. Then he happened on a solution. The Arabs, he suggested, did not have to win a war, they simply had to win an early initiative and enough time to allow superpower intervention; these would then be obliged to supervise and become the guarantors of a once-and-for-all peace. Sadat reckoned he would get the benefits of victory without risking a bloody and costly defeat, and he very nearly succeeded.

The Arabs' collective war council agreed on a surprise offensive along the entire length of their borders so that the Israelis would be unable to detect the direction of the main offensive and not know where to concentrate their counter-attack. The Syrians would use Soviet-style massed armour along the Golan Heights in the north, and the Egyptians would employ Soviet river-crossing techniques to bridge the Suez Canal in the south. The Israeli army and air force would then be split two ways.

The timing was crucial but as in all things Arab it was a compromise. The Syrians wanted a dawn attack when the sun was behind them and the Egyptians wanted it in the late afternoon for the same reason. But they did agree the date. It had to be in October because that was the month when tidal conditions in the Canal best suited a crossing and it could not be later because of flooding from rain and snow on the Golan.

They chose 6 October. It was the anniversary of the Prophet's victory at the Battle of Badr in AD 626, and it was also midway through Ramadan, the Islamic month of fasting. But most crucially it was the Jewish Day of Atonement – the holiest in their calendar, a day of rest and prayer, when the Israelis could be guaranteed to be at their least prepared. It is called Yom Kippur.

News of the attacks on both fronts broke the odd silence in Tel Aviv that October Saturday. People went to their doorsteps and their balconies, transistor radios to their ears, looking to the sky and nodding to each other. It was an exact repeat of that June scene six years before. Then they had called it the Six-Day War, when their own military had launched one of the most devastating offensives in the history of warfare. Now the avenging Arabs were attempting their own. Jerusalem Jews, fasting and praying, realised that something serious was happening when an Israeli jet fighter flew low over the city's flat roof-tops some time after seven that morning. On Yom Kippur nobody is allowed to use machines and nobody breaks that sacred law. But by noon all the rules had been broken and Prime Minister Golda Meir had assembled her War Council, summoning her ministers from their holiday beaches, farms and kibbutzes.

By noon Tel Aviv was chaotic. The streets were full of traffic, the barriers preventing cars from entering the Jewish areas of West Jerusalem on the holy day were removed, all army leave was cancelled and all men and women between the ages of eighteen and fifty left their homes and synagogues to report to barracks. That afternoon the air-raid sirens sounded for the first time in six years and families began filing quietly from their homes to the shelters.

In the Arab areas of East Jerusalem and in the occupied territories of the West Bank and Gaza, it was almost festive. Shops remained open and crowds gathered round radios to listen and cheer martial broadcasts from Cairo, Damascus, Amman and Baghdad.

We all thought then – and reported it so – that the Israelis had been taken by surprise. They were not. They had been expecting an offensive of sorts but they had not known when it would come. They had been quietly mobilising their reserves a week before when they went on a Phase Two Alert. Israeli intelligence had reported an unusual Syrian military build-up along the peace lines in the Golan, which marked the northern point of the Israelis' advance into Syria at the end of the Six-Day War. Israeli patrols had been criss-crossing the border on special missions, returning with photographs and information of Syrian troop numbers and the position and strength of their armour. General Moshe Dayan had recently returned from the Golan and had warned Prime Minister Meir of the Syrians' heavy concentrations of troops, tanks and artillery and of their Russian-built anti-aircraft missile batteries.

In the south, Israeli reconnaissance planes had brought back photographs from their high-level sorties which showed unexplained activity on the Egyptian side of the Suez Canal, and Israeli foot patrols reported much movement at night under arc lights behind the sand dunes that hid the Egyptians on the west side. Israeli intelligence agents also reported that Russian advisers and their families were quietly leaving Damascus and Cairo, an indication that Moscow had failed to persuade its Arab clients to stay their hand and was getting its people away before Tel Aviv or Washington could accuse it of complicity in war.

Sunday, 7 October, and the El Al flight out of Heathrow was full of accents – a cabin full of Americans, Canadians, Cockneys, Australians, South Africans – young men and women from every continent who had more in common than their age: a second passport embossed with the Star of David. Now they were returning to a homeland under siege and prepared to fight and die for it. They sang Jewish songs in a language which except for a few moments in their religious calendar was foreign to them. Yet at that moment it made them feel one and when the aircraft's wheels touched the tarmac at Lod Airport they cheered and clapped. Then they sank back in their seats and wept.

I was travelling with Gerald Seymour, the second ITN reporter (and now best-selling author), and our producer David Phillips who, like me, was returning to a second Middle East war in two years. By the time we landed in Tel Aviv it was agreed that Gerry should cover the Golan Heights and I should drive south into the Sinai Desert. As it happened, I had been given the short straw.

Early that Monday morning, with cameraman Brian Calvert, I left Tel Aviv and drove off into the desert beyond Gaza towards Suez to look for the war and the Egyptians. Gerald and his crew went north to Galilee and the Golan Heights to look for Syrians. Brian drove a large open white American car and nothing could have been more conspicuous to Egyptian planes overhead, or more hateful to the Arabs on the ground. There was no better or bigger target for small boys' stones, old women's ridicule and old men's spittle.

According to the bulletins on the car radio, the Egyptian army had crossed the Canal with no resistance and had advanced well into the Sinai, well beyond the Israelis' fortifications on the Bar-Lev Line. Their air force had attacked Bir Gifgafa over two hundred miles inland, and also El Tasa and Baluza to the north. The crossing itself was critical because it broke the myth of the Israelis' invincibility and showed the Arabs they could succeed and whatever happened later never took the edge off that. On the first day of the war the Egyptians fought their way across the Canal in dozens of places and by Monday they had managed to get ten bridges into service to bring armoured guns and equipment over in force. They had to withstand twenty-three Israeli counter-attacks and none was made with less than a battalion of armour. Yet they were unco-ordinated and all failed. Losses among the Egyptian infantry on the east bank were heavy but Israeli confidence had been badly shaken.

The desert was empty. We had been driving for five hours turning west and then south, leaving the known road for the sand, looking for tracks, scouring the horizon for telltale signs of war: fire, smoke, dust-trails, jet trails, searching, wishing, believing that if we drove deep enough we should sight the Egyptian spearhead with their tanks and artillery driving towards us, a division of Arab men and armour on their way to conquer the land of Zion.

We drove all that morning and into the afternoon and saw nothing. If there was a war out there we were not to see it that day. I thought of Gerry. By now he was almost certainly on his way out of the Golan with the first exclusive war pictures to be put on satellite that evening to London. A world scoop. Damn Gerry's luck. Damn the Egyptians!

The sun was now moving down towards Egypt and soon it would turn red; our shadows would stretch behind us and the desert would be black and cold. It was time to turn back. Brian slowly brought his large car round in a wide circle. Then I shouted and pointed. Brian stood on the seat, steering with his foot. We had been looking the wrong way for the wrong army. Five miles away we saw rising sand clouds, like a slowly-moving storm except that it was too long and too uniform. It was a convoy, an Israeli convoy, large and long, the first into the Sinai, and suddenly we were filming them, squadrons of British Centurion tanks leading open armoured personnel carriers spouting mortar barrels and heavy machine-guns, and trundling behind them lorries full of soldiers, lorries full of ammunition, lorries towing field-guns and howitzers and missile batteries. Here was the Israeli counter-attack, moving westwards across the desert to confront the Egyptians, to fight them and trap them, and finally and very bloodily, to turn them back.

Brian ran in all directions, filming everything from every angle: tanks belching black smoke, their tracks churning the sand, men cheering, men scowling, until I sighted the end of the convoy and jumped in front of the camera, shouting excitedly into the microphone, pointing to Israel with my left hand and Egypt with my right as if I were introducing a boxing match. I hesitated, spluttered, but Brian was already peering out from behind the camera with a finger across his throat, Cut, Cut, Enough! And so it was, more than enough.

We went back the way we had come, north to Tel Aviv, and how triumphant we were, slapping each other's backs and singing songs as the open car hurtled across the sand. But as we passed kilometre marker 280 we shut up. It was now well past five o'clock and another four hours' driving at least was ahead of us. We should arrive back in Tel Aviv and the television station at Herzliya too late to process, edit and satellite our film for that evening's *News at Ten*. We had great pictures, a great story, the first evidence of the Israeli counter-attack, the beginning of their fight to retrieve, but now it would have to wait until tomorrow, and tomorrow is always second-best. We had lost the first day of our war.

But I had forgotten some fundamental television truths: that there is no limit to a cameraman's recklessness when his film is at risk, nor to a film editor's ingenuity, sleight-of-hand and sprinting speed when a satellite is beckoning. Brian Calvert and John Harwood between them that evening provided the necessary, as men like them invariably do, and at ten o'clock London time ITN transmitted its world scoop: world exclusives from both fronts in the War of Yom Kippur.

*

The Sinai schedule was physically shattering. We left at about four o'clock every morning and took it in turns at the wheel. I brought an alarm clock and when it rang on the hour we swapped drivers, no matter what. As the Israelis began pushing the Egyptians back towards the Canal, so the war moved farther from Tel Aviv. Towards the middle of that first week the journey to the front took seven hours. We then gave ourselves two hours maximum to film our story before we began the seven-hour drive back again – aiming to arrive at the Herzliya television station at around eight o'clock. That gave us just enough time to process the film, edit and dub and be ready for the evening satellite feed.

Of course, it seldom happened that way. There were military roadblocks, military diversions, military cussedness. Sometimes we would stop to film an incident on the way or there were air attacks, punctures, a blown radiator, even a wounded donkey.

We had stopped to film what I described as a Centurions' knackers' yard. The British prime minster, Edward Heath, had decided that the simplest, quickest way to end the war was to withhold the supply of spare parts to the tanks that Britain had sold to Israel in peacetime. The sales spiel is well enough known to governments and gun-runners alike; that selling highly-profitable armaments equally to opposing sides is the best way to stop them ever using them. The Heathite view took the strategy a stage further: should the customer go to war – for whatever reason – you simply stopped the supply of spares, so that the guns ran out of shells, the infantrymen out of bullets and the tanks stopped rumbling. Then, supposedly, the protagonists would sue for peace and consciences were salved. Among the Israeli tank crews the name Heath was spat out with the same venom as Sadat.

But the British government, like the Arabs, had again underestimated Israeli ingenuity. Crippled tanks were towed to engineering bases set up in the desert and every usable part from them was taken and used on another machine. The engineers boasted they could make a new Centurion out of six shattered ones in two days. There was even a man whose final duty was to pressure-hose the inside of the rebuilt tank and clean away the blood and bone-splinters of the previous occupants.

We were close to Bir Gifgafa which Egyptian Sabres had attacked in the opening hours of the war, and while my crew filmed the knackers' yard I walked towards a line of houses ribboning out from the settlement. I saw the donkey in an alley, looking desperately for shade and final relief. Its front left leg had been blown off at the knee, its body was lacerated and bleeding from shrapnel wounds. It was dying slowly and agonisingly. I asked a soldier to shoot it. He shook his head. He would not, could not, he said, as if all the world agreed, shoot a donkey. It stood in front of me, trembling on its three legs, a buzzing mound of flies sucking at the stump of the fourth, a little blood and froth around its mouth and nostrils. I asked the soldier for his rifle, put the barrel to the donkey's ear and pulled the trigger.

The Sinai schedule finally beat us, so Gerry and I agreed to do alternate days and that Thursday I had my first sight of the Golan. We drove north from Tel Aviv along the fast coast road to Haifa and then turned inland to Nazareth and Tiberias, skirting the Sea of Galilee and past the Church of the Resurrection. Then we slowly climbed to the Heights.

In the Sinai we had had to search for war, looking for the plumes of smoke and trails in the sky that pinpointed an air attack, or follow a convoy hoping it would attack or be attacked. In the Golan it was different; there the war was everywhere, and we were engulfed in its debris. Below us was the Syrian army and beyond them it was possible to imagine you could see the shadow of Damascus.

On our first day we came under heavy Syrian bombardment and ran for the nearest cover, crouching between the enormous back wheels of a giant army lorry. A few minutes into the bombardment, with the shells landing happily a hundred yards away, we saw a soldier frantically waving and shouting at us. We ignored him. Whatever it was we had done could not be more important than what we were now doing and we pressed ourselves harder against the thick shrapnel-proof tyres. The soldier finally came running, ignoring the lethal barrage around him. But he was not angry, he was simply concerned. Crawling in after us, he explained that as he was the driver of the lorry he felt obliged to tell us it was packed with high explosive.

It is easy to suffer paranoia in wartime. Syrian shelling was accurate, yet indiscriminate. But to be attacked by Syrian MiGs twice when there was nobody else in sight – that did make me wonder if it was time to go home.

Chris Faulds, sound recordist Johnny Soldini and I were travelling towards the Heights. Johnny was driving. We had been passing convoys all the way along the road from Haifa but now the road was empty in both directions. Suddenly there was a black shadow over us like an enormous vampire and the shattering roar of jet engines. It was like being run over by an express steam train. Eye-witnesses later said the Syrian MiG had strafed us, which seemed unlikely and certainly unnecessary. After all, why should the pilot, whatever his mood, swoop so low to attack a blue – and obviously civilian – car?

Shocked by the sudden noise, Soldini drove off the road, tried to pull the car back on course at eighty miles an hour, hit the edge of the tarmac and somersaulted, landing a hundred yards ahead, upside-down. The roof of the car was flattened level with the seat-backs. Chris and Johnny, a trifle bloody, pulled themselves out upside-down, then hauled me, unconscious, after them. We were surrounded by a crowd soon enough, but we were not their concern. Shivering and shaking, I came to on a stretcher as I was being loaded aboard an army ambulance and I remember seeing the wheels and seats stripped off the Volvo and plastic bowls catching the last drips of petrol from the upturned tank.

That evening David Phillips, my producer, drove from Tel Aviv to the hospital. ITN, he said, was insisting I should be flown straight home. Instead, he brought me a neck-brace and a dozen red roses.

Some days later I was back on the road and in the Golan where, with the crew and David Phillips my surviving witnesses, another Syrian MiG attacked us, this time with rockets. We were driving towards Kuneitra when we saw it coming low behind us. We skidded to a broadside and jumped into a ditch as two rockets skimmed the roof and exploded in the sand fifty yards ahead.

The neck-brace became an embarrassment. To me, it was a badge of the war wounded and I felt rather pleased to be wearing it; but my editor, Nigel Ryan, was bombarded by viewers accusing him of cruelty. He sent me a cable: EITHER THE NECK-BRACE COMES OFF THE SCREEN OR YOU DO, so from then on, before I appeared on camera, I had to unstrap the brace. As it was my style in those days suddenly to surprise the cameraman by jumping on to a tank to interview a commander, or run alongside the troops to interview them, having to pause first to unstrap my neck-harness significantly reduced the drama of the day.

The Israelis were now advancing well into Syria, and above them was the protective umbrella of their air force. The Phantoms and Mirages fought off the scores of Syrian missiles and it remains one of the war's most indelible images – watching a missile trailing a jet fighter as the Israeli pilot tried to manoeuvre his way out of reach. Sometimes they were so high, the chaser and the chased were just thin looping whiter trails in the blue. Sometimes the trails moved off in opposite directions and we all cheered the escape, sometimes we saw the burst of orange and the ball of black smoke when they met. There was never a parachute. The pilots who died must, until that very last instant, have believed they were escaping. They were revenged in the most savage and terrible way. We were witness on one such occasion.

Determined to prevent any further Israeli advance towards Damascus, the Syrians had hastily reinforced, and a large convoy was sent along the Kuneitra road from Sassa. The lead vehicles were about to cross a wide bridge when it was suddenly attacked by a Phantom, whose single bomb took away the centre span. In the commotion and panic, no one saw the other Phantoms peel out from the clouds to begin their slaughter. They hit the lead lorries and those at the rear simultaneously so that the convoy could not go forward or back and those who tried to turn simply sank up to their axles in the soft sand. An entire column of lorries filled with men, fuel and ammunition was a stationary and unprotected target and the pilots casually picked them off until it was a line of fire, an exploding inferno. It was horribly clinical.

When we reached the smouldering wrecks we saw that no one had escaped. It was a convoy of grotesquely contorted corpses, some bloated, some black and brittle; skeletons with their helmets on.

We were on our way out of the area when we were waved down by Don McCullin, one of my generation's greatest war photographers. Nick Tomalin, the reporter he was working with on the

Sunday Times, had been killed some miles back when a rocket had hit his car. Don had helped tidy up the body and carry it away.

There was a moment when I believe the War of Yom Kippur might well have made me a rich man. My second crew – Jon Lane and Hugh Thomson – and I were in the Golan Heights in the final weekend of the war. We had reached an artillery battery on the ridge and filmed them working their guns, massive 155mm, their long tapering barrels pointing high, targeting the Syrian troops along the Damascus road. By the side of each gun was an enormous pyramid of brass shell-cases which the young battery commander, a lieutenant, said added up to four hundred and eighty. 'Or, looked at another way,' he said laughingly, 'two thousand dead Syrians.'

'You'll never know,' I said.

'If I knew for sure,' he answered back, 'I'd be disappointed. But hopefully we'll soon move the guns forward to give us a chance at Damascus. Then the killing will really begin!'

Picture the scene. Sunset on the Golan, the long slim barrels silhouetted against the glowing orange twilight sky, the battery crews stripped to their waists, scorched by the sun, glistening with sweat as they pulled another brass shell-case out of the smoking breech to swing another back in: the shatter of the explosion, the recoil of the barrel, the ground shaking, the smell of cordite.

'Hey!' shouted the lieutenant as we waved our goodbye. He stood there glowing, the gold Star of David hanging on his breast, white teeth gleaming from black stubble.

'Do you have a cigarette?' he asked.

Jon pulled a packet from his breast-pocket and threw it to him. Then with that deadly, magical backdrop he caught the packet, held it to his cheek and with the widest grin, he said to the camera: 'Ah! Benson!' And we knew we had just lost a million-dollar advertisement!

With the fighting in the north all but over, I went south into the Sinai for the final days there, deeper into the desert with the Israeli forces along the Bar-Lev, close to the Canal. We slept underneath the Centurions that night in shallow trenches in the sand to keep off the frost. A few hours before dawn we moved off to war and to what was to be the final battle. Jon and Hugh went in one armoured personnel carrier, I in another. It was a mistake to be apart and I regretted it. The lieutenant in charge of my APC warned me that his orders were to move directly to the Canal, whatever the Egyptians did, whatever the ferocity of their artillery bombardment. 'We expect to take many casualties,' he said cheerfully.

There were seven of us: the driver, the young lieutenant sitting by him, a sergeant, a corporal sitting opposite me and two others. The vehicle had heavily armour-plated sides, an open top and, bolted to the floor, a 120mm mortar. We and the other APCs in the squadron were providing protective fire for the tanks, which to me seemed absolutely the wrong way around. The Egyptian artillery spotters were already within sighting distance, watching our approach through their high-powered binoculars, brave men on their own, radioing to their battery commanders, some miles back, our exact distance and co-ordinates.

Our Centurions were meant to be ideal for the conditions we were fighting in, because their guns were gyroscopically controlled, designed to remain in a level firing position whatever the land contours. But even the Centurions could not cope with this desert; its dunes were steep mini-mountains. So our APCs had to move among and even ahead of them so that their mortars could bombard the Egyptian artillery batteries. It seemed so reassuring but that day the Egyptians were very determined and very brave.

I had come to witness the ending of the war. Suddenly I was certain I should not live to see it. The Egyptian shelling began furiously as we accelerated forward towards where the shells were landing. They were hitting the ground so close that, even encased in steel, we felt the desert shudder under us. We turned white with sand and fear.

I became a member of the mortar crew, pulling the finned bombs out of their tubes and passing them along the line to the sergeant, an enormous man. I remember the rhythm: Bomb to barrel . . . Drop . . . Close eyes . . . Hands to ears . . . Explosion . . . Bomb to barrel . . . Drop . . . Close eyes . . . and all the time the wild lieutenant screamed his orders at the driver, standing and pointing left and then right, as if he could see the incoming shells and was directing us safely between them. We did not speak to one another, but we knew we were about to be destroyed; it was on our faces. The corporal opposite me began to mouth a prayer and, not for the first time, I said mine. Then he stood up, pushed his way past the sergeant and shouted, but the lieutenant grabbed him by his shirt and sent him sprawling back.

'The madman's taken us ahead of the tanks,' the corporal said. 'We're leading them – just us. We're killed already!' The wild young man up front was intent on death and glory and we wanted neither. The boy by my side was crying and praying, nodding his head in short, sharp jerks as if to emphasise every word and every appeal for help. There was a quick succession of explosions nearby and then we stopped. The lieutenant turned and shouted. He was angry.

The corporal said. 'A tank has been hit. They're sending us a wounded officer. We must take him back. Thank God . . . thank God!'

The steel doors at the back opened and men, bloody themselves, pushed in a stretcher and the doors clanged closed again. Then we were turning, on our way back and out of range of the Egyptian guns.

The lieutenant had been denied his glorious death and he was furious, but no one listened any more. We watched the wounded man. His body was torn open, his uniform stripped, his left foot had been smashed, his helmet was cut open and I saw white and red inside. He began clawing himself and grabbed at his face. A nail caught his eye, and tore away the lower lid. The corporal held one of his hands and nodded at me to take the other. It took four hands to hold two, there was such strength in them, and in a man so badly maimed.

Every few miles the lieutenant shouted, 'Is he still alive?' And we answered together, 'Yes. Hurry!' We had the same thought: if the writhing man on the stretcher died, we would simply turn around and drive back into the war to die ourselves. Then the strong hand I had been holding so tightly went limp, the writhing, tormented body was still and the eyes unblinking. I looked at the corporal. We said nothing. The mad lieutenant shouted, 'Is he still alive?' And the corporal shouted back, 'Yes, yes. Hurry, hurry!' Twenty minutes later we arrived back among the concrete bunkers on the Bar-Lev Line. I was still tightly clasping the dead man's hand.

We returned to the Canal later that afternoon, but by then the battle was over. For miles we passed lorries with red crosses painted on their canvas tops taking the casualties home.

That evening we sat with the dirty, weary tank crews in the dank semi-dark of a bunker. No one spoke. The squadron commander, a colonel, a tall, slim, almost effete man, sat on his own, smoking, looking at no one. When Egypt's final surrender was eventually broadcast over the radio, there was hardly a murmur, but then that was not strange. They already knew the war was won. They had fought to its final seconds.

The colonel stood up slowly and painfully, as if every joint ached, walked stiffly to the opening in the bunker and looked out to the desert. He lit another cigarette. I went and stood by him. It was shortly after midnight and the night was crystal-clear, the air sharp, smelling of frost. The resolute, monumental Centurions were scattered about in no order, but they all faced west, their long gun barrels still pointing to Egypt.

'You must wonder,' the colonel said, 'why we are so quiet, why we are not celebrating the way you would.' He inhaled and blew smoke to the sky. 'Some of us, you see, have been to war against the Arabs three times, three times in twenty-five years. There are fathers here who have sons here. I am a father. I had two boys. One I lost in '67, in the June war fighting the Egyptians, and I thought this time the Syrians would take my other. So we have all fought the Arabs, and we thought we knew them. But they have never fought like this before, this time they were brave, now they are different. In the next war I will not survive, and maybe not my son. No, we will not live through another war, and I think not Israel. So we do not celebrate. Do you understand?'

I nodded but he was already walking away, the tip of his cigarette glowing red, into the still and silent Sinai battlefield.

It was 23 October 1973, the first hour of another peace. The Yom Kippur War had lasted seventeen days.

Having defeated the Egyptians, the Syrians, the Jordanians and the Iraqis, the Israelis have since had to fight the Palestinians in a tiny, bloody, endless internal war. Before the Palestinian uprising – the Intifada – began in December 1987, when in the weeks before Christmas Bethlehem became a place of slaughter, the Israelis had been preoccupied on their northern border with Lebanon and the PLO guerrillas who came across with such ferocity and so frequently on their suicide missions. Again and again the Israeli army and air force attempted to destroy the PLO training camps but, as the Palestinians had done some years before in Jordan, the military camps and the refugee camps were in the same place; to destroy one was to destroy both. Finally, the wholesale bombing of PLO bases in Beirut in 1980 and the annihilation of the refugee camps persuaded the Lebanese to wave Yasser Arafat and his men goodbye. On the last day of August 1982 they packed their bags, their hatred and their bombs and were shipped out to a new host: the ever-mischievous Colonel Gaddafi, international terrorism's godfather.

Not that anyone believed the PLO's departure would save Lebanon. For some years the Lebanese had, in their own special way, been painfully killing themselves, and for the most ancient of reasons. I remember the beginning in 1975 and then the sequel the following summer.

How rapidly they went about demolishing the capital, Beirut. It had been such a splendid city – pearl of the Levant, so painstakingly put together over two thousand years as the centre of Levantine mercantile adventurism, extravagance and a thousand promises. It had the magnificent Grand Mosque, it had the Bois de Pins planted by an environmentally-minded Emir to keep the desert back. It was a city of sweeping esplanades, elegant promenades, terrace cafés, café noir, cognac and francophiles to boot; it boasted the world's most expensive restaurants, among them some of the world's best; the grandest and most elaborate hotels and nightclubs, where visiting Arab princes and playboys could pay the casino's mortgage in one week's losses. There were wide tree-lined avenues where the world's most expensive cars ferried the world's most extravagant women; an endless and exotic souk where traders beat their breasts and pleaded with you to bankrupt them for the privilege of selling you a Persian rug for less than it cost to make. There was a harbour where the yachts made Monte Carlo seem a poor man's marina, a city with the Mediterranean at its feet and the mountains, snow-capped and ski-able, at its shoulders. It was a rich man's paradise, where more champagne was drunk in one night than anywhere else in the world.

Which is why perhaps, as the devout believe, it became the target of Allah's wrath, and why his servants became so manic and thorough in the way they went about destroying it. It was not always easy to know who was destroying what and why – the battle-ground became such a confusing mixture of ideologies, national-isms and religions with the Palestinians at the centre of it.

By the summer of 1975 I, among many, could report that the destruction of old Beirut was complete. Hotel Row had become a geometrical nightmare with acres of steel girders creating gravity-defying triangles and trapezoids sprouting from pyramids of rubble that had once been the fillings in between.

ITN report, Beirut. June 1975:
This has been called the year of pointless death. The harbour has been completely destroyed and over twenty thousand homes and businesses have been flattened or gutted. It is what disinterested defence experts might term a perfect example of 'limited warfare'. Modern construction techniques and mod-ern weapons create an altogether different kind of ruin. This is perfectly defined havoc. The devastation is awful, and it is not difficult to believe that thirty thousand have already died in the fighting. The soldiers of the left, ragged and filthy, patrol the streets where streets are defined. They sleep in cellars and eat when somebody remembers to send them bread and a barbecued lamb.

The looting of the burnt-out shops and hotels is long fin-ished. Now and again someone who lived here comes back to see what is left – and there is very little. Every bank that wasn't blown down during the bombardment has since been blown out by a stick of dynamite. At one, in the biggest bank raid in history, upwards of forty million pounds in sterling notes was taken.

This is the front line, a row of sandbags – in street warfare it is what you'd expect. During the past weeks, the sandbags have moved slowly forward as the right wing has given ground.

If the present attempt by the two sides to talk their way out of this war fails, this will continue until one of the two is destroyed and the rest of Lebanon too.

Prophetic, but it was not hard to get it right in Beirut then. Who would have guessed, all these years later, that there would still be men left to fight, and anything left to fight about?

The street warfare in Beirut that June was intensive and it became all the more confusing for us to report because of the involvement of the Syrians.

Beirut. June 1975:
Families hide in cellars and lift-shafts as the Syrian forces use Katusha Russian-built rockets in batteries of six. They are called 'Stalin organs'. The streets around SAIKA headquarters, which was taken by the Palestinians during the night, are littered with the dead of both sides. We are told that Syrian tanks are now within twenty miles of here and the artillery they are bringing with them is within easy shelling distance. So the war has new colours drawn. It is no longer left versus right or Muslim versus Christian. Now there is a joker in the pack, and it is called Syria.

I added a service message that we were attempting to get our film package showing the street-fighting to Amman in Jordan by road because the airport was now becoming very uncertain. I suggested they send a film editor and a producer to Amman as quickly as possible. The message was well timed. That afternoon we watched a Boeing 707 of Middle Eastern Airlines take off from the airport and begin its climb, then saw tiny brown puffs appear a little way ahead of it: it banked sharply, wheeled to the left and descended quickly to the runway again. A Palestinian gunner had sent his salvos sky-high and from then on the airport was closed.

The following morning I sat breakfasting with four other reporters – three Americans and a Frenchman – in the Commodore Hotel. This is in the El Hambra district and then as now is the headquarters of the International Press Corps, telex Beirut 20595 for reservations. It has never closed, no matter what the bombardment, and short of a direct hit probably never will. Its basement is the safest bomb shelter in the city, as countless journalists and television crews will vouch. It had a parrot, which sat on the bar and gave a frighteningly realistic imitation of an incoming howitzer shell, and also whistled the 'Marseillaise'. The hotel had a unique accounting system for those on expense accounts, converting bar bills to 'laundry' at no extra cost.

That morning, over our grapefruit and coffee, the four of us discussed the best way to get our war footage home. One, an American, said he would try driving to Damascus; another said he would drive over the mountains to Jordan. I said that I might go south to 'Dixie', which is what we called Israel whenever we were among Arabs. My companions considered the idea certain suicide. They said I would never get beyond the Palestinian lines to the border and even if I did I would never get back. Mines or Palestinian snipers would have me, one way or the other.

The risk was great, but so was the reward. If I did make the border and somehow persuade an Israeli to call our producer Peter Lynch in Tel Aviv to come and collect our film, it would be satellited to London that same day and I should have a world scoop. Nothing – at least, nothing then – seemed more important.

My cameraman was Paul Carleton, the sound recordist Bob Hammond. Paul was, and I understand still is, emotionally incapable of experiencing fear, and a trip to the border, he said, was a splendid idea. Bob, ever stoical, accepted the two-vote majority. So off we went and no one expected to see us alive again.

It took us some hours to get out of Beirut. There was a roadblock every half mile where we were searched, our camera gear unloaded, opened up and repacked by armed teenagers carrying a mixture of Russian and American weapons, wearing 'Kiss Me Baby' T-shirts and – even then – designer jeans. They enjoyed their roles, bullying and prodding us with their automatics. It is a chilling observation, staring into the end of a gun barrel, to note how tiny the hole is and wonder why its bullet can make such a big one. It has to do, I am told, with the way the gun designer makes the bullet enter its target at an angle, a little sideways for best effect!

Once away from the capital, we thought we had left the war behind, but we were wrong. As in Cyprus, where Turk and Greek had fought each other, village against village, family against family, in a nationalist vendetta, so it was in the Lebanon with Muslim fighting Christian, each anxious to use his knife, his garrotte or his AK47 to kill those he had known only to hate. We passed villages burning and bodies still smouldering, every door bolted, fathers and sons waiting inside, mothers and daughters already climbing the hills to safety.

But in the coastal town of Sidon we saw the worst. Syrian tanks had come down from the mountains and the Palestinians had surprised and attacked them. They were still on fire as we filmed them, turrets and tracks blown off, dead crews hanging from them, their bodies erupting with the heat. Even those who had survived had been shot or bayoneted as they tried to escape. It was a horrific slaughter and the Palestinians were jubilant. For our sake, a small Palestinian boy – he could not have been more than ten years old – pulled up a Syrian head and spat into the dead man's eyes. Mothers danced and screamed their delight.

At Tyre, another fifty miles on, I saw a coaster in the harbour, smoke drifting from its funnel. We found the harbourmaster, who quickly found the captain and yes, he told us, he was leaving in a couple of hours, and his next port of call was Cyprus. He expected to arrive early the next morning and he would be happy to take a paying passenger. Given the known risk of attempting the Israeli border, this had to be the better option. If Bob would carry the film to Cyprus, where there were frequent British European Airways flights, he could be in London the next day. It was a gamble we had to take. I recorded my new commentary to cover the new events we had filmed, and Paul and I drank warm beer in the harbourmaster's office until the coaster was a tiny dot on the shimmering horizon. Then we began the long and dangerous drive along the road we had come.

We were back in Beirut before midnight and an urgent telex was waiting for me from London. Where was my film? they asked. Why had I not met Peter Lynch at the border? I was confused. Had somebody telexed London on my behalf? Had London telephoned to find out what I was intending to do? Paul and I did the rounds of the various correspondents' rooms but nobody had made a call, nobody had received a call. The telex, they said, had only just come on line again and the telephones were still out of order. I had told only four other people of my intention to try for 'Dixie' and they were not likely to make that public – not in a hotel full of Arabs, in the middle of Beirut. Yet London knew I had intended trying.

I learnt later what had happened. Peter Lynch had been telephoned early in the morning by a contact in Mossad, the Israeli secret service, telling him of my intention and advising him to get to the border. So Peter went and waited for me to appear with the precious rolls of film. Someone at the breakfast table or somebody eavesdropping was an Israeli agent who had somehow transmitted a message to Tel Aviv.

Bob did not steam into Cyprus as planned. The coaster experienced one of the worst storms in the Mediterranean for many years, and they dropped sea-anchor to ride it out. Our film had already become history. As the Americans are so infuriatingly fond of saying, that's the way the cookie crumbles.

Some years later, when I was in Jerusalem giving a series of lectures at the university, I met an Israeli colonel who had spent some of his career with Mossad. He remembered the incident well, and the radio message from Beirut. 'Our agent,' he said, 'was not interested in your film, of course. We had simply to be alert to all traffic going north–south.'

'But you told Peter . . .'

'To help Peter. We like to think we have journalists in our pocket if we can do them a favour now and again.'

'You did me a favour, too.'

'Oh, no!' he said, and he laughed loudly. 'We were doing you no favour. We knew you would never reach the border alive. Believe me, not alive!'

Which is why I think fondly of that coaster and the storm at sea on the day we lost our world scoop.

It had been a thoroughly sour trip, and it was over. I vowed I would never return to the Lebanon again. I never did.

CHAPTER FIVE

Welcome to Cyprus!
July 1974

EVERY NEW STORY was a test and I was always anxious to leave while I was still running with it. I thought it was simply a matter of timing, as if chance and opportunity were of my own choosing. If I had any particular ability, it was to grab at luck and even on occasion to turn bad fortune to advantage. So it was in Cyprus in the summer of 1974.

Monday, 8 July, and John Mahoney, the shrewdest of all foreign editors, decided I should go to Cyprus. Four-line stories were appearing on the back pages of the national press reporting increased activity of the National Guard on the island. We agreed it was not a story that was likely to excite the editorial cabal upstairs, who decided what should and should not be on the daily news agenda, but nevertheless something unusual, something suspicious, seemed to be happening in Cyprus and it was worth the airfare to find out what. My report begins:

> *Nicosia, Cyprus. 10 July 1974:*
> What is evident is the sudden increase in the number of mobile patrols by the National Guard on the streets. In ten minutes on this corner of Metaxas Square we counted eighteen jeeps on patrol. Normally, I was told, you would see only about one an hour. Something is up.

The National Guard, formed ten years before to protect the island and its elected leaders, had now become a thorn in the government's side. That week, the president of Cyprus, Archbishop Makarios, had publicly accused the Greek government in Athens of trying to turn the National Guard into an army of occupation.

There were over ten thousand Cypriots in the Guard, mostly two-year conscripts, and it was by all accounts well organised and well disciplined and paid for entirely by the Cypriot government. It was equipped with Russian tanks, British armoured personnel carriers, field and anti-aircraft guns and with all the necessary communication back-up. But surprisingly, it was completely under the command of Greek nationals, officers who received their pay *and* their orders from Athens. Since the colonels' coup in 1966 relations with Greece had been strained, and President Makarios had decided the Greek officers should return to Athens and be replaced by Cypriot-born officers. Many of the former, he said, had supported the EOKA terrorists who had attempted to assassinate him in their fight for Enosis (union with Greece). In ten days, he said, the National Guard would be reduced by half and the six hundred and fifty Greek officers sacked. They would then leave Cyprus. A formal letter, he said, had been sent to Athens a week before.

That Friday, 12 July, we interviewed the archbishop in his splendid palace close to the River Pedieos. He was gracious, but answered my questions ambiguously; it was, after all, a sensitive time and it surprised me that he had agreed to give an interview at all.

At the end of it, as in most interviews, we did what we call in the trade a 'two-shot', that is, the cameraman uses a wide lens to show the interviewer and the interviewee together. It is a shot we often use to introduce the subject, leading into the first question and answer. Sometimes we use it to shorten an answer, a perfectly proper and long-used editing technique, and the archbishop knew this well enough. He was more familiar with television then than I was. So, simply to make conversation while the cameraman filmed, I asked him whether, considering the tension, I should stay on the island, and he replied, 'You are most welcome, but there is no need to stay. Nothing is going to happen. I am perfectly safe.' So home I went, carrying my filmed report with me, and it appeared on *News at Ten* that Friday evening. Early the following Monday morning, my telephone rang. It was John Mahoney. 'Are you sitting, Nick? If not, I suggest you do.' I did. 'There's been a coup in Cyprus,' said John. 'Archbishop Makarios has been assassinated.' He read me the agency copy.

Cyprus National Guard has seized and closed Cyprus International Airport and has taken over the Cyprus Broadcasting Corporation. There are reports that the presidential palace has been shelled and President Makarios killed. Fighting has broken out in Nicosia, Limassol, Famagusta and Larnaca.

That evening the world's television news bulletins repeated the interview I had done with Makarios the previous Friday, and they included the sound that had been recorded during the two-shot. 'Would you advise me to stay on the island, considering the present uncertainties?' 'You are most welcome, but there is no need to stay. Nothing is going to happen. I am perfectly safe.'

That Monday afternoon I was in Israel with cameraman Alan Downes and sound recordist Bob Hammond, and that evening Tel Aviv Radio broadcast a transmission it had picked up from a clandestine station in Cyprus carrying what was claimed to be the voice of Makarios. In Greek it said: 'I am alive. Yes, I am alive.'

A complicated situation became more so. The newly-installed president of Cyprus, a nominee of the Greek colonels, was Nikos Sampson, a car dealer and one-time assassin of British soldiers during the previous EOKA emergency in 1957, when the British had tried to keep the peace between the Turkish and Greek Cypriots.

The next morning, Tuesday, we chartered a light aircraft, flew out over the island and asked for permission to land. It was refused. That afternoon we did it again and again on the Wednesday morning. On the afternoon flight, because I insisted we should keep circling the island, we ran short of fuel and the pilot diverted to Adana on the Turkish coast, to refuel. As we landed, our plane was surrounded by armoured personnel carriers and we were arrested, searched and interrogated for some hours by military police and checks made with London to confirm we were who we said we were. We could not have landed in a more sensitive place at a more sensitive time and with hindsight it is astonishing they let us go, considering what was being prepared there at the time.

That Thursday morning we made our fifth flight over the island and again we asked the control tower for permission to land. The answer came back, 'Permission granted.' Once landed, we filmed the results of the coup's short and bloody street battles. Tanks and armoured personnel carriers flying the blue-and-white flag of Greece lined the road from the airport into the centre of Nicosia, lorryloads of troops waited at every street corner and surrounded the radio and television stations. Some houses had been demolished, others were barely standing. The walls of some government buildings had been neatly patterned by the snipers' succession of single bullets and from a distance looked like clever graffiti. Army jeeps and lorries were wrecked and still smouldering, tanks had torn up the gardens of the archbishop's palace where I had sat with him only a few days before. Some of the fiercest fighting had taken place close to the British Council and the Museum and there were still fires around the Post Office off Stasinos Avenue.

The Greek colonels appeared to have won and their killer puppet was now in charge. On the Friday afternoon, and under the impression that it was all over, I decided to hand-carry my film report to Tel Aviv, where my producer and film editor were waiting. I boarded the plane with Tom Fenton of CBS but half an hour later we were still waiting strapped into our seats, because the aircraft had developed a technical fault and the flight would be delayed. Exasperated, and more than a little cocky, I decided to stay in Cyprus and asked Tom if he would hand-carry my film package to Tel Aviv for me, to which he agreed. It was his unluckiest departure ever.

There was a party at the Ledra Palace that evening, though I remember little of it except that I finally crawled into my room at around three in the morning, in time to take a telephone call from Peter Snow, then ITN's diplomatic correspondent in London. Ever fond of cloaks and daggers, he whispered, 'Sources here tell me that THEY – you understand me, I can't be too explicit on the phone – THEY are coming in tomorrow, landing in the north at Soldana Bay.' He repeated it again, then the line went dead. I dropped the telephone on the floor and collapsed backwards on my bed. A landing in the north at Soldana Bay? Were the Turks coming to invade the island? But Snow had spoken of a landing in the north when Soldana Bay was east a little way along the Karpos peninsula from Famagusta. I smoothed out a map on my bed. Surely the Turks would come the quickest and most direct route from Adana to

Kyrenia. But Peter had said Soldana Bay. One of us had got it wrong. I tossed a coin, dressed, tiptoed down the corridor and woke up Alan, telling him in whispers what I planned to do. We would go directly north out of Nicosia to Kyrenia on the northern coast. We tiptoed in our stockinged feet past the doors of the BBC correspondents and crews and in the carpark we pushed our car out on to the road so no one, absolutely no one, should hear.

On the outskirts of Nicosia, passing through the Turkish-Cypriot suburbs, we saw families leaving their homes, hurrying for the shelters, carrying children and blankets and food. We did not need to stop and ask why. They had heard for themselves over the radio from Istanbul. The invasion had begun and we were a long way ahead of anyone else in covering it.

Then the car stopped: it phutted and faltered, kicked a few times and then rolled silently to a halt. We had, in a classic way, run out of petrol. It was difficult explaining to Alan and Bob why, only miles out of Nicosia, the petrol gauge was reading empty. One tries to be stoic at such times, and stoic we three were, for a while at least. Perhaps it was simply the shock of failure.

We walked back and after a mile came to a village. Perhaps we could pay somebody to drive us back to Nicosia, where we could hire another car. Then came the inevitable and final humiliation. A car approached. We stood humping our gear, and thumbed. The BBC crew and reporter John Birman replied with two fingers. A few minutes later the second BBC car passed and Michael Sullivan was just as generous. *C'est la guerre!*

Then we heard a familiar sound: heavy aircraft flying low, and then we saw them – waves of C-130s coming high above the village roof-tops. The Turks were coming by air as well as by sea, and a thousand paratroopers were popping white into the sky, mushrooming on to Cyprus: by happy default we were witnessing an airborne invasion.

An upstairs window opened and someone shouted, 'Hello, *News at Ten*' and a man in pyjamas was waving, a man who had woken up to a thousand parachutes filling the sky and an ITN crew standing in his garden. He was a student recently returned from the London School of Economics, an avid watcher of ITN's nightly news, and, in his front drive there was a brand-new Volkswagen.

He had driven us about a mile when we were stopped at a Turkish roadblock. Rifle barrels came through the windows, fingers firmly on the triggers, and our driver was ordered to follow a lorry full of Turkish troops, their automatics pointed at us, their prisoners. Some way further on, the road curved through a village where the main street became so narrow the lorry scraped the white walls of the houses on each side.

I had an idea and said to our young driver, 'Let the lorry get ahead and out of sight at the next bend. Then stop and we'll tumble out.' Which is exactly what we did. We ran through the village, down alleys and backyards and suddenly we were out into the fields, under the men falling. What I did next must have seemed a little surprising, given the circumstances. I stood and applauded them down, and as the nearest of them landed and gathered in his parachute I ran to him and shook him by the hand and said above the din, 'I'm Michael Nicholson of ITN. Welcome to Cyprus.'

It was not simply theatre. Imagine yourself a soldier landing in dangerous, hostile territory; in those final hundred feet you see below you a man with something large and black on his shoulder, pointing it at you, and by his side a second man pointing what we know to be a rifle mike yet to the soldier might be a rifle. But given there is a third man jumping up and down apparently delighted at your descent, well then, you might relax enough not to want to shoot.

We filmed them landing, we filmed them assembling, we filmed the red-and-gold Turkish flag hoisted triumphantly and then we followed as the brigade moved to a village called Guenelle within eyeshot of Nicosia, some few miles distant. Turkish Cypriots ran out of their bunkers and cellars to cheer them, and brought them food and water; children carried their packs, their ammunition, their rifles and machine-guns; and, as luck would have it, the very first officer I pointed the microphone at spoke English back to me. It had become that sort of day.

The Greek shells came soon after, and the Turks took their first casualties. We could not stay on open ground, filming artillery bombardment with nowhere for shelter, so we ran to a cluster of one-storey buildings and found cover inside the ovens of an old bakehouse. The shelling lasted another hour, some shells landing so close the blast took the tiles off the roof and shook the soot from the chimneys.

Turkish Cypriots from the surrounding villages became willing stretcher-bearers and in the short intervals between the shells they ran out – men, women and children – to meet the military jeeps and trucks bringing in the dead and dying. The village was taking direct hits, it was such a prominent target for the Greek gunners with its white stucco houses shining bright in the morning sun and it seemed only a matter of time before all those in the field hospital and all those treating them would be buried in rubble. Yet to our dismay a sergeant hoisted the biggest, reddest Turkish flag from the top of the roof. We moved out to a ditch some fifty yards away where a group of Turkish troops was taking cover. There with them was a disenchanted *Gastarbeiter* who regretted returning from Germany to visit his home with such poor timing. He was wishing himself back in the safety of Stuttgart.

Alan heard the new sound and recognised it first; it was anyway more familiar to him: nobody who had been to Vietnam could ever forget the very special sound of Huey helicopters. They came in low from the north, line after line, each one slightly higher than the one ahead, stepped up from just above ground level to a thousand feet. The first landed, troops fell out of them and the next took its place as the shells and mortars landed among them. I jumped in front of Alan's lens and, excited and not a little confused, began as usual by telling the time. I do believe that, in those days, had I not had a wristwatch, I should have been speechless.

Then suddenly the Greek guns were silent. Since early morning ten thousand Turks had landed on the island and were now spread out in a shallow crescent east and south of the capital and, given the order to advance, could easily take it. In the lull we could hear firing in the suburbs of Nicosia. What was Nikos Sampson prepared to do? He had been put into power to control an unarmed civilian population. But were the colonels in Athens prepared to fight this invasion force to keep him there?

The sun was red and dipping. It was time to go, time to return to Nicosia, to find a way to get our film to London, to find a way to leave the Turkish lines and cross no-man's-land to the Greek side. It was now past five o'clock and in an hour the sun would set; given the half-hour of twilight, we had ninety minutes to find our way back. If we were spotted carrying the cameras, at least we would be identified and that was some measure of safety, but in the dark we dared not move. We considered our chances of survival at night to be nil. We sat in our dugout and with an eye on the shadows agreed that the safest way was the quickest; we would simply walk back down the road we had motored along that morning. Trying to avoid patrols of either side was senseless, they would see us long before we saw them. Nor could we attempt to skirt the separate armies because we had no idea where they were.

So we walked the road to Nicosia. Within minutes – it had to be coincidental, since the Greeks would hardly waste their artillery on us – the shells began landing in the fields around us. We lay flat until the bombardment became less intense. Then we took our shoes off so we might hear better and whenever there was the soft distant thump of a gun firing we went down, waited for the shell to land, and strode off again.

No patrols stopped us, no sentries challenged. No one was expecting three dirty, ragged Englishmen to walk casually into Nicosia that evening: certainly not in their socks! That night, within sixteen hours of landing, the Turks had pushed their heavy armour and troops from Kyrenia east to Famagusta and west to Morphou to seal off the north-eastern part of the island. The government in Ankara had achieved what it had boasted it would do: create the Attila Line dividing Cyprus in two.

The Ledra Palace Hotel – the watering-hole for a generation of journalists who had come to Cyprus – was situated quite by accident in the middle of the 'Green Line', the *cordon sanitaire* that kept Nicosia's two hostile Cypriot communities apart. Fellow-ITN reporter Christopher Wain and his crew John Collins and Tony Pilkington were in the hotel that day: Greeks and Turks, they said, had been firing at one another from opposite ends of the hotel swimming-pool. Everyone had seen the paratroops land but from such a long way off nobody had filmed it. We kept our secret and told nobody except Wain and his crew what we had seen and what we had filmed. No one should know until our film was safely on its way to London. I knew well enough that in such situations, with so much at stake, journalists did things which in normal times and places they would find unthinkable. I knew, and by name, those few among us who in desperation and not a little spite might alert the Greek military, who would certainly not have allowed the film to leave Cyprus.

That night Wain and I and our crews sat in the dark, dank cellar of the Ledra Palace writing and recording our commentaries by torchlight, and planning what to do next. We had been told by a United Nations colonel that the UN force had commandeered the hotel for its own use (the UN invariably chooses the finest of every-thing for itself) and that he had arranged for a one-hour cease-fire to enable all civilians in the hotel including (and especially) all journalists to be transferred to another hotel on the safer outskirts of the city. We were to move at ten o'clock the next morning.

In our cellar headquarters the six of us worked out the details of a plan to get our film out of Cyprus. We had somehow to get to the RAF base at Akrotiri on the western end of the island. It was a journey of about sixty miles, in normal times less than a two-hour car ride. But the road went through countryside that was both Tur-kish Cypriot and Greek Cypriot. Villages would be blockaded, there would be many barricades, military and civilian; it was a highly uncertain expedition. I was for tossing a coin to see which of us should go, but Wain insisted he and his crew would try it. So we began our preparations.

I sent Alan to the carpark to siphon petrol from other cars and empty it all into Wain's. Running out of petrol once was unfortunate, a second time would have been carelessness! Bob Hammond found a large Union Jack, somebody else a white sheet and two pillowcases. The Union Jack was tied to the front bonnet of the car and the white sheet to the roof. One of the white pillowcases flew from the radio aerial as the flag of neutrality, the other became a shipping bag for our cans of film. We separated Wain's story from mine and hid them separately in the car. If one were found the other might not be. Food and water were packed, and I seem to remember a half-bottle of whisky went into the glove pocket.

At ten o'clock sharp, the United Nations colonel summoned all hotel staff and foreign nationals to leave the hotel. We could still hear sporadic firing in the streets and the thump of mortars, so it was like a Le Mans start in the carpark. Chris Wain and crew were the first out, but some of the cars, their petrol gauges recording zero, did not get beyond the front gates, and their occupants had to clamber in panic aboard other people's cars to take them to safety.

With the monumental good fortune that was ITN's trade mark in those days, Chris and the crew made it to Akrotiri just as a RAF VC-10 was taxiing to its take-off point. The timing was impeccable and hardly plausible. The pillowcase travelled SHOP – Safe Hands Of Pilot – and ten hours later was thrown safely down to waiting hands at Brize Norton airfield in Oxfordshire, where it was transferred to a helicopter and London. That night, at the end of thirty extraordinary hours, ITN broadcast its world exclusive.

Sunday, 21 July. Now the fear was of an all-out war between Greece and Turkey. The colonels in Athens sent the government in Ankara an ultimatum. It read: EITHER YOU HALT ALL ACTION IN CYPRUS AND PULL OUT INVASION FORCE BY TWO P.M. LOCAL TIME (SUNDAY) OR WE PROCLAIM ENOSIS (UNION WITH CYPRUS) AND GO TO WAR.

It was sent by Brigadier Ionnides by way of Joseph Sisco, the American assistant secretary of state, who was shuttling between the two hostile capitals. NATO went on full alert after reports that the Turkish navy and air force had sunk three Greek ships in a convoy trying to land troops and supplies at Paphos, at the western tip of the island. The Soviet Union declared a state of military alert and the Pentagon ordered ships of the Sixth Fleet to move to Cyprus, including the assault helicopter carrier USS *Inchon*, to be ready to evacuate the two hundred and fifty American civilians on the island. Four armies were now embroiled on the tiny island of three and a half thousand square miles: forty thousand Turks, fifteen thousand Greeks, nearly five thousand United Nations troops, including fifteen hundred Brits, and another eleven thousand British regulars – nearly seventy thousand men, and all within small-arms fire of one another, not knowing who would be first to spark the powder and set the island alight.

Alan, Bob and I went to Famagusta, which was under attack from the Turkish air force. We drove through the British army roadblocks around the base of Dhekelia and continued on through the Athna forest which was already filling with Cypriot refugees, until we saw what until the previous weekend had been the southern Mediterranean's Mecca for British holidaymakers. It was said that business was bad in Famagusta if you could see sand between the bodies on the beaches.

Famagusta had been only slightly less vulgar than the Spanish *costas*: crowded and gaudy, a place of lotions and chips, lobster-pink bodies under parasols and Watney's Red Barrel on tap in pubs with names better suited to Oxford Street. Now the entire town was deserted and the lines of breezeblock hotels were empty, two already gutted by rocket attacks. The only visitors were the Turkish air force Phantoms. We filmed all there was to film and left, back along the same route to Dhekelia and Larnaca, to join the Nicosia road to Limassol and Akrotiri, another white pillowcase flying from our car radio aerial.

I cannot recollect why, on that third day of the war, we did not take more care of ourselves. Perhaps it was the nonchalance that comes from a run of good luck. We ought to have recognised the warnings. Every village we drove through was empty, the shops and houses shuttered, one village flying the blue-and-white flag of Greece, the next – only a few miles on – the crescent moon of Turkey. Occasionally we were stopped at crossroads by armed men who demanded our passports. If they were Greek Cypriots, they were furious to discover we were English. Why was the British government doing nothing about the invasion, they asked. Britain was co-signatory of a treaty guaranteeing the sovereignty of Cyprus . . . why was Prime Minister Harold Wilson doing nothing? Was he a coward? We nodded back agreeably and even Alan, normally anxious for a political scrap, decided it was wise to say nothing.

We were a little over halfway to Akrotiri, a few miles beyond the Nicosia–Limassol junction. The road wound its way through steep, high hills, bare except for gorse and the occasional ragged olive tree. Suddenly there was a burst of automatic fire; Alan braked hard and the car skidded sideways. In the panic we crossed – I ran out of the car to the right, Alan and Bob ran left. I lay flat against the grass embankment as the firing continued, sporadic bursts from a light machine-gun. I could see the puffs of dust as the bullets splintered the rock forty yards away. Then it stopped. I called out to Alan. There was no answer. I started to crawl up the bank but I had not moved more than a few yards when the firing began again, but this time an aimed single shot, a sniper's round. I slid back down, and another bullet whistled as it passed above me. Twenty yards along the embankment I could see a culvert, a concrete pipe three feet high. I rolled towards it, then stopped as the sniper fired again. The sun was scorching, sweat dribbled into my eyes; I raised my hand to wipe it away; another shot, another whistle of wind. It occurred to me that perhaps the Greek or Turk was simply entertaining himself on a hot summer's day, sniping at a silly man who appeared not to know there was a war on.

You can sometimes feel an odd sense of safety under indiscriminate fire by convincing yourself that as a non-combatant it is not meant for you anyway. You are a spectator and like the Zulu *impis* who smeared themselves with magic potions to deflect the redcoats' bullets, you can persuade yourself that the little plastic card that spells PRESS hanging around your neck can accomplish much the same. But to know that a man is aiming at you, has you in his sights and is pulling the trigger only for you – well, that is altogether different.

I wondered how long he would play his game, and how he intended to end it. So I shouted the question as loudly as I could – difficult when you are lying face-down. The answer exploded in the dust a few yards away. I wondered if I might die there, if not by his bullet, then from sunstroke. It was only a few minutes past midday. How could I survive another five hours of this sun and heat?

After an hour of lying still, I believe I was beginning to lose consciousness when I heard a vehicle braking hard on the road above. The machine-gun began firing again as two British soldiers in their light blue United Nations berets came scuttling down the embankment. I rolled towards them and pointed to the hill above. The corporal near me shouted out his identification and, as I expected, the man on the hill answered with a single shot. The corporal demanded in loud, slow, clear English, that we should be free to leave. Again there was that dreadful whistle of air above us. The two soldiers raised their rifles and the corporal said to me, 'I can see where he is and he can certainly see us. Do you think he is having us on?' I nodded, and I must have looked very close to tears. The corporal paused, then shouted another order and together they dragged me up the bank into the back of their jeep.

Suddenly we were away, leaving the mad joker on the hill and his friend with the machine-gun firing after us and, as we agreed later, missing us in the most professional way. When we got to the next village, Alan and Bob were already waiting. They too had suffered in the sun, but, hidden from the sniper's sights, they had crawled further back along the road and Bob had said, 'We either die of sunstroke or some silly sod's bullet, and I think I prefer the quick way.' With that, they had got up and walked away.

Sunday, 21 July. The holiday island of sun and souvlaki, the package-tour paradise, had in seven days been turned by coup and invasion into an island where everyone was afraid. It was decided to evacuate the holidaymakers of all nationalities as well as the families of British servicemen, about fifteen thousand people in all. The order was given to bring them by convoy, by any means of transport available, into the sovereign base of Dhekelia in readiness for the evacuation to Britain. That morning Sir John Aiken, commander of British Forces, Near East, broadcast over the British Forces Network an appeal to both the Greeks and the Turks to allow the convoy to proceed safely.

> Its identity will be unmistakable. It will be clearly marked with the Union Jack and escorted by military vehicles similarly marked. My orders are that my troops will not fire except in self-defence.

So what was described as the mini-Dunkirk and the Great Trek was under way, hundreds of cars, vans and lorries, bumper to bumper, over three miles long, under the security of the British flag and British guns, drove the thirty miles to Nicosia, which was the principal assembly point, to Dhekelia and safety. To help those people trapped in the north, the aircraft carrier *Hermes*, the destroyer *Devonshire* and the frigates *Andromeda* and *Rhyl* steamed from their anchorages off Akrotiri to Kyrenia to stand by for evacuation. And at Akrotiri RAF Strike Command aircraft began airlifting the first of four thousand tourists from over thirty nationalities to Fairford in Gloucestershire and Lyneham in Wiltshire.

'ONLY THE BRITISH COULD DO IT,' wrote one reporter. It was a popular headline then, and few queried it.

Cease-fires were declared and broken, and attempts were made in Geneva and the United Nations to establish peace once again in the NATO camp – both Greece and Turkey were members. On Friday, 26 July, the colonels in Athens resigned, humiliated and humbled, their regime toppled by an absurd gamble. And that should have been that. But the Turks acted as if nothing had changed, and continued to build up the troops and armour on the island. A gigantic military shuttle service operated twenty-four hours a day between Adana and Kyrenia, along a protective corridor of Turkish destroyers and gunboats. As we drove westwards from Kyrenia we passed thousands of new troops, just landed, and ahead of them convoys of tanks and an assortment of vehicles carrying mortars, heavy machine-guns and recoilless rifles.

By the end of that first week the Turks had more than enough men and armour to occupy Cyprus easily, and that was their strategy: to establish a position of strength so that they could dictate the terms of the eventual peace settlement and draw the line which was to divide the island in two. In the no-man's-land of the new border they laid their mines, and their first casualty was one of our own. Three cars carrying pressmen were on their way to the village of Lapithos when they ran into a minefield. There was an explosion, and the BBC sound recordist Ted Stoddard in the first car got out to warn the others behind. He stepped on a mine and, staggering, blinded by blood, he stepped on another. Those behind watched and one cameraman, safely out of range, filmed his death.

I was pulled out of Cyprus that weekend, and sent to Greece, my foreign desk reasoning – more likely hoping – that, having been so humiliated in Cyprus, the Greeks would revenge themselves by invading Turkey. The only way they could do that, short of an air- or seaborne invasion, was through Thrace. So we sat there for some days waiting. But it did not happen, nor was it ever likely to. And my Cyprus adventures ended not with a bang but with a whimper!

The story should have ended there but, as always, the hotels have the last word. A week after I arrived home I had a letter from the manager of the Ledra Palace and, with it, the bill. He wrote:

> We hope that you had a pleasant journey home and that your stay at the hotel was an enjoyable one, **up to the unfortunate moment when the Turkish invasion broke out, for which I am sure we will all have a memorable experience.** I have invoiced your account up to the nineteenth of July. Thanking you in advance, we look forward to welcoming you back at the Ledra Palace on better conditions in due course.

That letter was dated 11 August 1974. They are still brokering for peace in Cyprus and we are still waiting for those better conditions to be welcomed back to the Ledra Palace. At the usual press discount!

CHAPTER SIX

Vietnam – Cambodia,
1969–75

Diary. Saigon, Monday evening, 28 April 1975:
It is all over and who would have guessed it would happen quite this way? Once we had been encircled by tanks with a white star painted on their turrets. Now there are tanks up the road with a red star, just waiting for the last of the Americans to leave. Then they will come trundling in and a flag with that same red star will fly above the presidential palace and Vietnam will be communist, one and all, like it or not. We think they are waiting until Wednesday to enter the city; that is May the first, the day of the Socialist International and Ho Chi Minh's birthday. We hope by then we shall be gone.

Early this morning they fired five of their large 122mm rockets into the city. One was a direct hit on the Majestic Hotel, a few hundred yards down the road from here on the river front. It destroyed the top floor and with it the penthouse suite, where the Saigon authorities had fantasised they would sit down with the communists and negotiate an amiable peace. They could not have been sent a more dramatic reminder that things will not be that way. The other rockets landed in Cholon, the Chinese ghetto, and a lot of people have been killed. A photographer who was there soon after has pictures: one shows a little girl who has lost her face, only her eyes show; in another, a father is holding the remains of his baby. Who was it said the survivors must envy the dead?

This will be our last night. By rights we should all get drunk but nobody wants to chance a hangover tomorrow, the last day of the war perhaps, though probably not an end to the bloodletting. People fear the worst. Wealthy Vietnamese fathers have been touring the hotels, offering wads of dollars and jewellery to any evacuating European who will sign a form promising to marry their daughters. It is the only way to get them out. A lot of dollars have been taken. I doubt if many daughters will be. One Vietnamese lady in the room along the corridor says she will poison herself tonight. We shall know tomorrow.

From my balcony I can see military police below in Lam Son Square making sure the curfew is obeyed, even now. They are still in their immaculate uniforms and white helmets. We once called them the 'white mice' but they at least have not run like so many units of the army, whom we have seen stripping down to their underpants. Beyond Lam Son is the statue everybody wishes the Vietcong had hit with their rockets – surely the world's ugliest monument to fighting men. Made some years ago in quick-setting cement by what one wag called the 'Saigon Realist School of the Grotesque', it shows two advancing Vietnamese soldiers. Today, an army officer stood to attention under it, saluted and shot himself in the mouth.

There are squads of cyclo drivers sitting and smoking on the steps of the National Assembly building, which the French built as an opera house, and on the far side of the square is the dilapidated and splendid Continental Palace Hotel we are all so fond of and will miss more than many things. In the morning I shall go there for my last Saigon breakfast to eat boiled eggs and paw-paw and listen to the waiter coughing up a night's nervous accumulation of phlegm.

Today my French crew, Jacques Chaudensen, Lucien Botras and I filmed the last fighting of the war, the very last, and we had it to ourselves. There must be around thirty international television crews here in Saigon but for some reason no one else turned up. Perhaps they have already packed, ready to go, their fighting done. It was on New Port Bridge, spanning the Saigon river on Highway One, the last the communist army have to cross to enter Saigon. A lot of men on both sides of it died today, but I am glad not to have missed it, now it is over. That is an epitaph and it is Vietnam's.

There was a violent thunderstorm that afternoon and during it South Vietnam's third president in eight weeks was sworn in. It had been my job to cover the ceremony, it was Sandy Gall's turn to film the war. He had arrived in Saigon a fortnight earlier. For nearly four months I had been covering the war both in Vietnam and in Cambodia on my own. It was rather typical of ITN, when the war was almost over, to send in a second reporter. There was not really enough war left for two to share, so Sandy and I took it in turns. One day he would go up the road looking for a fight and I covered the political angles; the next day we swapped. That Monday was his war day and in the morning he had got some action on the bridge which he told me about over lunch; I remember we shared lobster, strawberries, and some Chardonnay. Peeved by his little scoop, but promising to keep my date with the new President Big Minh, I left him with his bounty, detoured via the bridge and drove straight into a salvo of mortar bombs.

We went on our hands and knees and crawled most of the way up the rise, bullets pinging the rails, towards the most forward South Vietnamese troops. There was a tank and some armoured cars giving protection to the men behind and all along the edge of the bridge there were rows of M16 rifles, the helmets of their aimers barely visible beneath the shallow parapet. They were firing nonstop and the road was slippery with shell casings, the bullets from the other side hitting the top of the handrail three feet high. There was another explosion, a mortar, twenty yards from us and I could hear the shrapnel ricocheting off the sides of the armoured cars. Another fell a few yards nearer and we turned and tried to hack it back, crouched, heels touching our bottoms, like cossacks dancing. The dead lay just beyond the tank and there were some wounded too but nobody was bothering to fetch them. One man raised his arm in the air, hoping someone would see him. Someone did on the other side, and shot him dead.

We could sometimes see the Vietcong, hiding in the shadow of smoke from a burnt-out warehouse, just occasional glimpses of black pyjama suits as they ran with bombs to and from their mortar positions. We moved closer to them, following the South Vietnamese, until we were only fifty yards away. We jumped sideways and filmed from inside a pillbox as sappers ran close to lob their hand-grenades into the foxholes. There was a pause and then exploding dirt and bits of people everywhere. One sapper was hit in the throat by shrapnel from his own grenade. He sat down crosslegged, ignoring the crossfire, holding the blood with his hand. Then he let go and it sprayed everywhere. He fell on his back and was still.

The warehouse erupted again and the breeze blew the blue-black smoke our way, and out of the smoke people came running. How odd, I thought it was, that they should leave the winning side to come to us, the losers. A soldier ran past carrying a small girl through there seemed little point; her body was charred and her lips, nose and cheeks had been burnt away. Perhaps she was already dead, perhaps he was only carrying her away as an excuse to save himself. Then they brought out a stretcher and on it was a young woman dressed in black pyjamas. She was wounded and unconscious, and in the extraordinary etiquette of battle they had placed her rifle by her side. I could see no blood. They said her back was broken. VC, they said, smiling . . . Vietcong.

The smoke from the burning warehouse blocked out the sun, like a rain cloud, and Jacques said we must get faster film stock. So we crawled back to the far side of the bridge and ran to the car. Sandy was waiting there with his crew – Peter Wilkinson and Hugh Thomson – and he was angry. This was his war day, he reminded me . . . this was his bridge. I should hurry or I would miss President Minh's press conference. I said bugger Minh and bugger war days. This was the war's last day and it was anybody's now. We had the best of the action and we were going back to see if we could get even better. He could come, he could stay; it was his choice.

Both crews backed away as we stood face to face; it might have been a scene from *High Noon*. I was quite expecting Sandy to punch me and I would not have blamed him; but I was on fire and he saw it, so the sporting gentleman wished me luck, went himself to see President Minh and I went back into the smoke on New Port Bridge.

Thirty years before, almost to the day, American special forces – they called it OSS then – had parachuted into Vietnam to help an obscure resistance leader called Ho Chi Minh fight the Japanese. He was dying from disease and one of the medics filled him with drugs and saved his life. Such irony!

Twenty years later, in March 1965, three and a half thousand US marines went ashore on the beaches of Da Nang to defeat Ho and his army, the first American combat troops to set foot in Vietnam. By the end of the year they were joined by another two hundred thousand, come to win Uncle Sam's war to stop Ho Chi Minh and his fellow-communists from taking over Indochina. They came prepared to stand and fight, but this was not what they had expected. They had been trained in Texas and Virginia, Florida and California, but it had been nothing like this. They had not been told what Vietnam was like. They were infantrymen, ready for set-piece battles, behind tanks and artillery, a war of attrition, the kind of war Americans had fought in Korea, and the only way they knew. But it was not the way of their enemy, the Vietnamese communists. This war was going to be fought on *their* terms and where they chose to fight it.

The enemy would be invisible, hiding in jungles, hiding in tunnels, they would be the killer shadows, ghosting at dusk and dawn, an enemy at night, smiling farmers planting rice by day. The Americans would become maddened by the mystery of who they were and where they were: a sniper from the tree-line, the *mama-san* who did the washing, the child hiding a grenade. Vietnam would be an endless hallucination.

The Americans would discover Vietnam's genius for surprise and unique ability for defeating expectations. They should have read Kipling:

And the end of the fight is a tombstone white with the name of the
late deceased.
And the epitaph drear: 'A fool lies here who tried to hustle the East'.

They should have read their history too, and learnt from the French. Eleven years before, at Dien Bien Phu, the French suffered their only defeat in their Indochina empire. After a last, massive, desperate parachute drop, at the end of a two-month siege, they surrendered to the army they had trained in the country they had given a name.

That year, 1954, in their capital Hanoi, the Vietnamese celebrated what they thought was their independence with the man they thought had given it to them, the fervent nationalist and dedicated Marxist, Ho Chi Minh. They were not to know it but there was to be no peace in their victory; this was just the beginning. Ahead was another twenty years of fighting – and another million people would die in a ten-thousand-day war against the richest, strongest nation the world has known.

By the end of 1967, two and a half years after landing on the beaches of Da Nang, the Americans had turned South Vietnam into a vast military camp. Their forces had been increased to more than half a million men and they were still arriving. The war was now costing a staggering two and a half billion dollars a month. But where was the victory? What had happened to the generals' promises of a short, sharp war? So they persuaded themselves they were winning by simply adding up (and often doubling) the official number of communist dead and the 'body count' became a vital statistic in the propaganda battle; how else could they measure success against such an enemy?

The Americans' own body count was now more than one hundred and sixty a week – over eight thousand killed a year, with five times as many wounded and maimed. If they still had no clear idea of what winning meant, they knew what they were losing.

The lifesavers were the Medivacs, the medical evacuation helicopters. More and more Vietnam had become a helicopter war; there was no front line and the fighting was spread across the country. Never before in any war had helicopters dominated the action: the Loaches, the Chinooks, the Hueys and the Cobra gunships, the helicopters that took you to war, helped you to fight it and brought you back again, one way or the other. The generals claimed that no wounded man was ever more than thirty minutes' flying time from a hospital. It was the one promise men needed to believe.

Tay Ninh Province, February 1969.
We were on a tank operation in what is called the Parrot's Beak, close to the Cambodian border. It was at the end of the Ho Chi Minh Trail, a ten-thousand-mile network of tracks and roads that brought troops and supplies from the north. The American air force had tried to destroy it with B-52 saturation bombing and until I saw my first B-52 raid I did not comprehend what saturation meant. Each aircraft carried sixty tons of high explosive and there

were often ten aircraft in each attack; yet despite the tonnage, the air force failed and communist supplies continued filtering south. So they tried their close-attack fighter-bombers and their laser-guided bombs to knock out bridges and fuel dumps. The lasers were infallible and the pilots never missed, but still the communists came. So then the Americans saturated the trail from the air using multiple machine-guns, firing a thousand rounds a minute. They could lay a carpet of shells across an area the size of a football field in less than two minutes. And still the communists came: a hundred thousand men with a hundred thousand tons of war supplies a year beneath the cover of the jungle forests. To deny them that cover, the Americans tried to take the forests away by spraying them with a defoliant called Agent Orange. Twenty million gallons of it turned the jungle into a wasteland, a moonscape. The convoys were simply re-routed, but they never stopped.

We were told it was the biggest tank operation of the war, but then we were accustomed to American war superlatives, particularly those of Colonel Patton, famous son of famous father, who was commanding our operation. He was his father's lookalike, brash, stylish and with the same pearl-handled Colt .45 at his hip.

He led us through a Michelin rubber plantation, sitting astride the lead tank, smoking a cigar, as if he were in a victory parade along the Champs Elysées. The neatly-regimented rubber trees were bull-dozed flat, the avenue of devastation we left behind was many miles long and hundreds of yards wide. The American government paid Michelin for every tree knocked down, which made Patton one of the last of the great spenders. And the noisiest. The tanks and the accompanying tracked armoured personnel carriers roared and churned their way forward all that day, and helicopters gusted in and out, delivering more men and supplies. I was new to Vietnam but I did wonder how the colonel expected to catch the Vietcong unawares in such a way.

We stopped that first night, *laager* fashion, tanks in a circle, guns pointing out, in an area already cleared by B-52 bombs. It was like Ypres, the Somme, Passchendaele: four-foot-high sticks where there had been a forest of giant trees, craters and small hills which had once been flat land, valleys where there had been none before;

and all covered by a thick black-and-grey-streaked carpet of ash.

Just before first light, there was a commotion: small-arms fire and grenade explosions. We had, by chance, camped above a Vietcong tunnel complex. But instead of staying underground and safe, three of them came out firing at the tanks with their rifles. They were quickly killed. Colonel Patton ordered a tank to plough back and forth over the escape hole, and that was that. It was not! An hour later more Vietcong emerged, firing just as futilely at the great reinforced steel hulks. A flame-thrower was used to destroy them. The colonel then ordered a tunnel rat, an army specialist in tunnelling, to be sent below. We heard a single shot underground and we waited for him to poke his head out, thumbs up, execution complete. After a few minutes more they shouted to him but there was no answer. So they emptied phosphorus grenades into the holes. They slowly burn a man away. We heard no more.

Alan Downes filmed and I scribbled in my notebook: 'The Americans are criticised for the way they are fighting this war. But how do you win against such an enemy?'

Patton ordered the tunnels to be opened. He wanted to recover his tunnel rat but he was curious, too. So they scooped out his body, and other bodies too – Vietcong men and girls, still smouldering with the phosphorus – dragging them at the end of a piece of rope, always afraid they might be booby-trapped. They found some others farther away along the network but they were not burnt. They were wet and yellow with clay and they had all died in the same hunched foetal position, their hands clasped tight over their ears. Blood had congealed between the fingers. They had died of concussion, from the shock waves of the bombs. The B-52s had killed them.

Only one of them was marked in any other way. His stomach had burst into his lap. Young GIs, stripped to their waists, sat within the smell of him, spooning their breakfasts out of cans.

Colonel Cong was in his early fifties, tall, athletic, crew-cut, lantern-jawed, gung-ho and popular with his men, exactly Hollywood's image: he knew it and loved it, just as he did his nickname. He wanted to be remembered as intensely amiable, and told us he was a doctor of philosophy and read ancient Greek for relaxation. At one time in his career, he said, he had been closer to becoming a professor than a soldier. When the war was over, he thought he would probably return to his university in New England and finally retire as an academic.

He invited us for lunch and we ate astonishingly well. Not the combat rations heated over a kerosene stove we had expected but the choicest Vietnamese food freshly cooked by a Vietnamese chef who travelled wherever the colonel's tour of duty took him. We drank wine which the colonel shipped in from Bangkok.

He talked entertainingly and nonstop throughout the meal as he reviewed the world situation and talked of the war and how much better America could fight it. He had worked for 'Psych-Ops'. The American army has a penchant for abbreviating everything: it meant Psychological Warfare. He described how he would go 'psyching out the enemy', flying helicopters low over villages with loudspeakers hanging from the skids. The Vietnamese, he explained, worshipped their dead, so the boffins in Psych-Ops arranged for suitable ancestral voices to be recorded by Vietnamese actors in Los Angeles, ghostly voices that told the Vietcong they were not popular in the afterworld and should give themselves up to the Americans.

He had also been involved in the civilian pacification programme called 'winning hearts and minds', generally known by its acronym WHAMMO, which was a good indication of its gentleness and subtlety. It was an American attempt to win over the peasant Vietnamese by what the handbook described as 'postures of strength and humanity'. To help the posture, they flew portable flush lavatories and shower units to remote villages where people had been coping well enough for thousands of years. An army helicopter, sprouting machine-guns, landed at one village and GIs, with strict orders to smile, distributed seven thousand toothbrushes in four colours.

But Colonel Cong was no longer convinced that was the way to win wars: 'We've tried the soft option long enough and we're getting nowhere by gentle persuasion. All we've got to do is to grab them by the balls and their hearts and minds will follow. We've gotta do what the general said we should do . . . bomb them back to the stone age!'

We finished our excellent meal with coffee and cognac. Then shook hands, exchanged addresses and said our polite goodbyes. A helicopter was waiting to take us back to Saigon.

'Now,' said the colonel, 'it is time for recreation.' Every afternoon if the war kept its distance, he said, he went hunting Cong.

'Cong?'

'Vietcong.'

'Vietnamese?'

'You bet! Viets, Gooks, Slopes, Charlie, VC . . . any bastard out there who shouldn't be there.' He climbed into the small two-seater Bell helicopter.

Still uncertain, I asked: 'Anyone?'

'Anyone.' He strapped himself in tight and the pilot handed him a long-barrelled civilian hunting rifle which he laid across his knees. The rotors spun and he was away, waving merrily to us. We asked around, and his men confirmed it. Every afternoon, after such a lunch, and given the war had stayed away, the colonel flew across the Delta, looking for anyone working in the paddies below, anyone who took his fancy. Then he would direct his pilot to stalk them, to make them run, to make them stand perfectly still, to make them hide and make them cry, to do what he made them do until his sport was over. Then he shot them dead and returned to base much relaxed. Every afternoon . . . after lunch.

A man's got to have his bit of fun,' said our pilot as we skimmed the Mekong river. 'Yessir! This war would drive you crazy otherwise!'

It was the oddest thing, to return to Saigon after such experiences. Safely back from the bizarre, filthy clothes thrown to the laundry boy, a shower and a shave and then lobster and salade Niçoise at Ramuntchos, the French restaurant on Lam Son. Dolly girls, five dollars a body, another twenty later for the doctor, dance clubs providing the strangest partners whose jockstraps bulged from sequinned limb-clinging dresses, a night-time's whoring and drinking, business as usual. Saigon went dollar-crazy, competing for the GIs' time and money. When was there ever a war like it?

Saigon tried to pretend there was no war. Beyond the city's boundaries, the Americans had turned South Vietnam into a vast military zone, but in the capital the war had brought more opportunity for greater wealth. The Americans provided a constant flow of money, a dripfeed of dollars on a life-support machine guaranteed never to stop. The suspicion that it might came on the last day of January 1968, just as the Vietnamese were about to celebrate Tet – their lunar New Year. The American and South Vietnamese commands were caught completely unprepared as the Vietcong attacked them in thirty provincial capitals. In Saigon, the Americans fought to recover their own embassy, when a unit of Vietcong sappers, kamikaze-style, attacked the nerve centre of America's Vietnam operation. The suicide squad killed the marine guards and laid siege to the embassy. The Tet Offensive was under way.

Of all the battles to defeat the communists in their New Year offensive, the battle for Hue, the ancient imperial and spiritual capital, Vietnam's Mecca, was the longest and the bloodiest. The city was just below the demilitarised zone – the no-man's-land that separated north from south. The communists had stormed and taken it in one night and it was to take the marines nearly a month to get it back, in some of the bloodiest ground fighting of the entire war. They fought nonstop around the ancient walls for twenty-four days and nights. They lost men as they advanced, and lost more as their enemy forced them back again. Among the brave were the television camera crews who recorded those wins and losses.

On the twenty-fourth day, the North Vietnamese army withdrew from Hue just as suddenly as it had invaded it and when the fighting was over and they counted their dead, the US marines knew they had suffered their highest casualties of any single action in the war. Later, much later, I interviewed a communist sniper who had killed seven marines in Hue in almost as many minutes.

'I watched one man come through a hole in the wall. I sighted on him and fired and he stumbled. Then they sent in another man to fetch him and I shot him too. They sent out three more marines to pull the dead back. I killed one of them on the way out and another as they ran back. I could not believe they would show themselves in such a way. It was not until after the war was over that I heard the marines always recover their dead comrades and I was proud of them for that.'

When all the dead were counted across the country, the Tet

Offensive had cost the Americans nearly four thousand men. The communists, nearly sixty thousand. It took longer to count the civilian dead. When the rubble was cleared from the once-beautiful Hue, they found over three thousand bodies buried in mass graves, victims of the communists' three-week occupation. They had been shot, clubbed or simply buried alive – everywhere: in people's front gardens, in the parks, under stones in backyards, in flood drains. It was the worst political slaughter of the war. A South Vietnamese musician, Trinh Cong San, witnessed it and wrote a ballad which began:

> I sang on top of the dead,
> I saw, I saw, I saw beside a garden hedge
> A mother hugging her baby's corpse
> And a father his frost-cold child.

There were frequent horrific reminders of the atrocities committed by both sides. American search-and-destroy operations were as brutal, and often more indiscriminate, burning down entire villages to deny the communists food and shelter, whatever the innocents' suffering. 'Destroying to save' entered America's vocabulary of war.

The communists lost the Tet Offensive. So did the Americans. The Vietcong were never again a fighting force but they had scored a vital victory, because with their bodies, bulldozed into mass graves like scenes out of Belsen, was buried America's credibility. Three years of war and half a million soldiers and they still could not win it, could not end it. The strategy of attrition – send more troops, step up the firepower – was bankrupt. The combat GIs knew that what their generals were claiming did not match what they were seeing for themselves. Victories were hollow and their cost too high. All of a sudden the mighty American war machine was bogged down with nowhere to go.

Khe Sanh was such a place. It was a camp under siege, six thousand marines with no way out except by air or a white flag. Close to the border with Laos and the Ho Chi Minh Trail, the generals had pledged their president they would defend it, however long it took, whatever the price. It became America's Dien Bien Phu.

For more than two months, the marines were shelled and mortared day and night and they wondered why. After all, the base was no use to anyone any more. But television had made it a symbol of true grit and it became an American obsession. When finally the siege was over and the communists withdrew, despite the months of famous fighting and dying, the generals abruptly abandoned the base, on April Fool's Day. And when they had gone, the communists came back, moved in and stayed. Khe Sanh began as a folly. It ended as one more of America's Vietnam tragedies.

Their excursion into Cambodia was another, and the saddest.

I seldom went to Vietnam without visiting Cambodia too. The capital, Phnom Penh, was only thirty minutes' flying time from Saigon or, if you were possessed of a death wish, half a day's drive. I went there first in 1970, shortly after the CIA coup that sent the precocious Prince Norodom Sihanouk into exile and put the lamentable General Lon Nol in his place as head of state. The prince had, by default, allowed the North Vietnamese to extend their Ho Chi Minh Trail through Cambodia and the Americans wanted it stopped. The easiest way to do that was to spread their war across Vietnam's western border into the staggeringly beautiful land of the innocent and unsuspecting Khmers.

I remember vividly the first day they went to war on America's behalf and at America's behest. What might generously have been described then as an armoured column moved out of Phnom Penh along the road to Takeo where guerrillas of the communist and largely-unknown Khmer Rouge had been sighted. At the head of our column was a second world war French tank that was push-started by an armoured personnel carrier of the same vintage. Following them and towed by brightly-painted civilian lorries were some field guns left behind by the Japanese twenty-five years before. Then came the infantry, a straggling line of new recruits carrying the oddest assortment of weapons, few of which could ever have been fired. Marching briskly ahead of all of them, even outpacing the tank, was a bright-eyed boy of twelve, proud and erect, like the ancient Cambodian flag he was carrying: the golden temple of Angkor Wat on blood-red silk.

At the end of that fateful day, we filmed all that was left of the determined column: smouldering wrecks and the bodies of the jolly infantrymen who had walked so blithely to the war they were bound to lose. I saw an American photographer weep as he knelt by the body of the little colour-bearer. The flag was torn and streaked with blood. The American folded it into a square and covered the boy's face.

He was the first to die in a war that transformed Cambodia. Until that day it had known only peace; wars had somehow passed it by. It was a sanctuary of exotic landscapes, of gentle people, and with an ancient culture. The temples of Angkor Wat were counted among the world's marvels and the royal palace in Phnom Penh was one of the most exquisite in all Asia. The capital was a splendid gem of French colonial architecture with its wide tree-lined boulevards, the grandest hotel by a stern red-brick cathedral, countless orange-tiled and magnificent pagodas with saffron-robed, shaven-headed monks spreading out from them, with their begging bowls in their hands.

On Sunday afternoons, families thronged to the tiny park of tall palms which encircled the ancient burial place named after the widowed queen from whom Phnom Penh took its name. Children rode elephants there and their lost balloons tangled in the palms like a crop of coloured coconuts. Couples, young and old, promenaded along the esplanade or took a pleasure-boat trip up the Mekong river. Farther upstream in another park named Cheung Ek, pretty women in pretty summer dresses sat under parasols, took refreshments on the tea-room's filigreed wooden verandah and listened to the band playing Offenbach. Five years later the genocidal Pol Pot decided that Cheung Ek, representing such middle-class gentility, should be the site of his Killing Fields.

When the war began, the Cambodian army did its best to cope with the sudden invasion by the international press corps, with covert guidance from the American Army Information Command in Vietnam, who considered the war in Cambodia just an extension of their own, which it was. We assembled every morning at military headquarters in Phnom Penh to be briefed by the Cambodian army's senior intelligence officer on the war's progress – or not, as was usually the case. The major's name was Am Rong, which provided some amusing copy; but not for long, such was his integrity and our collective sympathy for his tiny country's plight. There was also a military censor who was responsible for checking all copy before it was telexed or cabled out.

The censor had his office opposite the Restaurant de la Poste. On occasions I would sit with a *café filtre* and croissant at a table under the awning on the pavement, listening to Cambodian music played on a flute by a blind old man. The sun was already hot by nine in the morning, but I would sit comfortably in the shade waiting for the queue of international newspapermen outside the censor's office to go before I went across the square to pay my respects and offer my script for his approval. Story after story would be scrutinised by this dapper little Cambodian army major and always he would stamp it 'Passé par censeur'. At first, of course, I would not type certain things in my script that I had already recorded on tape. After all, I could not expect this diligent Khmer to accept glib phrases like 'this Cambodian Fred Karno's army' or 'their armoured columns looked in the distance like Dinky toys and on close examination seemed to have the equivalent firepower'.

But as one defeat at the hands of the Khmer Rouge and their powerful North Vietnamese tutors followed another and casualties among the untrained Cambodian army soared, everyone recording the war on newsprint or film became more outspoken in their criticism of the way the innocents were being led to the slaughter by the unscrupulous Lon Nol and the fallible American generals. The French journalists found the censor most severe in his use of his blue pencil on any criticism of the government. But still the flower vase, hanging with exquisite bougainvillaea of all colours, shook on the table as the censor's rubber stamp of approval was hammered down on to my scripts and those of my fellow English speakers.

Then I discovered that he could not read English. French, of course, he spoke and read fluently. English he spoke a little too. But he could not read it, and because of the nature of the man and the people he belonged to, he was too proud to admit it. I kept his secret and our association continued happily. Café and croissants were still taken and the rubber stamp of approval was given -- right up to the day when the American army airlifted out those French and English-speaking journalists who wanted to leave, with the barbaric Khmer Rouge literally a stone's throw away across the Mekong River.

Cambodia was a dangerous war to cover. In Vietnam we were cosseted by the Americans, flown wherever the war was, given armed escorts on high-risk stories, drenched in information and flown safely home again. No war was ever so tailor-made for the communicators. It was not like that in Cambodia and it caught many reporters unawares, especially those who had been to Vietnam and somehow considered themselves veterans. When you go to war, more often than not you have an idea, ahead of time, of what you are going to find there. Sometimes you are guided by superstition, an omen, sometimes by a sixth sense you ascribe to experience. Like many, I learnt to ignore it at my peril. It was with me one morning in June 1970.

The Cambodians were fighting along Highway Three and taking heavy casualties near the provincial capital of Takeo, fifty miles due south of Phnom Penh. My American cameraman Marvin Farkus and I had been up and down that road all week. Every day the action was the same, only the words changed, but it was the only bit of the war we could find within driving distance of the capital and that was the first rule of survival: you always returned to the city before dusk. We had driven no more than twenty miles, to a village where we always stopped to buy coconut milk, a village which was always busy. Now it was deserted. We drove on slowly, suddenly aware that the road ahead and the fields and rice-paddies around us were empty too. Marvin began playing his ukelele; he always did when he was nervous. He had a small repertoire and when it was exhausted he recited endless Groucho Marx jokes.

We reasoned that the road must be clear. Three American television correspondents, George Syvertson and Gerry Miller of CBS, Welles Hangen from NBC and their crews had left Phnom Penh on this same road a good hour before us. Had there been problems we should have seen them returning; there was no other safe way back. So we tried to convince ourselves that they must be ahead and therefore the road was safe. But Marvin and I had worked together too often in Cambodia and in Vietnam and we knew the signs. No pigs, no chickens, no people, no go! If the American crews and reporters were ahead we could guess what it was they had found.

The next day we filmed what remained of the wreckage. It was about ten miles on from where Marvin and I had stopped and turned around. Syvertson and Miller, in the lead jeep, had been ambushed, and under heavy fire came off the road, probably hit by a rocket. Syvertson must have died there because his body was found in a shallow grave next to the burnt-out jeep. None of the other nine men was ever seen again.

During the two months of that late spring and early summer, twenty-four journalists, cameramen and photographers were listed as dead or missing in Cambodia. Among them was Errol Flynn's son Sean. He drove to and from his battles on a motorbike, with a bright red bandanna round his head and, like so many, sometimes with a head full of marijuana. We often passed Flynn and another who drove with him, Dana Stone, leaving Phnom Penh at dusk, the time when wiser men were coming back. They liked to be known as the 'easy riders'. We heard some time later that Stone had been hacked to death and Sean Flynn crucified, though it was never possible to know for certain.

I returned to wartime Cambodia for the last time in January 1975. My brief was to stay on after the cease-fire and witness the entry into Phnom Penh of the victorious Khmer Rouge. For the first and I think the only time in my life, I had a premonition, a conviction that I would not live to see it through.

The weekend before I left London, I bought my first super-8 film camera and took Diana and my two baby sons, Tom and William, to Southwold in Suffolk. I made Diana take pictures of me with the boys, and with such insistence she quickly understood why. I had somehow persuaded myself that I would not see them again.

Those of us who had been in and out covering the five years of the war thought we knew something of the Khmer Rouge. We described them as dedicated and merciless fighters, steeped in a confused ideology of communism and nationalism. We thought it was clear what kind of order they would impose, once in power. How little we knew.

There were no clues. No press men had ever been captured by them and released to tell their story. Right up to the end, there were many among us who believed that all those journalists who had gone missing since 1970 would one day reappear, alive and well, as prisoners-of-war. Perhaps if we had been less intrigued by the unseen, unknown Khmer Rouge and more observant of the Cambodians about us and what they were capable of doing to one another, we might have had a better idea of what was in store. Like, for example, their cannibalism.

A freelance Cambodian cameraman came to me one day offering some war footage – exclusive coverage, he said, of government troops capturing a Khmer Rouge. I offered him fifty dollars, the going rate. He refused. It was worth much more, he said, because it showed the prisoner being executed. I upped the price but still he shook his head. This was worth more because after they killed him they cut out his heart and liver and ate them. I said he should take his film to the Americans and he did.

It was, at the start, ritual cannibalism – a rite to celebrate the death of an enemy, believing as they did that if you ate the heart or liver of a man who had died bravely you inherited his strength and courage. Sometimes they would eat a slice of it raw and keep the rest to cook later. But as the war progressed, as food became scarce and the suffering and the hatred intensified, man ate man to survive.

The small town of Kompong Seila is on Highway Four about seventy miles southwest of Phnom Penh, close to the Pich Nil pass in the Elephant Mountains. In May 1974, the Khmer Rouge laid siege to the town and began to starve it into surrender. There were about nine thousand people in the town protected by a thousand government troops – all confined in the narrow valley with no way in or out. There they endured the longest siege since the second world war. It lasted nine months and ended only when the Khmer Rouge abandoned it for their final assault on Phnom Penh.

The defenders of Kompong Seila were under constant bombardment, on average three hundred mortar and artillery shells and rockets each day. They lived in dugout shelters and tunnels. Two thousand of them died and five thousand were injured, but such was their terror of the Khmer Rouge that they would not give in. At first they ate their buffaloes and cows, then their dogs and cats and finally birds and rats and lizards. For four months they survived. Then, when there was nothing else, they ate their first man. They dragged in the body of a Khmer Rouge shot dead on the perimeter and cooked it. A meeting was held and it was agreed that only the enemy should be eaten. They organised hunting parties, teams of four who went out at night working their way through the mine-fields and barbed wire to hunt and kill the communist soldiers. On one such expedition, the hunters brought back thirty bodies. The corpses were then expertly butchered and the best cuts, the but-tocks and fillets, given to the senior army officers and the hunters themselves. The rest, boiled in the communal kitchens and mixed with vegetables and chillies, was called 'man soup'.

By the second week of April 1975, the Khmer Rouge had sur-rounded the capital and were only waiting for the foreign embassies to evacuate their staff before entering to begin their slaughter. Most of us had already decided to leave: it was generally agreed that it would be suicide not to. Sidney Schanberg of the *New York Times* said he intended staying, but then we knew he was capable of saying many silly things very loudly and few believed he would not be on the evacuation flight like the rest of us. We were wrong. He stayed along with the British Journalist Jon Swain of the *Sunday Times*, and the story of their survival and of Sidney's Cambodian stringer, Dith Pranu, was the basis of David Puttnam's film *The Killing Fields*.

The Khmer Rouge were now so close they could bombard the city with their Chinese 122mm rockets when they chose. Their favour-ite target was the central market and their favourite time was mid-morning when it was packed with shoppers. It was the only place left in the city where there was food so the communists knew they could inflict the greatest terror and the greatest casualties. People had no choice and went there every morning, knowing it was the most likely place to be killed.

The rockets had not always been so effective. A year before, when people heard them approaching they fell flat; because the blast rose, they usually escaped with a few grazes. But when the war sci-entists in Peking heard this they went back to their drawing-boards and invented an altogether more efficient killing device. From then on, when the rockets burst open in Phnom Penh market, they unpeeled like an upside-down banana, spreading the white-hot shrapnel low into the unsuspecting crowd who had believed them-selves safe.

In those last few weeks, there were so many dead, they were piled in heaps with the market garbage and left to putrefy. They rotted in the morgues too because there was no refrigeration. The hospitals were so full, the ill, the diseased and the wounded found their own dark corners to sit in and wait for the end. We filmed stinking maternity wards where dehydrated babies sucked the nipples of women who seemed their grandmothers. We filmed men who sat and watched their life emptying out of the bleeding stumps of their amputated legs. We filmed people – once sturdy, handsome, beautiful people – shrivelling like wrinkled prunes because they had lost their blood and there was none left to give them. There was nothing left in those hospitals except the dying and the dead.

The remnants of the Cambodian army retreated fighting. There was no lack of dignity, those of us who watched it agreed. There were many senior officers and politicians who could have evacuated themselves but those with honour stayed, fatefully. Though there were some without it, who filled crates with gold and ancient treasures – much of it from the national museum – and took the last flight to Saigon and Hong Kong en route to Paris and California.

Now people were talking of surrender in days rather than weeks. Marvin and I went up the road for the last time for my last report along Highway One, the road that leads east to Vietnam. Somewhere along that road we had been told Cambodian troops were preparing for their last stand.

The road ran close to the riverbank. We passed a pagoda; its shiny orange-tiled roof had been shattered by the shelling and through the charred rafters we saw a towering headless Buddha. There were monks by the river, praying, and we stopped to film them. In their hands they held small turtles taken from the river and then ceremoniously freed again. It was a traditional thing to do at times of impending disaster. By giving freedom to another living creature the giver gained merit and release from suffering – not for himself but for the people he loved and in the life beyond.

When we reached the line of armoured personnel carriers, we had travelled only nine miles, that was how near the front line now was to the capital. The Mekong was on our left, a hundred yards away across the rice-paddies. The Khmer Rouge were entrenched beneath a tree-line ahead and to the right. It was quiet. We waited for some hours but there was no movement: each side watched the other a quarter of a mile away. I walked up the road, fifty yards, no more, and turned left towards the river, along a high narrow dyke that separated the paddies. I could see women on the riverbank loading sacks of rice into a sampan. For five minutes I was out of sight of the road and the army as I photographed the women and their children. They smiled. Nothing could have been more peaceful. I cooled my face and hands in the water and walked casually back across the dyke.

It might almost have been a signal for the battle to begin, because suddenly we were mortared. A line of explosions hit the road and came towards us. Engines roared and the armoured carriers reared forward, their machine-guns sweeping across the sugar palms that hid the enemy, cutting the trees in half. Troops ran between the moving armour, tiny men weighed down with ammunition packs, bandoliers and grenade harnesses and helmets too large that bounced on their heads; brave men, ordered to defend their city and now instead running towards their enemy in one last desperate attempt to chase them away.

We moved with them, filming, and felt no risk at all. The mortars were falling behind us and there was no incoming fire from the trees. Our soldiers were so confident, they left the protective armour and ran ahead, firing wildly. Then they were shot dead. As we watched they seemed to go down together, as if someone had shouted an order.

We were dizzy in the sudden confusion and panic. It took some seconds before we realised we were now being fired at from the front and rear, from the line of palms and from the road we had just left. The ground was exploding around us. I looked for any hole to hide in, saw one and dived but Marvin caught me by the shirt – and saved me. It was a well, very wide and very deep. So we crawled on our hands and knees, dragging the equipment between us, towards a copse of sugar palms where we could see huts. But at that moment we were seen and became targets ourselves. So we lay on our faces, pushing our noses into the soil, spreadeagled as flat as we could, and we listened in dread and with our eyes mostly closed to the war about us. Marvin said that someone was trying to kill him and he reached across and pulled my wrist, but I pulled it away. I was not going anywhere.

Then it rained, that sudden, heavy, dense, warm, blinding, blessed rain of the monsoon. The firing stopped, we ran to the palms, reached a hut and hid in the darkness between its stilts. A buffalo cow and her calf and chickens hid with us, and large rats sat and watched between our legs. I said that, short of a direct hit, we were safe. Marvin replied that that depended on who won out there. He had a knack of neatly summarising horror. But that was the option. The firing would stop and if it was the Khmer Rouge who found us, we should die more slowly and painfully than from any piece of their shrapnel. For the next two hours we tried, above the constant hiss of the rain, to gauge the volume of fire on one side and the other – ours and theirs – persuading ourselves that ours was winning. When the firing petered out a little before the rain did, we waited for footsteps and voices. None came, so when the sun came out, we did too.

We kept to the trees, crouching and stepping lightly, bypassing the dreaded fields of fire and what was scattered across them, until we came close to the road. Men were there talking, even laughing. We waited a little longer. Then we heard an armoured personnel carrier turning on its tracks, and we saw the flag above it through the trees: the golden temple on red cloth. Only then did we stand up and join them, the survivors of the last fight of the war. Few of them would survive the peace.

As Marvin retrieved the car and packed away the camera equipment, I walked back to the banks of the Mekong and across the dyke. It was hot and the ground was steaming. Through the steam I saw the bodies of dead Khmer Rouge sprawling out of foxholes each side of it. They had been there all that morning, hidden beneath a camouflage of branches and rice plants, waiting to attack. They had watched me pass within a few feet of them, so close they could have touched me, so close, had I seen any one of them, they would have killed me, silently and quickly, while I was down by the river, taking snapshots of mothers and their children, who knew it all and smiled so sweetly, so encouragingly back.

It would have been foolish to have remained in Phnom Penh until it was too late to leave. But it would not have been wise to leave too soon. Either way would displease London. But, as often happened in a quandary, my mind was made up for me.

Every evening I listened to my favourite programme and its famous introduction: BBC World Service and 'Lillibullero'. Night after night, it was reported from Vietnam that more provinces were being abandoned by the Saigon government; the red army was marching ever more certainly south to victory just as the other red army was about to do here. Was it time to leave this story for that? I did not dither long. Within a day I received a cable from my foreign desk advising that they were considering sending a reporter to Vietnam. I sent my cable by return: CONSIDER ME ALREADY IN SAIGON. SEND SUICIDE MAN HERE INSTEAD.

All that day I waited at the airport for a plane to anywhere. The choice was limited: Bangkok, Vientiane, Hong Kong. A Dakota was being loaded with wooden crates belonging to the evacuating British Embassy staff and with such care and security I joked that they must be smuggling out the treasures of Angkor Wat. The quip cost me a place. There was room, but when the doors closed I was left on the tarmac, growling.

That evening I thumbed a lift aboard one of the American rice planes that daily shuttled in food from Saigon. We took off just as it was getting dusk and, circling slowly, I got my last look at Phnom Penh in the yellow light below. Then we headed due east across the Mekong. The river was wide and the many small green islands were highlighted by the brown water. On them I could see the fires of the Khmer Rouge, their flags flying red. They were waiting for the order to cross and enter the capital to declare the nation theirs, waiting to begin the greatest slaughter since the Holocaust, for the sake of a macabre social experiment. Cities would be emptied, money, marriage, cars, churches, medicine, education – even the family – banned from existence; the genteel Tuol Sleng Girls' High School would become the torture prison and the tea gardens at Cheung Ek the Killing Fields; a million and more people would be murdered on the orders of one man. Pol Pot was about to attempt to make the future past tense, to try to stop the present in its tracks and begin again at Year Zero. It would be written: 'In Cambodia the unburied dead cry for vengeance and the living dead for pity. And cry, both, in vain.'

I watched those tiny flickering fires until they were lost in the haze of the twilight and I remembered the words of Neil Davis who had left Phnom Penh some days earlier. Neil who had known and loved Cambodia and knew better than most what was in store. We shook hands and said goodbye and there were tears in his eyes.

'Nick,' he said, 'the shits have won again.'

Half an hour later we landed in Saigon, where I joined my last war in Indochina. The American military had long gone from Vietnam. In 1972 Richard Nixon had promised, in his presidential election campaign, to get his troops out. He did, forcing the communists to negotiate a peace the old-fashioned way. At Christmas 1972 he ordered the bombing of Hanoi for the first time in the war. The B-52s, flying from their bases in Guam and Thailand, dropped over one hundred thousand bombs on the city. It was called the Boxing Day Blitz and it went on for eleven days and nights. Over two thousand civilians were killed and the Americans called it their most successful air raid in a war in which they had dropped over seven million tons of bombs – more than were dropped during the entire Second World War.

But it did the trick. The Americans got their peace on paper without further communist dawdling and they were soon on their way out. On 15 January 1973, American military operations against North Vietnam ceased and by the end of March the last GI was on his way home. It was goodbye Vietnam.

Once they had gone, the communists tore up the peace plan – it was after all only a piece of paper to get the Americans out; Hanoi knew it, Washington knew it; only the South Vietnamese, it seemed, did not.

By April 1975 the South Vietnamese army had abandoned the northern and central provinces, retreating south and fighting a furious rearguard action all the way. The North Vietnamese came after them just as furiously, bringing men and supplies to last them, if need be, a year of intensive combat. They would need enough for only another few weeks. Finally, the South Vietnamese battalions grouped around their last remaining city, Saigon, and prepared for defeat.

As the troops had retreated south so the people fled after them, filling the roads and tracks and disused railway lines, more than one and a half million in panic. In some places the line of refugees stretched for twenty miles, and where the roads were cut they turned to the coast, making for any port, praying for any vessel to take them where they might be safe for a while.

Jacques Chaudensen, Lucien Botras and I followed and filmed them all the way down that long thin country. We were with them at the docks in Hue as they fought and scrambled aboard barges and freighters, just as hours later we fought our way on to the last aircraft out of that city. Then they congregated at Da Nang and fought one another all over again, giving their babies away, even throwing tiny children on to the decks, preferring the dangers of the South China Sea in the arms of strangers to the enemy at their heels. And when Da Nang fell, they filled the ships bound for Cam Ranh bay until that too was taken.

Vung Tau was then the only seaport left and there they fought with soldiers to get aboard, troops who had deserted their posts and would soon throw off their uniforms too. We filmed those ships, so full they were close to sinking. But they did not leave Vung Tau because there were no ports left to sail to. They sat and waited, abandoned by the government that had abandoned the provinces they had once lived in. After months on the move, they had run out of places to run to. All roads leading into Saigon in that last week of April were unending streams of refugees which never stopped, day or night, a million people emptying the countryside, haemorrhaging, not really believing there was sanctuary ahead, knowing only that they were terrified of what was behind them. Nobody tried to stop them from filling the city; nobody could.

For a fortnight, they had been trying to get children out on evacuation flights – mostly war orphans and mostly from the many church and international charity institutions scattered in and around Saigon. They were filling a flight a day with two hundred children, some only babies still suckling.

Right or wrong, the evacuation was manna to journalists who had been reporting death and despair for so long. Suddenly there was a new headline to share: CHILDREN OF WAR ON MERCY FLIGHTS TO FREEDOM and, to no one's surprise, newspaper and television news editors back home were enthralled. The *Daily Mail* even chartered its own airliner to pick up babies for Britain, and its team came complete with baby baths, bottles, nappies, powder, and its editor Sir David English, immaculate in a dapper safari suit emblazoned with the words BAO CHI (the Vietnamese for press) which we residents assumed to be a precaution in case he was confronted by the Vietcong 'twixt his jet and the VIP lounge.

The last children to be evacuated out of Ton Son Nhut airport left aboard a giant American air force transporter: over three hundred and fifty children, including many babies and their keepers. We filmed them leaving, a sea of tiny expectant faces, strapped in for the short flight to Thailand, there to be shared out among the eager families worldwide waiting to adopt them. As I watched, I remember feeling that there was no right and no wrong. It was not a moral judgement. They had lost their parents; what did it matter that they lost their country in the journey to find a new home?

That what was what I would have written as the last line of my commentary, to go with the final shot of the enormous Starlifter lumbering into the sky over Saigon, taking away its precious cargo. But its wheels had hardly left the tarmac when it keeled over and exploded, the cockpit bouncing away from the rest of the fuselage and the fuselage from the wings.

We filmed from a distance. The heat was so intense, we could not get near the burning wreckage until the firefighters had doused it in foam. As we got closer, we saw them picking out the tiny bodies and piling them in a heap like a mound of waste. Soldiers fired at looters.

Sunday, 27 April 1975. The crew and I went on what we thought would be our last trip up the road in wartime Vietnam. The last big battle had been fought and lost at Xuan Loc a few days before: all that was left to do was to film the last retreat. Michel Laurent hitched a lift with us. He was a quiet, charming, brave and expert photographer working for Associated Press. He had been a friend since we had worked side by side in the Indo-Pakistan war four years before and he had won a Pulitzer Prize for his coverage there.

We travelled along Highway One, past the miles of despair, until the road was empty and we were stopped by incoming shells. We had reached the front line. We left the car dead-centre of the road and looked for foxholes to hide in. Seeing us, South Vietnamese soldiers jumped out of theirs and insisted we went into them. Such was their chivalry, even then.

The bombardment over, we walked forward until we could see the village of Hung Loc about six hundred yards away at the bottom of the hill. If the communists were there as we had been warned, they were keeping very still. The South Vietnamese sent in a few mortars. We saw them explode and waited for movement. There was none. I always carried binoculars with me, and I scanned the village. Michel said we should go down there and see for ourselves. He was nervous and anxious and I knew why. He had missed much of the last month of the war. He had been on assignment elsewhere in the world and the man sent in his place, a much younger photographer, had been determined to do well in his first major story. So Michel, coming in late, was desperate to match him. He was looking for his last great picture of the war and knew he was running out of time.

He pulled my arm. 'Come on, let's go! It has to be empty.' He could have gone on his own, but he was not sure. Nor was I and I looked a little longer through the glasses. Had I imagined movement down there? Had I seen someone, or was it wind in the trees or a timber falling in the fires? I asked Jacques and Lucien what they thought. They shrugged. They always did when they reckoned the decision was mine. I looked through the binoculars for the last time, then turned about and walked back to the car, Michel protesting, Jacques and Lucien quiet and probably much relieved.

There was another car waiting and standing by it was another French photographer; young and with little experience; Michel easily persuaded him to go with him to the village. We tried hard to dissuade them, but they drove off.

We were too far away to hear the explosions or the machine-gun fire. We knew nothing until it was over. But a South Vietnamese officer had watched it – had seen the car entering the village and then the ambush. He thought it was a rocket that hit the car. The young Frenchman fell out of the driving-seat, wounded, Michel stumbled out to help him and was then cut apart by the bullets. They left the bodies there until Monday morning. The next day the war was over.

29 April: the last day: 'There is no way that tree is coming down. If we are to leave we'll do it with dignity.' The American Ambassador, Graham Martin, looked down from his sixth-floor office at the thousands of South Vietnamese who had been surrounding the embassy since dawn. He was a sick and moody man since his favourite GI son had been killed in Vietnam. He had one last ambassadorial duty to fulfil: to get his staff out of Saigon without adding to the thousands of mistakes the Americans had made in Vietnam. He meant to do it in the proper fashion and he almost managed it.

The tree was a mighty tamarind that had been planted a century before by the French, who knew something about the problems of leaving Vietnam with dignity. It towered on the embassy front lawn and the CIA men had decided that it should be felled to make room for helicopters in an emergency evacuation. But Ambassador Martin was adamant: 'If that tree falls, all America's prestige falls with it. I have given my word to those people down there that we will not run away. Goddamn it, but if they see us cutting down our biggest tree, they'll know the helicopters are coming to take us, and everything we stand for, away.'

But the helicopters *were* coming to take away us and everything we stood for and everyone in Saigon knew it. This was Evacuation Day.

We heard that three thousand South Vietnamese whom the Americans had promised to evacuate were stranded at Ton Son Nhut airport. They were just about to board the C-130 transporters when the communists began bombing the airport with captured American bombs and captured American A-37 planes. The last two Americans to die in Vietnam were killed in that attack. The Vietnamese evacuees took shelter in the GIs' gymnasium and the cinema. There was still a poster up advertising the last film: THE DAY THE EARTH TURNED INTO A CEMETERY.

That morning we had our final briefing, or something resembling it, from a CIA man dressed like a cowboy with high-heeled boots and a pistol holster, looking as if he was determined to enjoy what was left of the war. He was also carrying an M16 carbine, which he never put down, and we took it to be our first indication that it would soon be time to say 'Goodbye, Saigon'.

He handed us all a pamphlet entitled SAFE which was not as we thought about worry-free sex but fifteen pages on THE STANDARD INSTRUCTION AND ADVICE TO CIVILIANS IN AN EMERGENCY. It contained a map of Saigon showing the assembly points when the RED ALERT came. It also suggested essentials to bring; these included: TWO CHANGES OF CLOTHES, A RAINCOAT AND UMBRELLA, A SEWING KIT, CAN-OPENER, MARRIAGE CERTIFI-CATE AND WILL.

We would know there was a RED ALERT by a coded message transmitted over the American Forces Radio, which would say: THE TEMPERATURE IN SAIGON IS 112 DEGREES AND RISING. Then Bing Crosby would sing WHITE CHRISTMAS. We were then to go to the assembly points – ours was the Bank of America – in an inconspicu-ous way that did not arouse suspicion and create panic. It was not, of course, that simple. At the last minute of the eleventh hour, my French crew, Jacques and Lucien, decided they would stay in Sai-gon. The French ambassador had announced that he and his staff were remaining and had offered sanctuary to any French citizens who wanted to stay too. 'Many are,' Jacques said between puffs on his cheroot, 'and some journalists among them.' I protested. I shouted. I may even have suggested with the help of some unkind old English expletives that they should abandon their *savoir faire* and do as they were bloody well told. After all, if they stayed, it meant I would have to stay too, which frankly no longer appealed to me; four months was too long. I had had enough.

In all the years I had worked with Jacques I had never known him lose his temper and he kept it then. He blew evil-smelling blue smoke over me instead. The communists, he said, would not harm the French but they might be unkind to the Americans, and to the North Vietnamese the British and the Americans were the same. 'Anyway,' said Lucien, 'the story is not over yet.' He was right; it was not. I would have to stay.

I had of course forgotten Sandy Gall. I found him in his room packing, ready to evacuate. When I told him the news, he did what I hoped he would do and what his reputation demanded. There would be no tossing of coins, no drawing of straws. As I had been the first into Vietnam, well, then, I should be the first out – it was only fair, old man! It was as gentlemanly as that. So he unpacked his bag and typewriter and as an honorary Frenchman walked off to join his new crew, leaving Peter Wilkinson, Hugh Thomson and me feeling much relieved and not at all guilty. That was to come a little later.

Come the alert, someone at the embassy lost Mr Crosby and 'White Christmas' was never played. So, doing what Americans do in moments of crisis, they ignored their rules and sent four highly-conspicuous coaches to pick us up. Worse still, they were driven by embassy staffers who had never driven a coach before or even driven in Saigon. Ours took us wildly to Ton Son Nhut airport, ignoring our shouts that it was on fire and the desperate voices over his own radio telling him the security situation there was out of control. We heard over that same radio that some of the coaches had made it into the airport but we got only as far as the first gate and were quickly turned around by military police who sent a burst of automatic fire a yard above our roof. Across the road the bill-board read: THE NOBLE SACRIFICE OF ALLIED SOLDIERS WILL NEVER BE FORGOTTEN.

We went instead to the harbour. There were two enormous barges on the river, sandbags piled up in a six-foot wall around the decks to protect them for the run down-river to the sea. Realising his mistake, our driver tried to turn around, but we were besieged by panicking Vietnamese who clambered on to the roof and sat on the bonnet. Our driver held the wheel with his left hand and fired his M16 carbine out of his driving window with the other but no one seemed to hear: there was gunfire everywhere now. So he let the clutch in and out sharply and we bounced our way back out through the gates.

A woman grabbed the rim of the side window, pleading with us to open the wire anti-grenade grid. Her fingers were locked through the mesh and she was holding two tiny children hard against it. She screamed in English: 'Take them! Take them!' Their little faces were distorted and they cried and struggled. She tried again to pull out the grid, lost hold of the children and dropped them. They fell under our rear wheels. For an instant she looked into the coach, expecting to see them, unable to believe what she had done. Then she looked behind at the road and what was lying there and she too fell away.

At last we were across the road from the American embassy and there was America's ignoble Dunkirk. Thousands more Vietnamese had been queuing there throughout the night, ignoring the curfew: the wise, the wealthy and those with any known American connection – pleading, demanding the one-way ticket out on evacuation planes that were still supposed to be flying into Ton Son Nhut. 'Don't panic,' men in Texan boots and hip-holsters shouted from the other side of the high steel gates. 'You have nothing to fear.' For as long as anyone could remember in Vietnam, Americans had been shouting the opposite: Ho Chi Minh was the brother of the devil, communism was barbaric. They had once dropped leaflets in Hue and Da Nang which read: BEWARE! THE VIRGIN MARY HAS FLED SOUTH, FOLLOW HER OR BE SLAUGHTERED BY THE BARBARIAN COMMUNISTS. Now the 'barbaric communist' tanks were just a few miles up the road and a Texan was telling everyone they had nothing to fear.

But the people clawing the gates were those who had believed in the Americans, who had worked with the Americans and fought for the Americans, and they did not hear him. They began to climb the walls to get in and we did the same. We fought and clawed our way toward the hands of the marines who were hauling only Westerners over the top. And we did fight and we did claw. I was not proud of what I did that day. No one who was there can feel anything but shame at what they did and what they allowed to happen to others around them. Marines lined the top of the wall by the back gate on Hong Thap Tu, pulling us all up and booting down the rest. They lunged with their bayonets at young girls, knocked children unconscious with their rifle-butts, stamped with their boots and broke the fingers of those who reached the top. But they pulled us up.

One of the marines shouted and pointed to a young Vietnamese in the crowd below who was aiming his American M16 rifle directly at him. An American cameraman on the ground in between began filming – first the gunman, then turning to focus on the marine, the target. An order was screamed and three marines jumped down and charged the man, grabbing his rifle and knocking him unconscious with it. Then they turned on the cameraman, knocked him down, took his camera, held it high above their heads and smashed it to pieces on the ground close to his head.

A platoon of marines stood at the side gates, a line two deep, in helmets and flak jackets, sweating, looking very grim, their M16s at the firing position. They had orders not to fire unless the mob broke through, and that could not be long. The steel bar holding the lock was bending with the weight of bodies; people pressed so hard that their feet were not touching the ground, their eyes were bloodshot and their faces had turned blue. A grenade exploded close by but no one turned round for fear of losing his – or her – place.

We could hear and sometimes see the American staffers wreck ing the embassy, helped by the CIA cowboys. One reporter saw crates of champagne smashed open with fire-extinguishers and bottles of whisky poured over the expensive carpets. Typewriters were thrown through windows three floors up, all done in the spirit of scorched earth – just to be cussed to the incoming conquerors. Somebody had issued an order that the pictures of America's famous hanging on every wall should not be defaced. It was unthinkable they should be left behind, and yet they were too bulky to carry. So with solemn civilian salutes and using bundled up Old Glories as tinder, US presidents past and present were piled on the floor and set on fire. Ambassador Martin was told he might take away his own personal Stars and Stripes and an autographed photograph of Richard Nixon, but he must have forgotten or changed his mind because when it was all over the next day they were found in the filth on the embassy floor.

We heard that the first wave of thirty-six marine and air force helicopters had taken off from the carrier USS *Hancock*, one of forty ships of the Seventh Fleet waiting twenty miles off the coast in the South China Sea – about a hundred flying miles from Saigon. F4 fighter-bombers had also left the US base at Utapao in Thailand to provide cover for the helicopter shuttle.

We queued with a thousand others; the Vietnamese who had somehow made it, as well as American civilians, workers, nuns, priests, the press and other foreign nationals, standing at the edge of the swimming-pool waiting for the helicopters to come. An American colonel distributed C rations and baby food to people who had not eaten since the night before. Two births were reported and, in one case, Vietnamese crowded around the woman in labour to hide her, in the belief that the Americans might refuse the extra passenger.

The first of the giant Chinook helicopters hovered in gingerly some time after three. It must have been the only occasion in my working life that at a critical time I did not look at my watch. When we reached the head of the queue, the loadmaster shouted for us to run, then to go back, then to come again. For some seconds we were actually running in a circle. Then as we cantered across the lawn we could not see. The Chinook had raised dust and dirt and a little of the green pool-water, but the air was suddenly white, as if it were snowing. The embassy's documents had been hastily shredded and left in open bins for the helicopter's downdraught to spread, and we were enveloped in tiny strips of white paper. It was like a New York ticker-tape welcome, instead of a Saigon goodbye. We lifted off with the war's secrets all around us.

We could see the Caravelle Hotel and the presidential palace and then we followed the Saigon River. We could see the desperate armada of sampans, ferries, fishing trawlers, military patrol boats – all heading for the sea and whatever liberty they expected to find beyond it. The communists were watching them from both banks but were letting them go, just as they were letting us go. I saw a crescent of fire: New Port Bridge was burning. The South Vietnamese had poured petrol on the tarmac, hoping the wall of flame would delay the tanks a little longer. It is the last image I have of wartime Vietnam. Then our pilot swung us due west for our rendezvous with the Seventh Fleet in the South China Sea.

We flew for an hour until we saw the ships below, streams of grey in a shining sea; aircraft carriers and assault ships, destroyers and frigates. The message came back from our pilot that he had instructions to land us on the USS *Okinawa*, a second world war carrier, but that it was busy down there and we were in a queue and would hover for another fifteen minutes, maybe more. 'Busy' did not adequately describe what was going on. It was chaos mixed with madness. Admiral Gayler, charting the operation from his headquarters in the Philippines, had not prepared himself for a mass evacuation threatened with disaster by mass desertion. South Vietnamese pilots had commandeered helicopters at bases in Saigon and the Delta, had flown their families to the carriers and dumped themselves on their decks. Then, when there was no space left, the navy simply bulldozed the helicopters overboard, dozens and dozens of them. Some of the renegade pilots hovered for so long, waiting for a space to put down, they ran out of fuel and crashed into the sea alongside; many drowned before the rescue launches could reach them.

At last it was our turn to bump down on *Okinawa*'s deck and I think we cheered, it being our impression that the worst was over. We were wrong again. As we ran out beneath the spinning blades, we were directed to the rails of the ship and told to stand in line. Then a very tall and very muscular black marine sergeant ordered us to drop our trousers and bend over. One by one he went down the line and putting a condom over his middle finger, which was as large as a frankfurter, stuck it up our anuses.

Someone dared to ask why.

'Looking for dope, man!'

'You expect to find it up our bums?'

'Some boys will stick it anywhere.'

He found me troublesome. 'Man . . . but you've got a tight arse.'

I replied: 'Sergeant, if you had been through what I've been through today, you'd have a tight arse too!'

And that is how I ended my war in Indochina.

CHAPTER SEVEN

Angola,

1975–78

'The Land at the End of the Earth'

SOUTH AFRICA was now my home and southern Africa my beat. With my family I lived in Johannesburg.

I first went to Angola in 1975, at the time of that country's independence or, more accurately, its abandonment by the Portuguese after four hundred-plus years of colonial rule. In the struggle for independence, three separate factions had uneasily fought together, but after the hysterical flight of their colonial overlords the three armies began to fight one another. The Marxist MPLA, under a poet-academic president dying of cancer, grabbed power through the barrel of a gun, leaving the FNLA, led by a former taxi-cab owner-cum-gangster called Holden Roberto, and Dr Jonas Savimbi's UNITA to fight against it.

The Americans preferred the taxi-cab man to the doctor, whose credentials, one might have thought, would give him the edge. Savimbi was, after all, the leader of the Ovimbundi, the largest single tribe in southern Angola, which provided him with such a powerful constituency that, given a free democratic election, he would have been swept to power. Dr Savimbi is a highly intelligent and persuasive man with a doctorate in philosophy from Lausanne University. He had an impressive *curriculum vitae*, but the CIA decided that he was not to be trusted, because although the doctor insisted he was anti-communist, a devout nationalist, a proven political and economic pluralist and sympathetic to the West, the CIA knew he had been trained in guerrilla and psychological warfare in Cairo, Moscow and China. That of course made him a red, and better a hoodlum taxi-driver than a red.

A Measure of Danger

I remember the night of Angola's independence celebrations in April 1975. We were in Huambo, a large centre-of-country city on the famous Benguela railway which, in better times, had taken Angola's wealth to its Atlantic ports. The football stadium was bedecked in all the flags of Africa to honour representatives who never bothered to turn up. All the beer and whisky they never drank was consumed instead by the thousands of UNITA soldiers. On that Independence Day, I listened to the screams of kid goats having their throats cut on the stairs outside my hotel bedroom in readiness for the feast that no one except UNITA attended. The plane that brought us in from Lusaka (it belonged to Tiny Rowland) was shot up by wild and drunken soldiers as it prepared to take off again, and by evening they were roaming the city, looting, raping and killing. In the football stadium Dr Savimbi, shouting into the microphone above the din, pulled out his revolver and held it high, saying that he would personally shoot dead anyone caught on the rampage. We filmed what we could and then wisely kept to our rooms. The booze ran out and soldiers began to gather around our small hotel, looking for more. They began shooting at the street lights; but stone-cold sober and with the best telescopic sights they would not have hit them.

With us was Evan Davies, once Churchill's bodyguard. He was one of my mentors on Africa and has remained a good friend since. His advice that night was that we should not stay in our rooms, where he had hidden the odd bottle or two of whisky, but go downstairs, confront the drunks and humour them. My only counter-proposition was that perhaps we should lock ourselves in our wardrobes.

The street lights were still on, but enough bullets were being sprayed at them to black out Las Vegas. The soldiers gave each of us a gun and ordered us to fire at the lights too. I pointed the rifle in the general direction of the street, wondering what the odds were of hitting a master control switchbox at a range of a couple of hundred yards. But I pulled the trigger and the district was suddenly blacked out. It had the required effect. With the streets in darkness the soldiers stopped their bawling and brawling and very quickly became better humoured and almost respectful. One by one they lowered their guns and one by one they sat down; some even fell asleep. My shooting accident had tamed them. So we went back up the stairs to my room, stepping carefully over the stripped goats' carcasses, and did to those bottles of Glenfiddich what the drunkards downstairs had intended to do themselves.

Next morning those soldiers who had recovered consciousness were squatting around a large puddle of rainwater, in the middle of which was floating a dying fly. Each soldier in turn was spitting at it and betting on his aim, and the bets grew larger as their phlegm landed everywhere except on the tiny black target. Recognising me as the magical marksman, they insisted I should join them and the banknotes, worthless anyway, were heaped on the ground as they opened a separate wager on me. I squatted, drew spittle, cocked an eye, raised the nose and spat. The fly disappeared under the weight. I had never done that before. I have never done it since. Spitting at dying flies has never been much of an occupation of mine. Maybe it was the novelty that gave me such precise aim; the range, I seem to remember, was about ten feet. It was simply another impressive fluke but I should like to think that to this day there are Angolans who tell their sons of a young, red and raw-skinned Englishmen whose magic green eyes could send a bullet straight and true and whose spitting tongue was lethal.

That luck stayed with me in Angola – astonishing luck – until at the end it made a one hundred and eighty degree turn and almost sank me.

My visit to Angola that year lost Dr Savimbi a vital victory and a crucial ally. It all began, I remember, over my fascination with a man's leg, a white leg in a place where legs should only have been black. We had been promised a tour of the main areas under UNITA's control, areas clawed back from the MPLA government forces. We landed at Silva Porto and cameraman Alan Downes, sound recordist Jon Hunt and I were billeted in the residence of the former Portuguese governor. It was very splendid, with exquisitely tiled floors and moulded plaster ceilings, an ornate filigree cast-iron stove, and a table-tennis table.

There we waited and waited and waited. Waiting is a favourite African pastime. Waiting for something to happen offers a respectable reason for doing nothing, which is perhaps why Africans are so addicted to queues. But I was a hyperactive Caucasian with a job to do and two days table-tennising in a governor's mansion was two days lost. So leaving Alan and Jon at their seemingly eternal deuce, I walked to UNITA's headquarters at the airfield and wandered from empty room to empty room until I heard voices. A door was open. I saw an official at his desk. I entered, and very quickly the door was held firm, blocking me, but I had already seen the leg: a long, tanned leg with khaki sock up to the knee; tucked into the elastic garter was a comb.

'I believe the South Africans are here,' I reported when I got back to the governor's house. It was a stunning discovery, and the implications were outrageous.

Alan was doubtful. 'He was a South African simply because he wore long socks?'

'Yes,' I said. 'Or Rhodesian. No other white man in Africa dresses that way.'

'He's an arms dealer. Or another journalist.' Which was possible, though it did not explain the look of panic in the UNITA man's eyes or the foot in the door. Whoever had been behind it, whoever's foot it was, was somebody I should know nothing about because – and I was certain – above the khaki-stockinged legs was the khaki uniform of an officer of the South African army. It did not mean, of course, that the South African military were there in any numbers but, having sighted one of them, all we needed to do was to find his friends and we had something of a sensational story to send home.

I was exhilarated. It was like sailing close-hauled on a fast wind or skiing in a brave mood: when there seems to be nothing, absolutely nothing you can do wrong. How easy it would be for me now to pretend that what happened over those next few days was the result of the efforts of a determined, diligent, inquisitive journalist. It was not. It was, at least mostly, astonishing good luck, and my ability – no, our ability, because Alan and I had done it before in Cyprus – to turn bad luck to advantage.

The next day we passed a small convoy of camouflaged Panhard armoured cars with white uniformed troops in the turrets. We saw more at the airfield, white soldiers in a civil war where black African was supposed to be fighting black African, and deep inside Angola where white Africans were supposedly a common enemy.

Crossing Cunene River, Angola, 1978. (*page 187*)

The morning after: the return from Angola – with Diana, November 1978. (*page 198*)

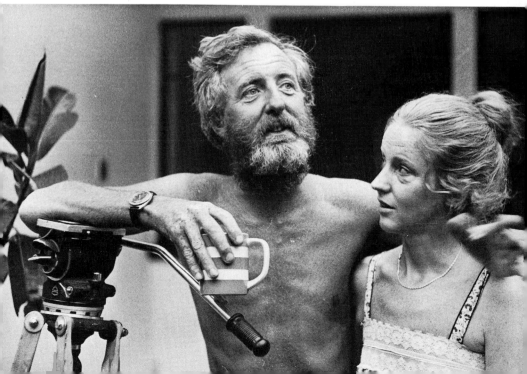

Another marine casualty, Hue-Tet, 1968. (*page 149*)

Nicholson (*l*), cameraman Jacques Chaudenson (*r*), Vietnam 1972.
The sound recordist was later killed in the Laos offensive.

It had been arranged that we should fly to Lobito on the coast because UNITA was anxious we should see how far they had advanced. Soon, they said, they would be marching into Luanda and victory. But their enthusiasm for us to go with them worried me. Why were we being allowed to stay if the South Africans *were* fighting alongside UNITA? A report from us confirming it would be enough to kill Dr Savimbi's military ambition. Perhaps I was wrong? Perhaps I was assuming far too much. Perhaps things were not what they seemed. But within a day, Alan got our proof with the only pictures of the South African army that ever came out of Angola. Thanks were due to our UNITA pilot's secret romance.

The pilot was Angolan-Portuguese and had decided to stay on when the other Portuguese had fled. We soon found out why. He flew us in UNITA's Fokker Friendship (it was their only aircraft then), but instead of going directly to Lobito he announced in mid-air that he was diverting to Cuito Cuanavale farther south. He had, he told us, urgent personal business to attend to. We landed at Cuito Cuanavale airstrip and a bus took us into town. On the way we were stopped at a roadblock manned by white soldiers, twenty of them, standing and sitting around their Panhard armoured cars. One who had words with our pilot was unmistakably South African. There were no identification marks on his uniform, not even the badge or mark of rank; even the man's name – normally stencilled over the right-hand breast pocket – had been inked out. Had it not been, I should have expected to see van Heerden or Botha or van der Merwe. Nor were we looking at mercenaries, but neat, spruce, young men with clipped hair and pressed uniforms – conscripts, who made up the bulk of the South African army. So unexpected was the roadblock that we lost that chance of a picture. But we would come back down this road and each of us knew well enough what the other was hoping: that the South Africans would still be there to stop us again.

The pilot sat us in the lobby of a grubby hotel while he attended to his private business and returned an hour later, a little flushed and out of breath, with a pretty mulatto girl, half his age. We boarded the bus again, Alan and I pushing and shoving to make absolutely certain we got the front seats and, with hugs, kisses and tearful farewells over, the pilot boarded too.

Alan was prepared. As we sat in the hotel I had watched him angling the camera on his shoulder, establishing its position by the angle of his forearm and the weight on his hand, so that by using the wide-angle lens he would be able to film with his face turned away from the viewfinder, giving the impression he was not filming at all. We had agreed the form. Once we reached the roadblock, I would try to leave the coach to talk to the soldiers. I would not be allowed to, of course, and I would then create a commotion to divert attention and give Alan time.

It worked. As I wrestled with the pilot and the driver, as Alan shouted abuse at me and at them, I could see the take-up spool on the camera slowly winding: the evidence we needed, recording on celluloid. Soon the pictures would be shown on every television station throughout the world, and reprinted as a photograph in nearly every newspaper.

Our priority now was to get out of Angola and back to Lusaka, where I could alert London to the story and ship out our precious film. Eventually I made contact with John Mahoney, our senior foreign editor in London, and had some difficulty in explaining what we had, on a public and possibly monitored telephone line. I did not know Zambia's attitude to South Africa's involvement, but I knew Tiny Rowland was involved in a very practical way. His money and his jet were being used to ferry VIPs – political and military, black as well as white, African as well as South African – between Angola and Pretoria. He backed South Africa's involvement in Angola and he would not have been pleased with our film, knowing the damage it would do to his friends and his interests there.

Our film was dispatched for safety to London, but I did not send a commentary. I could not. I was still not certain. Twenty white soldiers do not make an army and it was simply not enough to believe they did. I needed more proof, more back-up. What I needed was another witness, and from our separate sources, we could then establish the story's credibility. Historically, our editors back home were famously sceptical of unconfirmed 'exclusives'. I made contact with Fred Bridgland, the Reuter correspondent in Lusaka. I had never met him but I told him something of what I had seen and suggested that he went with me into Angola on the understanding

178

that he would not release his story until mine was transmitted by ITN. He agreed. It was, after all, an offer he could hardly refuse.

I arranged his flight and two days later we boarded the Lonrho executive jet for our short flight back into UNITA-land. But we went by an altogether different route; my luck was still running. We touched down at a South African air force base close to the Caprivi Strip and the most forward military base in what was then South-West Africa. Our pilots, both British, warned us to keep out of sight.

What we saw out of the windows was all the proof we could have wished for. The airfield was full of military hardware: armoured cars, light tanks, field guns, howitzers, mortars of all calibres, jeeps, ammunition trucks and troops – all being loaded aboard lines of unmarked Hercules air transporters. This was obviously the South Africans' main transit and supply base for their forward units operating across the Okavango River. They were indeed fighting deep inside Angola, committed in a war to put Dr Savimbi into power. It was a sensational discovery and I felt cross with myself for not having had the confidence to go it alone. I should never have told Bridgland.

I knew what effect my disclosures, once transmitted, would have on the war. The South Africans would certainly have to pull out. Savimbi would otherwise not survive international and especially African wrath. But without Pretoria's support he could not hope to win his war. It was a personal dilemma because I wanted Savimbi to win, and was loath to make public a story that could do him such damage. But I had, of course, no choice.

The day my report was transmitted by ITN, the day Bridgland filed for Reuters, the forward units of a Tiger Battalion of the South African army were reported within ninety miles of the Angolan capital Luanda, less than a day's drive away.

The day after the story the order was given to abort and Tiger Battalion began its retreat to its bases across the Okavango. Savimbi had come as close as he ever would to taking power and the South Africans had been denied victory in their first military adventure into Black Africa. And all because of a little inquisitiveness and an infatuated middle-aged Portuguese!

Some years later I learnt he had eloped with his mulatto sweetheart. He had simply put her in his or rather UNITA's plane and flown to South Africa seeking political asylum. I believe he is there still, which is surprising when you consider how little his hosts have to thank him for.

Sunday 6 August 1978: A hotel in Kinshasa, Zaïre, and we are about to fly the long, arduous way to Angola. No quick dart this time in Tiny Rowland's jet from Lusaka. Ten days, UNITA had said – a trek to southern Angola to meet Dr Savimbi again and report on his battling guerrilla army. Ten days, the foreign desk promised. But in that southern winter/spring of 1978 it was to take 110 days.

The colonial Portuguese called southern Angola 'the land at the end of the earth'. They knew it well. It is a vast, deserted, desolate land of sand, scrub and sparse forest, separated from the Kalahari desert by the broad and slow-moving Okavango river which, like so many things in Africa, goes the wrong way, winding east away from the Atlantic into Botswana where it wastes itself in the Okavango swamp . . . one of Africa's last remaining wildernesses.

We had kitted ourselves out in Johannesburg for our short sojourn, Tom Phillips, Micky Doyle and I, and flew Swissair to Kinshasa, the capital of Zaïre. This had become UNITA's external headquarters and re-supply base. The Americans had at last realised that the taxi-cab gangster Roberto was paying no political or military dividends and had switched their support to Savimbi. Zaïre's President Mobutu had been encouraged by Washington to do the same.

We were met that evening, as promised, by UNITA men. There were no passport formalities, no visas, no customs inspection; we were simply hurried from the steps of the aircraft to a truck hidden behind a hangar and from there to a small hotel in the hills overlooking the city. When we were not even asked to check in, we began to appreciate the sinister implications. Officially, we had not arrived. Should anything unforeseen, unfriendly or unfortunate happen to us, were we not to return to South Africa, there would be no one to blame. We had simply not arrived. UNITA had provided itself with the best possible alibi. Micky Doyle, our sound recordist, said he would scratch his initials and the date on the wall of his bedroom, in the style of the Count of Monte Cristo, to give some clue to any who might come looking for us.

Before dawn the next morning and still preserving our 'non-existence', we were hustled aboard UNITA's Fokker Friendship and kept well out of sight at the next refuelling stop at Lubumbashi. After a full day's flying we arrived at an airport close to Jamba in the south-eastern corner of Angola and in the light of a full moon and a sky full of stars we boarded a lorry already packed with troops, to begin the long night's journey northwards – a hundred and twenty miles – for our rendezvous with the good doctor.

We drove nonstop all night through forests without tracks, a single dimmed yellow headlamp pitched ten yards ahead. The trees were so dense and the canopy above so thick that only occasionally did we glimpse the clear, starry night we knew was up there. The lorry was packed so tight with men and supplies it was possible to sleep standing up, which I did for what seemed only minutes at a time. But suddenly it was dawn and we saw the first flickers of red light in the eastern sky, and behind us, which confused me because it meant we were driving west when I had assumed we were travelling north. The soldiers around me were still asleep, wrapped in dirty blankets and sacks which once must have held flour and now covered their faces in a fine dust and gave them the pallor of death as they shivered in the frosty morning air. They were an odd assortment of shapes and ages and the only things they had in common were their shiny new calf-length boots, which I recognised as standard US army issue, and their rifles, the Soviet-made AK47. Two large wooden crates filled with ammunition were secured at the front of the lorry. These further illustrated how many interested parties there were in this war, because the stencil markings, though clumsily disguised, were from France and from South Africa.

Our group leader was a young man called Ben who spoke understandable English, and excellent French and Portuguese. He had been training as an interpreter until the war sucked him in. He was also shivering with the cold but he said that within an hour the sun would be warm and we would stop to exercise and have food. We would also have to hide because helicopters with Cuban or East German crews would be out searching. This was why, said Ben, we could not travel by day and why we always had to move under the cover of the trees. The helicopter pilots would otherwise be able to see the broken grass our tracks had made and to plot our route.

Beneath the trees we were safe; convoys travelled that way all the time. It was Dr Savimbi's Ho Chi Minh Trail. The route was through sand and although we made deep furrows with our four-wheel drive the wind smoothed out all but the deepest. The boughs on some trees were broken and leafless and the trunks of others scarred, evidence that this was a busy route for the doctor's war traffic.

Our driver, whose name sounded like Pop-eye, said he was having problems with the fuel pump, so with the ingenuity that became UNITA's trademark he strapped a five-gallon jerrycan of diesel over his driver's cab with a gravity feed line running directly to the engine. It would mean we had to stop every two hours to change cans. Every distance was spoken of as time, not in miles or kilometres; that is the way in Africa. While Pop-eye worked, we tucked into our first Angolan breakfast, a plate of boiled maize mixed with corned beef. It was to become our daily and only ration.

Late afternoon we started off again across a vast plain of high elephant grass and the occasional msasa tree. It was still light and I asked Ben about the helicopters. But now it was safe, he said. The helicopter pilots had to fly back to their base in Serpa Pinto, three hundred miles to the north, and had to leave while it was still light or they would never find their way back. It was an advantage, and he said it with a smile, having foreigners to fight. They were afraid of the country because they were strangers to it.

He sat on the edge of the lorry sniffing the air left and right. I wondered what he could smell above the stench of the sweat around us. Was it wood smoke to tell us we were near a camp? Or was he using his nose the way wild animals are supposed to – like ears, to pick up any movement in the bush? And there was movement. We saw a dozen kudu, large white-striped and spiral-horned antelope, and some smaller deer, duiker perhaps. Some of the men raised their rifles to shoot them but Ben ordered them to sit down, which they did immediately. He smiled and assured me yet again that we were safe. But he was wrong.

Next morning, shortly before daybreak, our lorry was ambushed by Cuban and MPLA forces with machine-guns and grenades. Our driver skidded and skewed sideways into soft sand and the wheels spun. The noise and commotion were frightening, the men's rifles were on the floor, hidden in the tight mass of bodies. Tom and Micky were trapped in the front cab with the driver, watching everybody jump from the lorry; some were killed as they ran. I saw nothing for the first few minutes, hiding between piles of backpacks, lying as flat as I could, pressing my nose into the filthy floor as bullets hit the side. There was a loud explosion and shrapnel skidded off the cab roof – a mortar or more probably a rocket. The crates full of ammunition were a yard away.

There were AK47s all around me and I had the urge, quite suddenly, to grab one, stand up and fire back. How dangerously contaminated we are with Hollywood's fantasies. What an absurdly pathetic target I would have made for the professional ambushers beyond. Is that how men earn their posthumous medals?

Nothing moved in the front cab. For twenty minutes – it seemed much longer – I lay still, not daring to move, sweating out my heroics. Then I heard a call and the driver's cab door was forced open. Our commander, having run with the rest, had returned for us. The ambushers had left, he said, but they might return looking for the lost or wounded. So, shouldering our packs, our camera equipment, our food and water, we scurried off, ten of us, into the bush.

We walked for the rest of that day, distancing ourselves from our ambushers and any reinforcements they might helicopter in. That night we lit a small fire, but when the UNITA men fell asleep we did not feel brave enough to move out into the blackness to find more wood. So we sat and shivered, miserable and cold, not a little uncertain of our future and unable to believe that we were where we were or how we had come to be there.

Our commander had told us that in the three years he had been fighting in this sector of the war it was the first time his or any other UNITA convoy had been ambushed. Never, he said, had the Cubans or MPLA been so far south, and he could not understand why they had come now. Could it be us? I asked. We were, after all, the first television crew to travel so deep into UNITA-land and this was a critical time for both sides. Worldwide publicity about UNITA was something Angola's President Neto and his MPLA government would be anxious to prevent. The commander only smiled, and I was never sure whether it was meant to be 'Yes' or simply a gesture of sympathy, knowing better than we the ordeal ahead.

We walked for another three days and part of some nights, the night walking necessary if we were close to known SWAPO camps. The South-West Africa People's Organisation was fighting the South Africans for the independence of Namibia. Their guerrillas provided Luanda with intelligence on UNITA's movements in return for weapons and food. In turn, Dr Savimbi's men told the South Africans the whereabouts of SWAPO camps and trails in exchange for generous supplies. SWAPO and UNITA were constantly harassing each other, with the former causing by far the greater number of casualties.

When we finally reached a camp, exhausted and filthy, we assumed it to be our rendezvous with the doctor and that night, after a wash in the river and a shave by torchlight, a meal of corned beef and *sadza* (boiled ground maize), I ringed the date in my diary: 30 July. In nine days' time I was due to take Diana and the boys on holiday to Malawi.

But Doctor Savimbi was not there. We were not within a hundred miles of him. When news of our ambush was radioed to his headquarters he abandoned our rendezvous altogether. New arrangements would be made, because security was paramount – not ours, his. The next morning, we were told we could not expect to meet him until, at the soonest, two weeks hence – or three – maybe four!

The Cuban and MPLA forces began an offensive that August. Every day spotter aircraft flew over and the four hundred men and women with us stood absolutely still, quiet and safe. The huts were well camouflaged beneath the tall trees and fresh leaves and branches were replaced every few days to match the canopy. More worrying were the helicopters which came lower and hovered as they searched for any movement, any mismatch of colour beneath. Some came so close, it must have been tempting to try to shoot them down, but in those days UNITA did not have the kind of weapons necessary to ensure certain kill. Small arms, even a machine-gun, could not damage the machine effectually; some of those inside might be killed but there was always the risk that they would radio the attack and its position before the helicopter was brought down. Later, UNITA had ground-to-air missiles which guaranteed a quick and total kill and Cuban air surveillance ended.

Once the offensive began, we started our travels again, accompanied by twenty or so guerrillas who, as the days grew longer and hotter, became bearers for our heavy equipment and supplies. Some were boys, only twelve years old, carrying their own packs weighing sixty pounds and more for twelve, sometimes sixteen hours a day. We could not have managed without our bearers. My own rucksack was light anyway. I had packed a sleeping-bag, washing kit and a change of shorts, shirt and trousers. Underpants had a high market value among the guerrillas and in that first week I exchanged a pair for a groundsheet and in the second another pair for a tattered bush-hat to keep the flies from my eyes and the sun from my neck.

On one desperate day, we lost half our bearers to another guerrilla group going the opposite way to blow up a bridge. So we had to carry our own packs and our own gear and every ounce became a pound and every pound more and more unbearable.

Day by day we became fitter. In the first few weeks we stopped every few hours to rest, simply unable to cope with the pace and heat. We could not stop emptying our water-bottles – the more we drank, the thirstier we became and once they were empty, we went into a frantic, at times hysterical panic when no one could tell us how far ahead the next water-hole was. One day when Tom and I had finished our water early we could hear a little slopping about in Micky's bottle. He was very disciplined, astonishing for a man whose appetite for drink was legendary. It was a torture to be so thirsty and to hear the water so near. I drew my own spittle until there was no more to suck, I even scooped the sweat off my forehead and stomach and licked it off my palms, which only made things worse. To complete the agony, we stopped that night in a forest of charcoal. Everything had been burnt to a cinder and we made our beds in it. Tom and I watched Micky and his water-bottle, waiting for him to drink. He did not, and how we despised him for it; how we loathed his resolution, his discipline and serenity. I wept a few desperate tears that night, bitterly reflecting that I was wasting the only water I had. Of all the days and nights we had so far endured, and we were now into our twenty-eighth, that was the most difficult. We were black with charcoal dust, in this land at the end of the world; dirty, sweaty and wretched without water. Our day's toilet was simply to comb the fleas, flies and other insects out of our hair. Finally the moon rose through black pylons of charcoal trees in the petrified forest. The air cooled and we fell asleep.

Next morning when we woke our thirst had gone and before it could develop again we had arrived at our next water-hole. It was just that: a hole in the sand, seeping black water, with strands of slime and heaven-knows-what in it. But chilled Perrier could not have tasted better. Micky drank the last few drops from his bottle and then fell to the ground and guzzled his fill. Later he told us it was those few drops of water that had kept him going. He might not have managed otherwise. It was a lesson I remembered well, and despite many more long and waterless days the sound of half an ounce of water slopping sweetly in my bottle was enough to keep hate and hysteria from humbling me again.

We learnt to make our daily routine more comfortable and to ensure our survival. We learnt how to scoop a bed in the soft, sandy soil, how to clear the ground around our sleeping-bags of grass, weeds and creepers and smooth the soil flat to re-route snakes and scorpions. We were told we must always keep our sleeping-bags inside-out during the day; before we bedded down, we turned them back the right way, so that any snakes, spiders or scorpions hiding inside would fall out. We learnt how always to stuff our boots full of grass, tightly packed, to stop the same lethal things sneaking in, attracted by the heat and sweat. The precautions were not infallible. Micky laid out his sleeping-bag too early one evening and found a cobra coiled inside as he crawled into it. On another evening, as I was sitting watching the flames of the fire, wishing myself a thousand miles away, Tom shouted a warning and I turned to see a large white scorpion approaching, its deadly tail arched over its back. I hit it with the knuckle-head of my walking-stick as Tom shouted again and pointed to a black mamba undulating towards me. In two nights there we killed twenty-seven scorpions and five snakes.

We saw many snakes, mostly cobras and mambas, and they were a greater danger than the distant, unseen Cubans. One bite from any of them and our journey would have ended in the most painful way possible. We had no serum, nor did any of the guerrillas we ever met. Their attitude was simple: a snake-bite was not inevitable; it was just bad luck and a certain end to your war.

If Tom and Micky were a bit nonchalant about snakes it was because they knew little of their killing potential. I wished I were as ignorant, but a year before I had visited a snake farm a few miles south of Pretoria and had eavesdropped on a briefing session on snake-bites. It had been short and cruel, delivered by a man fondling a cobra in one hand and with a middle finger missing, a casualty of the same cobra's bad temper. Behind him on the wall was a cautionary tale by Hilaire Belloc:

> She died, because she never knew
> These simple little rules and few; –
> The snake is living yet.

'Snakes,' he said, 'do not make unprovoked attacks. If you come across one, stand still and let it pass. If it's a rearing cobra or a black mamba, don't run; they'll beat you. Try to identify your snake. You'll know better how to treat it. If it strikes and recoils it's a puffadder. If it hangs on and chews, it's a backfanged snake. If it coils before it strikes it's either a cobra or a mamba.' He went on, 'The symptoms of an adder or viper bite are severe pain, swelling and blood in the saliva, vomit and urine. A black mamba bite results in drooping eyelids, loss of control of the jaw and tongue, drooling and slurred speech, mental confusion and death. A *boomslang* bite ends in bleeding all over the body under the skin.'

I remembered too his final bit of advice: 'Don't pretend you're in the movies and try to suck out the poison; you'll only kill yourself. Put a plastic bag between your lips and the wound. You probably won't save anyone but that way you won't kill yourself.'

Much of our bad luck was of our own making. We had been six weeks and six days in Angola and were still chasing the good doctor, when we crossed several rivers running parallel with one another and for only the second time since we had arrived in Angola our feet touched water. We were told that we should cross rivers by wading them, carrying our packs, and especially our boots, above our heads. Keeping them on, we were warned, kept the feet

wet and softened the skin, and now that we were walking sometimes forty miles a day it would not do to develop blisters. But we
had a fear of contracting bilharzia, a disease of the blood caused by
worms carried by snails living in slow-moving tropical rivers. It is a
debilitating disease which, untreated, leads inevitably to death.
Micky decided to keep his boots on and within two days his feet
had blistered and turned septic. He could not walk.

We could not go on; we could not stay. The skin on his heels had
turned bluish-green, the blisters were tight with pus, his ankles had
begun to swell and he was developing a fever. So we laid him on his
stomach, Tom made his knife razor-sharp and I pierced the blisters,
released the pus and carefully cut away the rotting skin at the edge.
Tom stood over us twirling his shirt to keep off the flies as I washed
the wounds with the only antiseptic I had, a miniature bottle of
whisky (compliments Swissair). We had no other medicines except
two aspirin tablets so I crushed them into a fine powder, pressed it
as gently as I could into the raw flesh, then bound the wounds with
leaves and camera tape. We hid his feet inside his sleeping-bag to
keep off the flies, dust and creepy-crawlies.

Micky would not be able to move for a week, that much we knew,
yet our group commander insisted we could not stay. To remain,
he said, risked being discovered, and he appeared to take some
pleasure in telling us that in this war neither side took prisoners.
That afternoon, the commander and three of his men left us, and
early the next morning they returned with an ox trailing a wooden
dugout canoe. The sand was so soft and deep, it was impossible to
use a wheeled cart so the tribespeople used a crudely shaped hol-
lowed-out tree. Micky was carefully loaded aboard, covered from
head to septic feet in groundsheets, and our journey north began
again.

But we were not good doctors. The feet only appeared to have
healed. On the fourth day – and I was cleaning the wounds twice a
day – we saw that the toenails were turning black and the skin
around them green. We tried to help Micky walk by cutting off the
heelbacks of my spare pair of shoes, making them into slippers, and
for a while it worked. But sometimes the pain was such that for
hours at a time our UNITA escort took it in turns to carry him on
their backs. One afternoon he collapsed unconscious. Our com-

mander said it was probably heatstroke, but we knew it was not. We carried him into the shade and eased off his shoes; his feet were beginning to rot. We despaired. How long would it take for the poison to circulate? We thought we knew the answer and there was nothing, absolutely nothing we could do.

Then we met the doctor or, more accurately, the medicine man. He was old and thin, with spectacles and a boy scout's hat and in his bag we saw lint and iodine, bandages and creams and we were delighted. But he used none of them. Instead he gave his patient a drink the colour of tea and Micky's pupils grew blacker and larger, his head sank back and he stared, unseeing, at the sun. The medicine man, his bifocals perched at the end of a long thin nose that dripped, spread out a dirty towel, monogrammed with the name of a hotel in Luanda, and with the unsterilised blade of a knife carefully cut the black nails from the ten diseased toes. It took half an hour or more but Micky never murmured and when it was done another different-coloured potion was poured into his mouth and the magic was done.

The miracle man left as abruptly as he had met us, walking briskly off into the bush to catch up with his group. I cannot remember even thanking him.

That day our escorts built a small camp around us and by dusk a dense jungle had become a camouflaged clearing of ten huts. There we intended to stay while Micky convalesced. It took nearly a fortnight. That night he lay on a bed especially built for him, drinking juices from berries and roots especially crushed for him, eating the barbecued meat of a small deer which had been tracked and shot, I suspect, also for him.

No one suffered more for such a mistake or endured the consequences so bravely. Micky eventually recovered but never walked easily again. The pain had an astonishing effect: at the beginning of our trek Micky, the older, less fit man, had trailed. From now on he led.

On 14 September, one month and one week after we had begun our journey to the hinterland, we met Jonas Savimbi.

We entered the camp, leading our line of bearers, to be greeted by a thousand chanting women – women soldiers carrying automatic rifles and grenade launchers, the straps cleaving their enormous breasts, and all singing in glorious harmony UNITA's anthem. In a circle around them, women camp servants, dressed in the red, green and black colours of UNITA, arm-in-arm, were swinging from side to side in time with the rhythm and providing the descant; and beyond them a thousand or more men, some in uniform, some in half a uniform, some only in vest and shorts. As we came nearer they too joined in the singing, and stamped the syncopation.

The singing suddenly became a humming, and an avenue was formed for us. No one beckoned, no one spoke a word, but we saw the way we were expected to go. I walked slowly and as measuredly as I could to the end of the avenue of women, where a tall, broad, black-bearded man in uniform was waiting, surrounded by his bodyguards and a small forest of rifle barrels. I introduced myself and held out my hand. He took it.

'Welcome!' he said. 'I believe you're a little late.' I agreed that we were.

It took us less than a week to do what we had come to do, which was just as well because the camera batteries went flat on the last day. But we had our story. It had caused more *angst* and more pain and certainly taken more time than anyone had bargained for, but we had done what we had been sent to do. No television team had been here before – not this far into UNITA-land, to film this army and its leader so freely. Savimbi even offered us a chance to accompany sappers who were travelling farther north to sabotage the Benguela railway, Angola's lifeline to the sea, the most important and the most vulnerable of all Savimbi's targets. The round trip, he said, would take two months. He quite understood that we preferred to go south, and home.

Three weeks later and another four hundred miles of walking, and on the very day Savimbi had predicted we reached the Okavango and made camp. There we waited for the South African army to arrange a safe crossing, expecting to wait two, possibly three days for radio contact to be made and the route agreed. On day four, we assumed there had been some delay in checking our identities, confirming our credentials with the government's Press Bureau in Pretoria; perhaps even with ITN in London. They checked all right, and when they were satisfied we were who we said we were, they radioed: UNDER NO REPEAT NO CIRCUMSTANCES WILL NICHOLSON AND TEAM CROSS INTO SOUTH AFRICAN TERRITORY. THEY WILL RE-ROUTE AND EXIT ELSEWHERE.

That night the three of us lay awake, listening to the whine of a hand generator as the radio operator sent his messages north to Savimbi's headquarters. All next day we waited for the reply and tried to understand what had gone wrong. Tom and Micky suggested many theories but they were only being polite. We all knew well enough why; there could be only one reason. The South Africans were having their revenge. They had discovered that I was the same man who had exposed their military adventures in Angola three years previously. And here I was asking for their help.

I put it to both of them: we would try the South Africans again. We would ask UNITA to radio them but requesting a crossing only for Tom and Micky. I would remain and trust UNITA to find me a separate way out. It seemed a reasonable idea but Tom and Micky would have none of it. Micky forbade me to mention it again. We had come a long way together.

We became very careful with each other, careful not to create even a mildly hostile atmosphere, sensitive to a careless word or a selfish attitude. We were especially careful not to trespass on possessions or territory. For instance, once each had selected a spot on the ground for his bed, it and the area around it became as personal and private as if it were enclosed by a fence. We had our own areas for our daily ablutions. A tree became our piddling-post and a large area of ground around it for that other daily task, and no one ventured near it. There was no intrusion. It was basic, essential etiquette and so vital did we believe it to be to our survival that in all the months we lived so closely together, despite the physical and psychological strain, we never argued. We had our moods but they were private things, not to be imposed, not to be shared. All in all, we did well.

We were prepared for bad news from Savimbi's headquarters. Another week, perhaps two, then probably out across the Zambian border to Lusaka. But the news was much worse. Our commander came to us with a scrap of paper; on it was scribbled the decoded message he had received from Savimbi. We were to go north again, to a camp halfway to Luso, another fortnight's march, and there we would stay and wait while UNITA secured a suitable landing strip. So we went back the way we had come so confidently and expectantly a few days earlier. I developed a severe pain in my groin. I had three pain-killers; one, I had been advised, was ample. I swallowed all three and soon I felt no pain at all, no despair, only the happy feeling that I was floating and that my feet need never touch Angola again. Such pills! How much better I might have coped if I had brought a hundredweight.

On the sixth day we met a brigade of UNITA guerrillas with their general, on their way to the camp we had left. The Cubans had bombed it, and the general told me it meant the beginning of the expected Cuban-MPLA offensive. 'You were lucky,' he said, 'to have left it in time.' 'No,' I said testily. 'We are most unlucky. We had hoped to leave it for good.'

His troops moved through the bush in a line half a mile across and behind them on the centre track, like a long snaking tail, came the bearers – small, light-skinned men, so elegant, so different from the heavy-limbed Ovimbundi, they might have been Bushmen. They took nearly an hour to pass us, each little man, naked except for a wrap of dirty cloth around his middle, carrying an enormous pack on his head, easily his own weight again, a convoy of gentle pygmies, humping UNITA's food, ammunition, high explosives and mortar bombs to war. Many would never return this way again.

The sixth of October, and exactly two months since we had left Johannesburg. Was anyone worried about us? What was ITN telling our wives? Were they telling anybody anything? Had we been listed missing in action? Did anyone care? We felt lost, and we felt forgotten.

Every evening, with the heat and flies gone, we listened to the BBC World Service, and its ever-glorious 'Lillibullero'. We listened as the season of cricket passed into the season of football, two popes died, Liberal MP Jeremy Thorpe was tried for murder, Kenya's Jomo Kenyatta died, Egypt's Sadat met Israel's Begin in the spirit of Camp David, P. W. Botha became South Africa's president, the Shah declared martial law in Iran, a poisoned brolly killed a Bulgarian defector in London and Mao's 'Little Red Book' was denounced in Peking. But we did not hear of a British television crew who had disappeared without trace in the Land at the End of the World. We had, as Tom put it, been written off. Then the radio's batteries died on us and there was no more news from England.

We were now a burden to UNITA. What had begun as a public relations initiative to launch themselves into world television had become an embarrassment and now a danger. Valuable radio effort was being devoted to us when it could have been better used, and men were being kept guarding us when they were desperately needed elsewhere. The attitude of our escorts, our captors, changed, and we were nervously aware of it; like the noise and images of night, everything took on an exaggerated sinister meaning. How easy it would be to kill us and report that we had died in crossfire, or of dysentery, malaria, snake-bite or even suicide. Micky reminded us of our anonymous arrival in and departure from Kinshasa.

I was to learn many months later from a source close to Dr Savimbi that his senior commanders were advising him to do precisely that: to get rid of us. There was no prospect, they argued, of getting us out other than by an arduous three-month march to the northern border with Zaïre. Savimbi apparently said it was not and never would be an option. Instead, he said, the plane that brought us in would take us out and he ordered us to march south again. Africans have enormous reserves of optimism!

It was at about this time that ITN in London began to stir. A story they had estimated would take ten days had already taken two months and they had yet to hear from us. Over the years I had often heard my paymasters talk about the heavy responsibility of sending men away on potentially dangerous assignments and the struggle they had with their consciences. For those two months, consciences appeared to be on hold.

Towards the end of September, Mike Morris, the foreign editor, who had first sent us to Angola, was himself sent to Paris for a meeting with UNITA's representative Chitunda, who after some hours of bluster confessed he knew as much about our whereabouts as Morris. The British Foreign Office, who might have been expected to advise in such circumstances, even if it could not give any practical help, turned its back with the comment: 'They got into the bloody place . . . they can get themselves out.'

UNITA offered its Kinshasa-based Fokker Friendship, but it was discovered that the plane could not fly because its weather radar was defunct. ITN would have to pay for a replacement. Morris flew with the equipment to Kinshasa to see it installed. Reporter Tony Carthew was sent to Lusaka to check out the possibility of hiring a private aircraft and a pilot willing to take the flight. Another reporter was flown down to South Africa to make similiar enquiries there.

Nothing of our predicament appeared in the British press. ITN's editor David Nicholas had appealed to the separate newspaper editors to keep the story on ice until we were out – if we came out. Nicholas was quoted later: 'To admit our crew was missing in Angola where a civil war was escalating could only jeopardise their safety.' I have yet to appreciate this logic. Nicholas began to assemble his aircraft surreptitiously at various southern African airports, and it was said that at one point he had so many on standby he could boast the third largest air force in Africa!

On the last day of October – a Tuesday – our UNITA commander came to our hut with an odd message from London. When I read the one-liner there was no doubting who had sent it: WHAT IS THE NAME OF YOUR NEW DOG?

It was from Mike Morris. Some months before, he had visited my home in Johannesburg. I had just acquired a new dog from the local pound, a lonely wolfhound, abandoned by its owner and about to be put down. Morris had sent his request through the relay of UNITA radios, knowing only I could answer it. We realised that at long last something was on. They were planning to come and get us but first they had to be convinced we were alive. I replied: THE NAME OF MY NEW DOG IS BADGER. But somewhere along the line of hand-generated radio transmitters some hyper-suspicious operator, believing it to be an enemy code, turned it around and sent it back to us. Furious when our commander asked me to write something different, I shouted, 'Forget the bloody dog – just tell them to set up the beers!'

And that was precisely the message he sent, word for word. ITN received a garbled version of it but, knowing something of my temper, they were convinced. The rescue attempt was on.

We had now become prisoners of the flies. They, not the Cubans, had become our worst menace. During the day they attacked our eyes to suck the moisture, or they settled, dozens at a time in a seething black mound, wherever there was sweat. We could only eat covered in a groundsheet, where we sweated and suffocated more, so that eating was sometimes not worth the bother. Trees turned black with them, they hid the sun and we could not hear each other talk above their din.

We called our last-but-one camp Fly Camp and there we were confined from sunrise to sunset inside a hut measuring six feet by four, with our sleeping-bags blocking out the light to keep the flies away. For ten days we sat in the dark. There was no other way to cope. We did our ablutions at night – a dangerous excursion. Our guards had dug a pit and covered it with branches and leaves so that only a discreet hole was left. But when we poked our bottoms into it we were bitten by flies. Micky, ever inventive, made a lavatory lid with a film can, which happened to be about the diameter of the hole, and made a handle out of camera tape. It was a great hygienic and environmental improvement.

Three days after we had left Fly Camp we were caught up by a UNITA soldier who had bravely tracked and chased us all the way. He brought us what he thought we had accidentally left behind. From his rucksack he proudly pulled out our lavatory lid, a filthy, flyblown film can!

We moved southwards, and more of God's tiny things were added to our daily torture. We were attacked by tsetse flies which carry sleeping sickness, and with the beginning of the rains came the malarial mosquitoes.

As we left Fly Camp we were told that it was essential we should be at our final destination before 22 November – three weeks away. Then and there, it was promised, a plane would come for us. Twenty-one days of fast marching later – sometimes we were covering more than forty miles a day – we arrived on time at a place called Coutada do Mucusso, which we estimated was about a hundred miles equidistant from the Zambian and Namibian borders.

We called this Hyena Camp. In a grand welcome, the resident UNITA guards shot and cooked a wildebeest and we stuffed ourselves. It was the first meat we had tasted in three and a half months and we were violently sick. That night, because the soldiers had not bothered burying the carcass, we were visited by a pack of hyenas.

Growling and slobbering, they make the most terrifying noise of any African animal. They roamed the camp, sniffing our doorways; we could smell them, they were so close. Cubans and snakes, scorpions and tsetse, paled beside them. The African is more afraid of the hyena than of any other animal. The South Africans produced anti-SWAPO propaganda posters showing hyenas eating babies and it was a common South African military interrogation technique to put a suspect in a cell with a caged hyena. There was seldom need for physical torture.

We had hurried to be on time for our aircraft. Four days later we were still waiting for it. Every morning we carried our bags and equipment three miles to the airfield, a bumpy strip of dust amid elephant grass, that had once been a Portuguese rancher's private landing ground. There we waited, looking north in the direction of Zaïre for that tiny speck in the sky which meant freedom; just before dark we trekked back to the camp. Every day the journey seemed longer, the waiting more wearisome and the return to camp more hopeless, a hopelessness made worse because we had begun to talk about Christmas. We also began to discuss, secretly, the prospect of escape. What if we crept out of the camp and walked to Zambia? We could make it in about five days. We began to think of how we could collect food and water without arousing the suspicion of the camp commander, we studied the map, deciding on the best and most direct route. We were determined that whatever else we did, whatever the options, Christmas in Angola was not one of them.

It was, with hindsight, an absurd idea and we must be thankful we never got the chance to attempt it. Four months in the bush had made us proficient and we would probably have reached the border. But I doubt whether we would have got far beyond it. Unknown to us, Joshua Nkomo, leader of ZIPRA, his Zimbabwe nationalist guerrilla army, had training camps in the very areas we would have had to cross. We would probably not have survived them.

Saturday, 25 November. We had been 'missing' for one hundred and ten days and this was our fifth evening by the airstrip, the end of another long day's waiting. A plane was coming, we had been told almost every hour, and we needed to believe it would come. It was just as well that we did not know how very nearly it did not.

The rescue flight had originally been scheduled for 22 November, but as the Fokker Friendship taxied from its hangar in Kinshasa a wrongly-feathered propeller sheared from its engine. There was worse news for those at ITN mounting the rescue operation. UNITA informed them that because of renewed Cuban activity we could only be kept at Hyena Camp for another three days; then we would have to be moved. The window was closing. Another aircraft had to be found. Peter Snow, who was then ITN's diplomatic correspondent, knew of a private Hawker-Siddeley jet in Johannesburg and John Suchet went to see the pilots, both British: Roy Matthews, a former Royal Air Force pilot, and his co-pilot Johnny Adams of the Fleet Air Arm. Suchet explained the problem in detail. The risk of being shot down, especially by Cuban MiGs, was emphasised, but both agreed to go on what they later described as 'the most lunatic mission of their lives'.

They flew first from Johannesburg to Kinshasa to pick up the UNITA pilot who knew the exact co-ordinates of the strip at Coutada do Mucusso where we were waiting. They then flew directly south to Lubumbashi, still in Zaïre, to refuel where the attempt was almost called off. Matthews and Adams produced their credit cards to pay for the fuel, but the airport manager refused to accept them. He wanted dollars only. The two pilots just managed to scrape enough together to pay the bill. Before they closed the door, Tony Carthew pushed a case of beers aboard.

I stood peering into the dark blue northern sky, certain I could hear the sound of an approaching plane. I could see nothing, but then I was looking the wrong way. It was coming from the south, wisely making a wide circle round the nearest Cuban MiG base at Luso. I cheered but that had an unexpected effect on the UNITA guards, who raised their rifles to aim. Shouting hysterically, I ran to each of them, pushing their guns down: 'It's our plane . . . our bloody plane . . . for Christ's sake, don't shoot!'

The white jet came towards us slowly, less than fifty feet high as the pilots checked the condition of the runway before they climbed and banked to begin their descent. Then, in what seemed in those frantic few moments the final deliberate act of sabotage by persons unknown, and with dust spewing from the jet's tyres as it hit the ground, I saw, sitting in the middle of the strip, a family of wild pigs. Our guards saw them too and crazily opened fire. Certain they would hit the jet instead, I ran on to the runway to scatter them, arms flapping and wailing like a banshee.

It took only a few moments to get aboard. Few people, anywhere, could ever have been in such a hurry to leave. We were barely in our seats when we were airborne; exalted, we forgot to look out of the windows to the land we had crossed and crossed again, the land we had traversed for more than one thousand five hundred miles, the land that had been our home and our prison and very nearly our burial place. When I did look down, I was surprised to see it gone. I had lived with it so long, perhaps I thought it would never go away. Below, in the first light of the moon, I saw the broad Okavango, shining silver, and behind it only a shadow. Angola was already a memory. Within the hour ITN got Carthew's coded telex: ALL CHICKENS SAFELY BACK IN THE NEST.

We landed at Rand airport, just outside Johannesburg, shortly after midnight. On the tarmac was a familiar face to welcome us – Sandy Gall carrying a bottle of Dom Perignon.

But in the way of things, ITN had quite forgotten to let Diana know we had landed. The first she knew was a knock on the front door. And there, in the dim porchlight, she saw an almost naked scrawny brown man with a mass of wild hair, a wide ginger beard and a walking-stick.

Early the next morning, two little boys aged five and six crept in and stood by my bed to inspect the odd figure showing through the twisted duvet. I felt a little finger dabbing my dirty legs, another stroked my beard.

'It's got sand in its ear,' said Tom.

'It's got toenails like a chicken,' said William.

'Is it really Daddy?' they asked.

They were not convinced. But then, as Diana said later, four months is a long time in a little boy's life. It is indeed!

CHAPTER EIGHT

Rhodesia

Born 1890; died 1980; aged 90.

ITN's Johannesburg bureau was the first international television bureau in South Africa, beating the BBC by six weeks. It was 1976 and the beginning of what we all believed was the Black Revolution; for months there had been turmoil, with riots in the Cape and worse in Soweto.

As it turned out, the Revolution was delayed. The South African government contained it. But a bigger story in British terms was developing north of the Limpopo, which was to hold our attention and keep me employed on and off for the next four years. Rhodesia was always known as the blessed land of Cecil Rhodes. His dream was that all Africa, from the Cape to Cairo, would belong to the British crown in his lifetime: 'We English are the first in the world and the more of it we inhabit, the better it is for the human race.'

The Rhodesians never doubted it and for nearly a century they enjoyed one of the world's best climates and the privileges their petty *apartheid* gave them. They were convinced that Africa's post-war winds of change would never blow their way and when inevitably they felt the draught they simply turned their backs on it.

In 1965, with their Unilateral Declaration of Independence, they defiantly spat in the eye of the British government. It was the first successful rebellion by a British colony against the crown since the American Revolution two centuries before.

Black and white Rhodesians began their undeclared war against each other in 1972. Black nationalist guerrillas, based in neighbouring Zambia, began to attack across the Zambesi valley, along the northern border, raiding white farms and terrorising villages in the tribal trust lands. But it is a wide open valley, very dry and very hot, and more guerrillas died of thirst and exposure in crossing it than were killed by Rhodesian army bullets.

Then Soviet Russia took a hand and the little rag-tag armies of Joshua Nkomo and Robert Mugabe grew into better trained and supplied battalions. Mugabe's Zimbabwe African National Libera-tion Army, ZANLA, established its bases in Mozambique on the eastern border and in 1975 began infiltrating across the Pungwe river and over the Inyanga mountains, in a sustained campaign of guerrilla warfare. From then on, the white Rhodesians, ferocious in their war for survival, knew they would lose. Their leader, Ian Smith, had once said there would never be black rule. 'Not in a thousand years!' he had promised. It came within five.

It was not difficult to travel to Rhodesia's landlocked war. Occasionally dangerous, even fatal, but always possible. If you flew from South Africa, you needed a strong heart because, to minimise the risk of being blown up by a ground-to-air missile, airline pilots had devised a spectacular way of landing, descending in such a fast tight spiral over the city it felt as though the aircraft was in an uncontrollable spin. They called it the 'corkscrew'. When they took off they hedgehopped at full throttle until they were well away from known guerrilla areas. Hedges were not high in Rhodesia.

The other way in was by road, either at Plumtree on the Bot-swana border, very rarely used, or from South Africa across the Limpopo River at Beitbridge. Driving was always frightening, especially at dusk. It was the guerrillas' favourite time for ambush. The puncture was a popular way with them, a sharpened piece of thorn tree driven into the tarmac at an angle to oncoming traffic. Few people survived to change their wheels. They were dead and the guerrillas away into the dusk and the bush long before the army helicopters came.

The wise and the timid travelled those wartime roads in armed convoy. These were often a couple of miles long and at school holi-day times had an almost jamboree feel about them. The morning convoy to South Africa left Fort Victoria for Beitbridge at seven sharp every morning. Open trucks mounted with heavy-calibre Browning machine-guns were placed at intervals all the way down the line and leading the way was a 'Hippo', the nickname of Rhodesia's own design of mine-sweeper.

Those who would not or could not travel with the convoy drove with the threat of ambush at every bend and hill rise and with the nagging suspicion that every bump in the road ahead, every spread of mud or cow dung, was hiding a land mine. The guerrillas heated a steel barrel over a fire until the rim was red-hot. Then they hammered the rim's circle into the tarmac, made soft in the hot sun, and lifted it out, like a cowpat. They scooped out the earth below, put in their mine – about eight inches across – then replaced the circle and covered it with a light layer of earth and leaves. It was so easy and so often fatal. And yet there were times motoring those wonderful Rhodesian roads when nothing seemed more unlikely.

They are long straight roads: you can often see a half an hour's drive ahead and they are landscaped with frangipani and bougainvillaea and tulip trees. It is a country of grand contrasts and yet so compact that between breakfast and elevenses the bush changes to mountain and back again; by lunchtime you will have passed prairies of maize and vast fields of tobacco and towering clumps of massive multicoloured boulders which balance on a pinhead above slow, broad, brown rivers with signposts on their banks warning: BATHING IS SUICIDAL BECAUSE OF CROCODILES.

It was like travelling through an enormous park, the land was so neat and well-cared-for. Every ten or fifteen miles there was a layby and a picnic area with readymade barbecue spits, tables and benches. Occasionally, in one of them, the tarmac was black and uneven, clumsily and hastily repaired. Somebody, perhaps only a week or so before, had come in to rest or eat and had driven on to a mine.

One of my very first stories in Rhodesia was about mines and one man's unlikely way of coping with them. My report was datelined Mount Darwin, at the north-eastern corner close to Mozambique. A farmer there had boasted a unique mine-sweeper which he had called Major. He had discovered mines on the dirt track that led from the main road to his house, so every morning Major was brought out to test the track for safety. Major was a sixty-three-year-old house servant. Totally obedient and possibly ill-informed, the old man went down the track banging a heavy shovel on the ground as the farmer covered him with his rifle, a safe thirty yards back. Major survived the war; the farmer did not.

I knew of another who did not survive the peace. He was a Rhodesian legend and believed, in the way of legends, that he was indestructible. His name was Boss Lilford. In the early, heady days of UDI, he was called Mr Rhodesia, partly because he owned a great deal of it and partly because he sponsored the Rhodesia Front Party in 1962 and made Ian Smith its leader. Like so many white settlers across southern Africa, he believed Africans were fit only for servitude.

I first met Boss Lilford when he was having problems with poachers. His roaming herds of cattle were being depleted in the vast area he owned, which was called Triangle, in the country's south-eastern corner. Some of his prized stock were dying of disease because Robert Mugabe's soldiers were blowing up the dips, but many more were being rustled and taken across the Mozambique border to provide food for the camps there. The Rhodesian government and military had launched campaigns to stop it – dropping tons of printed posters by air, threatening death to rustlers and anyone sheltering them. As always, the poor villagers got it both ways: if they did not help the guerrillas they were killed; if they did, they died just the same. But nothing stopped the rustling; the herds were spread too far and wide for effective policing.

So Boss Lilford decided to do it his own way, which he invariably did when the law failed him. He advertised for bounty-hunters. First to come were two men who said they had once served in the French Foreign Legion. They were enthusiastic and for a while successful but they overestimated the limits of even Lilford's power and had to scamper across into South Africa after getting drunk one night and setting fire to a village with everyone asleep inside it. Then came some Belgians who claimed to have had experience of shooting and killing in the Congo and Biafra, but they too proved unreliable and created domestic problems for Lilford by poaching, raping and sometimes smothering the daughters of his farmhands.

Eventually, a British ex-paratrooper called Harry arrived in Triangle. Harry had come to Rhodesia from Liverpool a year earlier, having left the British army for reasons he did not wish to talk about. Perhaps he confessed to the Rhodesian army recruiting officer because he was turned down. However, knowing Boss Lilford and his losses, the officer sent Harry to see him. Harry told Lilford he was not intending to stay in Rhodesia. It was too full of blacks, and he hated blacks more than he hated the Irish, and Liverpool was full of Irish. Everywhere he went, he said, was full of people he hated. Lilford pointed out that Triangle was ideal for Harry because, unlike Liverpool, he would be paid for killing the people he did not like.

He was paid astonishingly well. For every poacher he shot dead, he got five hundred American dollars from the government and the same from Lilford. All he had to do was patrol at his whim any one of the likely guerrilla routes across the territory and anyone seen near cattle between evening curfew at six and first light the next morning could be shot on sight. Harry simply had to cut off and present the man's left ear to collect his thousand-dollar bounty. Only, he was reminded, the left ear. The Belgians had been cutting off both and claiming double bounty.

For a while it worked very well. Harry, being thorough and a good shot, came back from his murderous safaris with a pocket full of black left ears and within a few months had become a wealthy man, carrying his bounty money with him in a body-belt. He was an effective and reliable killer and Boss Lilford might eventually have changed his low opinion of the British. But Harry had a weakness which proved his undoing. He was too kind-hearted.

It happened at Mbire Hills, near the Esanby Dam, less than forty miles from the Mozambique border. Harry had set himself up for the night on high ground. He had been told by local police to expect movement from the east where a small band of guerrillas had been sighted. It was a cold night and Harry sipped from a flask of brandy and wrapped a blanket tightly around himself. At around ten o'clock he heard movement in the bush two hundred yards away and he put away his flask; the sport was about to begin. Curfew was now four hours old, so whoever was out there was legitimate game.

With only a slender new moon for light, Harry could just make out a solitary figure meandering towards him. Then it stumbled, laughed and began to sing. Harry picked up his rifle. He could see an old man wearing a dirty white nightshirt down to his knees. Such an easy target, a drunk, hugging a clay pot probably still half-full of maize beer; he had probably been to a wedding or a funeral or both; Harry knew they often held them on the same day to save the expense.

The old man was now less than fifty yards away. Harry paused to watch him do a jig, then pulled the rifle into his shoulder and took aim. But then, just as he applied first pressure on the trigger, he hesitated. Something worried him; something was not right. What was it the old man was singing? It was not a Shona tribal song, nor any one of the Chimerenga hymns of freedom and revolution sung by the guerrillas.

Later Harry told me: 'I had him full square, dead centre of his bloody great nightshirt and was just about to give him one in the chest when I realised what he was on about. It was "Old MacDonald had a Farm". I couldn't do it, could I? I mean, how could I clobber the old lad singing a song like that? Even if he *was* a blackie!'

Harry returned the next morning without his pocketful of ears and unwisely told his story to Boss Lilford, who promptly took Harry off the payroll. Harry left Rhodesia and I never heard of him again. He might now be rotting in some mercenaries' prison; he might have returned to Liverpool and learnt to love the Irish. But wherever he is, and remembering the old Rhodesia, he must know how unwise it would be to set foot in the new Zimbabwe.

Boss Lilford survived the war and the first few years into the peace. But national reconciliation, as it was called then, was not intended for him. In 1986 he was ambushed and murdered close to Triangle: one of many, many scores had been settled.

The Rhodesian government very seldom refused entry to journalists, nor did it exercise censorship in the normal way. It did not demand to see journalists' copy, photographers' pictures or television film, but if a story was judged to be deliberately, maliciously wrong or unfair, whoever reported it would be banned from entry the next time round.

The Rhodesians controlled the flow of information about their war in an effective way and one many governments have copied since. They simply denied access. The Ministry of Information gave many of us what they liked to call defence correspondent status, but that offered only the privilege of the occasional briefing from any one of a dozen brasshats, committed to telling us nothing that mattered. What our special status did not provide was access to the war zone, to be taken with the Rhodesian forces into the fighting, to report the course of the war, to gauge who was winning or losing. That was the logic of denial: the government could be relied on to confirm the wins; it could not afford to have independent witnesses report the losses. Like Mrs Thatcher at the time of the Falklands war, the Rhodesian government believed that the less said the better.

Although I reported the Rhodesian war for four years, I was only under fire a few times. That did not make it less harassing. Quite apart from the ever-present threat of land mines, there was the trauma of being late witness to killing; coming to a smouldering wreck of a car, the bodies inside contorted by the heat and turned black; the mounds of warm ash, village pyres, where entire families had been forced at gunpoint into huts doused in petrol and set on fire. A witness was often left alive, with his tongue cut out so that he would never speak his terror.

The tribespeople lost whichever way they turned; beaten by the Rhodesians if they did not supply information, burnt alive by the guerrillas if they did. I reported the story of one village headman who was loyal to the government. One afternoon, guerillas came and demanded food and beer and as his wife was preparing it he cycled off to tell the security forces. The Rhodesians sent in their bombers and the entire village was destroyed. When the headman returned, there were no survivors; his wife and children had been killed. Overwhelmed with grief and guilt, he went away and hanged himself.

The white farms were like fortresses. They were surrounded by high double wire fences, with the corridor between as a dog-run or laid with mines. At night, floodlights lit up the bush well beyond the perimeter fence, and after dinner the black servants were put out and the gate was double-padlocked. Farmers and their families, including their children, slept with a rifle or revolver on the bed with them. There was much to fear. The guerrillas killed in a terrible, random way. No one was spared; there were no exceptions, no mercy, no matter whether the victims were black or white, woman or child.

Exactly that horror came one night to an idyllic little mission in the Vumba mountains on Rhodesia's eastern border with Mozambique. It was a pretty and holy hamlet where missionaries and their families had come to live and teach the Bible despite the war. It was called Elim Mission, and was quite undefended. The nearest security forces were at Umtali, fifteen miles away, just the kind of soft target Comrade Mugabe's 'freedom fighters', high on ideology and marijuana, relished. No one escaped at Elim. Wives were repeatedly raped in front of their husbands and then made to watch their husbands murdered before they too died. Mothers were stripped, raped and bayoneted as they held their babies. The smallest children had their skulls crushed. Next morning we found torn-up Bibles by the bodies.

I came under fire once in the most absurd way. It would have made a ridiculous obituary. We were filming Cyril – an unlikely name for an unlikely man with an unenviable occupation. He was once one of Mugabe's ZANLA guerrillas but had been captured and persuaded to change sides, though we never discovered how the Rhodesians did it. Cyril was paid to tour the tribal trust lands with an armed escort, trying to persuade people to renege on the units that moved secretively in and around them. He would lecture, sing and dance a bit, then towards the end of his performance he would run into the audience and drag out boys and girls by their ears, acting the part of a guerrilla commander pressganging new recruits. Then, as he marched them away, he was ambushed by Rhodesian soldiers hiding behind boulders. That was the message. Mugabe could not win: the security forces were everywhere and all-seeing. It was great entertainment when entertainment was scarce. On that day it was also high drama.

As the Rhodesians went about their mock ambush, real bullets hit the rocks around us and ricocheted into the crowd who, suddenly aware it was not part of Cyril's act, panicked and scattered. The Rhodesian soldiers ran for cover but by the time they could replace the blanks in their rifles with live shells, there was no one to shoot at. A unit of guerrillas had been watching Cyril's performance from the hills above, and they had decided to exact their dues and go. There were no casualties except for a few red Rhodesian faces. It was, everyone agreed, an embarrassing propaganda defeat and Cyril's road show never went on tour again!

Not that it mattered. The government's war to win hearts and minds, white and black, was already lost and the Rhodesians were coming to terms with defeat. They had survived so long only because South Africa had provided them with food and fuel, military hardware and some military back-up. But now the South Africans were themselves under attack from within. Soweto was rioting, the Americans were applying a credit squeeze, the world was threatening increased sanctions, and the Russians were beginning to sell vast amounts of gold which threatened South Africa's profits. Not surprisingly, Pretoria decided that the rebels across the northern border could not be bailed out any longer. One Rhodesian politician called it the turning of the screw. Another, more aptly, said it was the tightening of the noose. South Africa was suddenly the Judas and the war was all but over.

At Christmas 1979, Robert Mugabe, hero and fashionable Marxist, returned home. In Salisbury, the statue of Cecil Rhodes on Rhodes Avenue was smashed to pieces, streets were renamed and blacks were served for the first time in the bar of Meikles Hotel. The thousands of guerrillas from both Mugabe's and Nkomo's armies surrendered their weapons to British troops specially flown in to supervise the cease-fire. The Rhodesians laughed and said they could not do it. British soldiers and one British policeman did it.

On 19 April 1980, Prince Charles represented the Queen at the independence celebrations. He watched the Union Jack lowered in the magnificent gardens of Government House and stood to civilian attention as the red, black and green flag of the infant Zimbabwe was hoisted in its place. Then he went to a rock concert in a football stadium and listened to Bob Marley. With him was Zimbabwe's first head of state, a man with a name unfortunate to European ears: President Banana.

During the war the whites always had hope. In the peace there was only despair. To be governed by blacks was more than most were prepared to accept and a hundred thousand and more hid their jewellery, gold and silver in their cars and drove across Beitbridge to start another life somewhere else. Jack Malloch decided he would take a different way out.

I had met Jack many years before in the Nigerian-Biafran war. He was one of many mercenary pilots flying for the Biafrans on the night-time supply drops at the Uli airstrip. He had teamed up with another buccaneer, an ex-Harrovian and fellow-Rhodesian, Alistair Wicks. Jack was a very large man in those days, so bulky he was nicknamed 'Minnesota Fats'. He was also considered a fine pilot and had flown Spitfires in the Royal Air Force in Italy and North Africa during the second world war. Another member of his squadron then was a Flight-Lieutenant Ian Smith. Jack made a thousand dollars a night on the Biafran runs and just as he was about to retire to Rhodesia he had the beginning of a long streak of bad luck.

One night, on the return flight from Uli with Wicks, he had engine trouble and was forced to land at Lomé in Togo. Suspicious because there were no markings on the aircraft, the police searched it. They found automatic rifles on the flight deck and they might have overlooked that but, stashed behind the radio transmitter, they found seven million pounds in Nigerian banknotes. The two were promptly marched off to prison, sans money, sans aircraft.

Within a year, Jack had bounced back and was flying again for the Biafrans, but the jinx flew with him. His chief engineer, a Canadian, disappeared one day after returning from Uli with the Biafrans' monthly payroll for all the pilots – a quarter of a million dollars in cash.

When I met Jack again he was already established as Rhodesia's top sanctions-busting pilot. That was not something I or anyone else was allowed to report, but what I could and did film was Jack's consuming hobby, a Spitfire Mark 22. It had sat on a concrete plinth at the gates of the Rhodesian air force base at Old Sarum, but Jack had bought it and over the years, collecting spares on his secret travels and employing engineers from Air Rhodesia, he had completely restored it. It was immaculate and worth a million pounds sterling. It was, he said, his old age pension.

One day, some time after independence, Jack rang the airport. They were to get the Spitfire ready, he was taking it 'for a ride'. He arrived wearing his original wartime flying jacket, helmet and

Michael Nicholson with Don McCullin, Vietnam 1973. It was so hot the tarmac had melted into the dying mens' wounds.

Pol Pot's killing-fields, where once there had been tearooms and parasols. Cheung Ek, Cambodia. (*page 152*)

HMS *Antelope* dies in bomb alley, San Carlos, Falklands, 1982. (*page 243*)

The British Harrier went the other way and the Argentinian Skyhawks hit *Sir Galahad*. Bluff Cove, Falklands, 1982. (*page 257*)

goggles. They watched him from the air traffic control tower as he soared high above the country he adored, lazily rolling and looping and peeling off in the classic, magic Spitfire way. They heard the famous Merlin engine roar as Jack pushed full throttle and climbed sharply into the mass of billowing white cloud that gathered so punctually over Salisbury every afternoon. Then he dived until he hit the ground.

The rover's life in Africa ended just before Christmas that year, when ITN decided it was time for me to come home. But we were in no hurry to leave Africa. Four years of sun and the good life had spoilt us. Professionally, it had been an exceptional time for me and the busiest of my career. In my first six months, the crew, Charles Morgan (later of Morgan Cars), Hugh Thomson and I had eighty-nine stories transmitted by ITN; that is an average of one every two days and probably ranks as an ITN best.

My patch stretched from the Cape to Tamanrasset in the Western Sahara. I covered the east coast from Mozambique to Ethiopia and the west too, including Togo, Nigeria, Ghana, the Ivory Coast, right down to Namibia, and most of the Africa in between. Uganda and Idi Amin, the madman I once upset and who warned he would personally cut off my head if I returned; Kolwesi, in what was once the Belgian Congo, now Zaïre, where I filmed the worst massacre I have ever seen – and I have seen many: white families killed by Katangese rebels, wrecked cars heaped with father, mother and children, hacked to pieces; women raped in the streets, grotesque in *rigor mortis*; and the House of Death, where seventy-five men, women and children, families all, had been machine-gunned down, three deep in a room twelve feet by twelve.

Yet I could return home from such horrors, pick the boys up from school, eat pizzas by the pool and talk of cricket and classwork in the happy paraphernalia of family life.

The four of us had had four wonderful years growing up together. We had travelled to all the corners of southern Africa: from the Cape of Good Hope to the Kalahari desert to Fish River Canyon and the Skeleton Coast. We had stayed on the Wild Coast and Port St Johns on the Transkei shores of the Indian Ocean. We had been to the Inyanga mountains in the east of

Rhodesia, through Lake Kariba to Victoria Falls and the mighty Zambesi in the west. We had swum in the crystal-clear waterfalls in the mountain forests of Swaziland and tobogganed across the ski-slopes on the roof of Africa in the kingdom of Lesotho.

The prospect of catching the British Airways jumbo at Jan Smuts Airport and arriving the next morning at a grey and probably strike-ridden Heathrow did not appeal. So we drove home. What we did not need and could not carry, including our animals – three cats, two dogs (including the famous Badger) – went by sea. We four jumped into our Range Rover (M-registration) and with only a five-year-old Michelin map to guide us drove the fourteen thousand miles across Africa.

It took us nearly six months. I wish it had taken longer. We went the eastern route, across the Limpopo river at Beitbridge into Zimbabwe, across the Victoria Falls bridge into Zambia, then Malawi, Tanzania, across Serengeti into Kenya, to the coast at Mombasa, Mount Kilimanjaro, across Masai-land and the Ngorongoro Crater and north to Sudan. We followed the Nile as far as we could until we reached Khartoum; then the nightmare of the eastern Sahara and into Egypt by the back door; to Luxor, Cairo, El Alamein, Alexandria and the ferry to Greece. We took the easy tarmac way to the English Channel and home. All of which is reported in greater detail in my book *Across the Limpopo*.

It would take a much braver man or woman to attempt that journey today. Africa, little by little, has closed in on itself. Many things combine to make it increasingly a hostile place. Sandstorms and floods, ripped tyres and aggressive tribesmen, quagmire and quicksand, heat, thirst, lion, cobra, elephant and scorpion are not the most dangerous hazards for today's overlander – patience, care, luck, enthusiasm and a little understanding of the internal combustion engine will see the intrepid adventurer through. But he has no protection whatsoever against the land mine and the Kalashnikov automatic rifle, which now deface so much of that sad and beautiful continent, with its grim record of coup and conflict.

I have been privileged to work and play in Africa on and off for over twenty years. In those few months of travel ten years ago, my family and I were other people in another existence. We shall not again see Africa as we then saw it.

CHAPTER NINE

The Falklands,
April–June 1982

We go to gain a little patch of ground that
Hath in it no profit but the name.
Hamlet

HAD IT NOT BEEN for a pregnant cow I doubt I should have gone to cover the war in the Falklands. When the Argentinians landed and hoisted their flag over Port Stanley in that first week of April, I was holidaying with my family at Ullswater in the Lake District. We were out walking for the day when we met a large, very pregnant and bad-tempered cow and in my wisdom I suggested we turned around and went another way. That took us back close to our hotel and as we neared it a messenger came running up the track towards us with urgent instructions for me to telephone London. Had I left it many minutes longer, the foreign desk would have called the next reporter on the list and I should have been told to carry on walking.

The House of Commons, said the excited voice at the end of the line, had just ended an emergency debate – the first weekend sitting since the Suez crisis. Tory backbenchers were demanding a task force be sent post-haste to the Falkland Islands and to the excuse that they were too far away, Edward du Cann had replied: 'Let's hear no more about how difficult it is to travel long distances. I don't remember the Duke of Wellington whingeing about Torres Vedras!'

A limp former Tory foreign minister had suggested that the very least Britain should do was to ban Argentina from the World Cup. Rising as ever to the occasion, the prime minister promptly ordered a task force to be assembled and sent to the South Atlantic, and I was offered a place on one of the ships. Within half an hour, as Diana and the boys nonchalantly continued their afternoon trek without me, I was on my way by car to a private airfield near

Carlisle where an ITN chartered aircraft was waiting to fly me to Southampton. From there a car took me to Portsmouth docks.

The next morning, Tuesday, 5 April, I went aboard the aircraft carrier HMS *Hermes*, my home for the next six weeks in the eight-thousand-mile journey to the other end of the world. The quayside was packed with mountains of supplies and vehicles, men and weapons. It had all happened in two days. Someone, somewhere, had got it right.

No one and nothing at that hour could have persuaded me that we were going to war, and I was not alone. I stood on the poop deck of HMS *Hermes* as we steamed out of Portsmouth harbour, past a booming brass band, a forest of Union Jacks on the quayside and a tiny armada beneath and all around us, and I felt a bit of a cheat. 'We'll be back in a fortnight,' I said to a young lieutenant-commander and he nodded back and said he would put money on it. As we sailed it was broadcast that Lord Carrington, the Foreign Secretary, had accepted responsibility for Britain's diplomatic unpreparedness and had resigned. We said he was the first and probably the last casualty of the Falklands crisis. That feeling, that the politicians and the generals were simply playing first division bluff and counter-bluff, stayed with us – the sailors, soldiers, marines and pilots – until we dropped anchor at Ascension Island, just below the equator.

Of course, we went about our daily tasks as if war between us and our former allies was inevitable. We were obliged to live in a constant state of battle readiness and became familiar with the naval shorthand that in emergencies would, we were promised, make a life or death difference. We practised days and sometimes nights. We were ordered to fire-drills and submarine attack alerts as if they were the real thing . . . running up and down ladders to action stations, learning to close and reopen hatches at double speed until our chins and our knuckles were bleeding. We cursed and sweated inside asbestos head-masks and gloves and staggered like stupid drunken men in our heavy orange-coloured rubber survival suits as everyone around us solemnly acted out an Argentine air attack.

It was hard work, playing at being soldiers and sailors. It created its own spontaneous melodrama but it was also menacing and disconcerting. I was a novice aboard. I had never sailed with any navy before, but as I was buffeted and bruised by men running in opposite directions down single-lane galleyways, as I fought my way through watertight hatches, as I waited in a long queue to climb or descend a single stepladder, as I searched for my gas-mask and helmet taken by someone who had lost his, I began to feel the first dread of a disaster at sea. If this was the way we should save ourselves, then many of us could consider ourselves already dead.

Leaving Ascension Island, halfway to the Falklands, our war games suddenly became more earnest. Our captain, Lynn Middleton, responding to a warning from British military intelligence that the Argentinians might attempt a gas attack, ordered that all men with beards should shave them off. We novices could not fathom the reason until it was explained that the gas-masks would not fit bearded faces tightly enough. There were many disgruntled sailors that day, among them men who had worn beards all their service lives. Brian Hanrahan, the BBC reporter, was among the casualties.

Every evening, we heard BBC World Service report the latest diplomatic efforts being made to resolve the crisis peacefully. Alexander Haig, the American secretary of state, was tirelessly shuttling between Washington, Buenos Aires and Number Ten Downing Street, and on some nights the radio reports said he might succeed, that we might well be turning and sailing for home. I remember the faces of disappointment among the young soldiers and sailors and especially the Harrier pilots that they might be denied their war. I remember the cheer at dinner the night we heard that the junta leader, General Galtieri, had rejected a final telephone appeal for peace from President Reagan.

Our Harriers flew every day and half the nights too, intercepting imaginary Argentine fighter-bombers. Our faces were scorched by their jet blast and because we lived our cramped lives aboard in a cabin directly under their landing deck, our nights were deafened by their screams. The Sea King and Wessex helicopters patrolled the ocean around us searching for similarly non-existent Argentine submarines and a thousand Royal Marines spent their days clambering over the carrier's superstructure attacking the imaginary enemy in their Falklands bunkers and firing thousands and thousands of rounds of ammunition into the sea.

Every contingency was prepared for it seemed, except us. Someone had overlooked how best to deal with the press.

We were given, as is the custom, junior officer rank. This allowed us to live, eat and drink in the wardroom – a privilege long bestowed on the press-at-war though we have always suspected that it has to do less with concern for our comfort than with keeping us away from the non-commissioned ranks and their indiscretions.

We had been obliged to sign the Official Secrets Act (I gather I am still bound by it) and were also given a tiny green booklet entitled: REGULATIONS FOR CORRESPONDENTS ACCOMPANYING AN OPERATIONAL TASK FORCE. It had been printed in 1956 for the Suez invasion, and began:

> The essence of successful warfare is secrecy. The essence of successful journalism is publicity. No official regulation can bridge the gap between two such incompatible outlooks unless goodwill and commonsense are resolutely brought to bear by both sides. A satisfactory liaison calls for complete frankness on the one hand and loyal discretion on the other and mutual cooperation in the task of leading and steadying public opinion in times of national stress or crisis.

We were urged to read it and appreciate its message, which we did, especially the bit about complete frankness. Much bad humour, wastage, spite and resentment might have been avoided had those who issued the booklet also taken the time to read it.

From the beginning, the Royal Navy wanted us left behind. Not for nothing is it known as the Silent Service. My impression was then that they would dearly have liked to sail away from Portsmouth at night, win their war and return as silently, hoping no one had noticed they had been away. The prospect of chaperoning bumptious, noisy, irreverent journalists did not appeal. Admiral Sir John Fieldhouse, commander-in-chief, like generations of military men before him, considered journalists to be the 'newly-invented curse to armies' and he was on record as quoting a former second world war censor; that if he had his way he would not tell anyone there was a war going on until it was over. Then he would simply say who had won.

It was Mrs Thatcher herself, and her press secretary Bernard Ingham, who countermanded the navy and insisted the British media should accompany the task force; albeit properly tamed and muzzled. From the moment we left Portsmouth, there was a determined covert campaign to silence us. It was directed by Sir John from his comfortable war bunker at naval headquarters HMS *Warrior*, hidden among the mansions of the stockbroker belt in London's suburban Northwood, and it was enthusiastically obeyed by most officers aboard *Hermes* and her sister carrier *Invincible*. One signals officer received a coded signal even as we were passing the Scilly Isles. It contained the single word: DIET, which decoded meant STARVE THE PRESS OF INFORMATION. It was to become an obsession. We coined a new phrase: information oppression.

There were seven of us aboard *Hermes* including the BBC's Brian Hanrahan, and another five on the second carrier, *Invincible*. More followed in *Canberra*, the commandeered Cunard luxury liner, making thirty journalists in all, including two television crews, one from the BBC and one from ITN. Some months before, over six hundred journalists, including thirty-two television crews, had been invited to attend British army exercises in West Germany. But now this was the real thing and the military had decided this was not to be a news war.

There were no foreign press aboard the task force ships, not even our allies the Americans, and when a disgruntled CBS News threatened to send its television crews in their own chartered ship from Miami, the Royal Navy signalled the network's headquarters in New York to warn them that their ship and everyone aboard it would be blown out of the water if they came anywhere near the Falklands.

By the end of April, the two carriers, *Hermes* and *Invincible*, had been joined by sixty Royal Navy and Royal Fleet Auxiliary vessels, which included destroyers, frigates, assault ships, tankers, troop carriers and hospital ships. And with them came another forty civilian ships, an assortment of tugs, ferries, container ships, freighters, cable ships, tankers and fishing trawlers. Chasing them were the two liners *Canberra* and the *QEII*, packed with troops and supplies. Out there too, though we never knew where, were our roaming hunter-killer nuclear submarines. It was the largest British fleet to have set sail since the second world war. Towards the end of April I radioed this report to ITN:

The task force is now assembled.

The carriers *Hermes* and *Invincible* are now surrounded and protected by their own destroyers and frigates, themselves enormous missile platforms. One of them, HMS *Broadsword*, carries the most advanced missile system in the world. In general weaponry the Argentinians cannot compete. The Royal Navy weaponry officers tell you so and they quote chapter and verse from the service manuals to prove it, though they concede that so much depends on who fires first. The Argentinians, surely, must have thought we'd never make it. Over 8000 miles through the tropics into the Arctic seas and every rendezvous punctually kept. The refuelling at sea, the supplying at sea, the exchange of food, ammunition, men, supply ships, tankers, and assault ships joining us on schedule on the day, sometimes even on the hour, until at last their admiral, Sandy Woodward, could signal London: WE ARE NOW ASSEMBLED. It was the day we hit the roaring forties, with the temperatures moving fast towards zero, and now war is only an order away. Our squadrons of Harriers patrol on full alert. Aircraft are in the sky constantly day and night searching for the violators. Pilots sit in their cockpits on deck on two-hour watches around the clock, ready to launch themselves and their deadly cargoes at what is now only referred to as the enemy. The 1000-pound bombs, the torpedoes, and the Sidewinder air-to-air missiles are now familiar furniture on the flight deck. No aircraft, Harrier jet or helicopter, leaves the carriers unarmed. All the anti-submarine Sea Kings carry torpedoes and depth charges and the khaki-painted helicopters transporting men and supplies, ship-to-ship, carry a machine-gun and a gunner. And as if to announce our arrival into the exclusion zone, Harriers from *Hermes* dropped the first of their lethal cluster bombs in a practice run alongside us, bombs which explode a hundred feet above ground, spattering everything, everyone below, with white-hot shrapnel. So close do we now feel to war that the ratings aboard have joined the Blue Berets; a volunteer force made up of cooks, stewards, stokers, all those not on action stations, trained to use rifles and machine-guns as back-up. They are the ship's Home Guard and there was such a rush of volunteers that there weren't enough instructors to cope. The enthusiasm surprised nobody.

So close to war, I had said, but I could not have known how near. At 0700 Greenwich Mean Time on the first of May, *Hermes* led the task force into the total exclusion zone to establish the British sea and air blockade. Forty minutes later, while it was still dark, a Royal Air Force Vulcan bomber attacked the airfield at Port Stanley with 21,000 pounds of high explosive. From *Hermes'* bridge, looking east to the Falklands, the sky glowed red and some minutes later we heard the voice of the bomber pilot, climbing high above us, radio a 'good morning', followed by a code-word. Operation Blackbuck had been a success. Or so we thought.

From the start, the joint chiefs of staff had worried about the threat of an Argentine air attack on the British fleet. Someone proposed the RAF should bomb their bases on the mainland but a few sums on the back of an envelope were enough to squash that. It would take seventeen Victor inflight refuelling tankers to get one Vulcan bomber to southern Argentina and back – because the tankers themselves would need refuelling as they circled in mid-Atlantic waiting for the rendezvous; and to allow for errors and mis-meetings, two extra tankers for each bomber would have to be in the air as standbys. Nor was it any good sending only one bomber. It is incredibly difficult to hit a narrow runway from two miles up unless you are using 'smart' bombs with someone on the ground guiding them to their target by laser. One bombload would not be enough to knock out the airfields. As there was only a fifty-fifty chance of even one of the twenty-one bombs the Vulcans carried hitting the runway, four bombers would be needed. That meant seventy-six tankers. The RAF did not have that many.

So the proposal to attack the Argentine mainland was abandoned. Instead it was decided to attack the runway at Port Stanley, to stop the Argentinians using it as a refuelling stop for their fighter-bombers and their Hercules re-supplying the garrison. The operation was codenamed Blackbuck. On the last day of April two Vulcans took off from Ascension Island. The lead bomber turned back after only three minutes in the air. A cockpit window refused to close and the aircraft could not be pressurised, so the crew of the second bomber, XM607 from 101 Squadron, went on alone. Ahead of them was fifteen hours of flying, seventeen refuelling rendez-vous and a diet of ham and cheese sandwiches and coffee. The bomb-aimer, Flight-Lieutenant Bob Wright, not needed until the Vulcan was approaching Stanley the following morning, settled down to read a paperback: it was called *Birds of Prey*.

Just before four o'clock in the morning Falklands time on the first of May, and one hundred and fifty miles from his target, Wright was alerted. The pilot, Flight-Lieutenant Martin Withers, had begun his descent to three hundred feet to escape Argentine radar detection. Forty miles from Stanley, as he climbed again to go above missile ceiling height, the Vulcan's early warning system began wailing; the Argentinians had spotted them. Withers, who still had another minute of climb before he was out of range of the Tigercat missiles (sold to Argentina by Britain) switched on elec-tronic counter-measures to jam their tracking radar. Three minutes later, at ten thousand feet and safely above missile range, they saw the lights of Stanley, and three miles out to sea bomb-aimer Wright made his final checks: bomb doors open, flying straight and level, target co-ordinates matched. At 4.23 he released his twenty-one bombs, 1000 pounds each, ten tons of high-explosives in all, falling towards the runway at quarter-second intervals. Withers turned his bomber in a wide circle. There was no flak. No missile trails. Only an orange-red glow. He radioed Ascension and spoke the single word 'Superfuse'. It spelt success.

Some hours later, midway between the Falklands and Ascension, the crew tuned their radio to the BBC and were astonished to hear that news of their raid was already being reported on the World Service. They were still only halfway home.

Operation Blackbuck cost over one million pounds; the British public considered it worth every penny. And perhaps it was in the way it raised British public morale and thoroughly depressed the Argentinians. Such long-range bombing by the RAF from

Ascension was something they had not reckoned on. But the raid didn't stop them flying their planes off that runway. Argentine Hercules transports, with their short landing and take-off capability, continued bringing in troops and supplies right up until the final forty-eight hours before the surrender.

We played our part of course in convincing the people back home that it had all been a huge success – we, the impressionable and thoroughly misinformed British press aboard *Hermes* and *Invincible*. Later that May Day, we were shown high level aerial reconnaissance photographs of the runway. 'There,' said our briefing officer, poking his finger at them, 'see how it's been absolutely wiped out . . . direct hits.' It had not, but not being specialists in the interpretation of photographs taken from ten thousand feet, we were persuaded it was: for the first and not the last time we were victims of deliberate official misinformation. And because Brian Hanrahan and I innocently passed it on in our broadcasts, so were the British public and the World.

The Argentinians, though, had the last laugh. Other air attacks were made on the airstrip by Sea Harriers; after each one the Argentinians hastily built circles of mud on the runway which from the air looked like bomb craters. At night, before their Hercules transports came in, the mud craters were cleared, then put back again before dawn. It was a simple ruse which foxed our military right up to the day they saw it for themselves.

The Sea Harriers from *Hermes* and *Invincible* made their first attack on the runway that same May Day, three hours after the tired but happy Withers, Wright and crew had left. We stood on the poop deck of *Hermes*. It was very cold and still dark and we could hear the crews on the flightdeck below positioning the aircraft, hooking up the power cables, loading the cannons, bombs and missiles, scampering from machine to machine with pencil beams from tiny torches, men looking east for the first touch of light.

Brian and I had already been to the air-crew briefing, at least that part of it that was considered safe for us to hear. It was like any briefing room in any Ealing Studio second world war production. Everyone looked so exactly right for the part – lounging, joking, smoking, cravated – embroidered squadron insignias proudly worn on the sleeves of the neatly-tailored suits of the flying warriors, precisely-folded maps in clear plastic, pencils chewed, mugs of tea, the smell of aftershave, white kid flying gloves, things said I knew I had heard before. It might all have been scripted: young bloods scenting their first war.

By the time they climbed into their cockpits, it was dawn, the sea and sky so identically grey it was hard to see the join. Bernard Hesketh, the veteran and exceptional BBC cameraman whom Brian and I shared (at Portsmouth it had been said there was space for only one television crew aboard), recorded them one by one as they taxied to their catapult position and then flung off the end – what they call the ski-jump. The Harrier can lift off vertically and hover in any direction, and it is the only aircraft in the world that can fly backwards. But it uses so much fuel doing it and its range is so limited that despite its unique versatility it had to be catapulted the way all generations of carrier aircraft had been before it.

The first wave hit the airstrip at Stanley and the second attacked the runway at Goose Green near Darwin, a hundred and twenty miles farther west. Over their radios, the pilots reported intense ground fire and one Harrier was hit, though not seriously. Soon they were back overhead in formation, victory rolls and all. It was, as somebody nearby said, a wonderful show, as if none of it was for real. But then for those of us who had been left behind so little of it was. Thirty minutes before they had gone loaded with bombs and missiles . . . now there was nothing beneath their bellies. They had killed.

Suddenly it was all Hollywood again; cheering flight crews, thumbs up and grins inside the cockpits, scripted still, right down to the announcement by the task force commander, Admiral Sandy Woodward, whose fiftieth birthday it was that day; lines spoken by him but surely written for Olivier or Todd by Coward or Rattigan: 'We did not want this fight,' he said to his victors as they climbed from their planes. 'I had hoped we could put it off. But we have shown our colours and this has been our day.'

It is what in my trade we call 'good copy' and Woodward knew well enough how to deliver it. That evening, with our reports read and edited by our censor, Captain Middleton, we were flown by helicopter to a nearby Royal Fleet Auxiliary supply ship and over the marine satellite radio (Marisat), Brian and I, then the task force's only broadcasters, sent our reports of that first day of war to London and via London to the world. They were lengthy and vivid; after all, how could we fail with such a tale to tell. Brian broadcast first, which was to become the routine because, except for odd occasions, the BBC evening news was an hour before ITN's *News at Ten*. It was a simple and practical courtesy and, as I had long discovered, courtesy in the early days of war can prove very cost-effective.

Since we were reporting the same scene from the same ship, it was not surprising that our reports were similar, give or take a memorable line spoken earlier by lieutenant-commander Rupert Nichol on the bridge. As the Harriers returned, rolling triumphantly in the sky, he, sensing the drama like all of us, remembered a British wartime film: a squadron commander waited anxiously in the control tower in an East Anglian Bomber Command aerodrome, watching his Lancasters return from a raid on Berlin, counting them down as each one lumbered safely home. At our side Nichol repeated the screen words aloud and to Brian Hanrahan, on his first war assignment, they magnificently captured the moment.

When I die I expect my epitaph (scratched in cement) to read:

> Here lies the man who did not count them out.
> Nor even did he bother to count them back.

Later that day, Harriers of our combat air patrol intercepted and shot down two Argentine Mirage fighters and a Canberra bomber which had flown from the mainland to attack the fleet. Later still that day, the first units of the SAS and the Royal Navy's equivalent, the SBS, were put ashore on East and West Falkland by helicopter. We had been twenty-six days at sea and the war had begun.

The next day brought the single most brutal action of the entire war. At four o'clock that Sunday afternoon, Commander Chris Wredford-Brown, captain of the nuclear-powered submarine HMS *Conqueror*, without warning and without challenge and knowing his target was outside the exclusion zone, fired two torpedoes at the Argentine cruiser *General Belgrano* from a range of three miles. There were over a thousand men aboard, including young recruits whose average age was eighteen. *Conqueror*'s first torpedo hit the cruiser on her port bow, the second hit her stern where many of the crew were asleep. Within a few minutes the ship was listing fifteen degrees to port and the order was given to abandon ship. Seventy self-inflating life rafts were thrown into the sea and men ran down its hull to get to them. But some of the rafts had been punctured by shrapnel and others turned turtle with so many clambering to get aboard. Others were sucked under the ship because the men's hands were so covered in oil they could not hold the oars tightly enough to row away. The selfless and the bravest went back into the sea and swam, pulling the rafts behind them; others tried paddling with their hands. When the *Belgrano* sank, stern first, the survivors sang their national anthem. Only the badly burnt did nothing; they sat in a state of deep shock. There had been no warning of the attack and many had been in their bunks, so they were not wearing anti-flash masks and gloves. A survivor tells of one who was so badly burnt he was forced to crouch on his knees for thirty hours until the Argentine rescue ships arrived. He died an hour later, one of the 321 men who lost their lives that afternoon.

The *Sun* distinguished itself and shamed journalism by publishing a photograph of the sinking *Belgrano* with the headline GOTCHA. A cable was sent from the fleet to the *Sun*'s editor asking for copies of his rag, which were urgently needed as lavatory paper.

A great deal has been said about it since, blame given and blame shared. It was claimed that the *Belgrano*'s two destroyer escorts, and possibly the *Belgrano* herself, were carrying Exocet missiles and even outside the exclusion zone represented a real threat to the task force; that the captains of the two accompanying destroyers fled after the attack and did not wait to pick up survivors. In fact it was *Conqueror* which fled, chased by the destroyers; they hunted her for two hours with sonar and depth charges.

In my mind there is no doubt the *General Belgrano* was doomed as long as she was at sea. The task force commander, Admiral Woodward, and those giving him his orders, intended sinking her wherever they found her. It was said that the order to attack was given that Sunday only because the cruiser and her escorts were '. . . closing on elements of our task force which was only hours away'. Yet, two days before, on 30 April, in an off-the-record interview aboard *Hermes*, Sandy Woodward told me: 'There's a cruiser sniffing around and I'm going to bloody its nose.'

Bloody it he did! Two days later, the Argentinians took their revenge and *we* bled.

Diary. HMS Hermes, *4 May 1982*:
Warned we can expect air attacks following *Belgrano*'s sinking. Action stations Red Alert piped 1310 hours. Enemy planes detected 118 degrees. RAF Vulcan makes second raid on Stanley airfield. Also our Harriers have another go. One of our planes is missing. . . Nick Taylor's. Why him? 1420 hours HMS *Sheffield* hit by single Exocet fired from Super Etendard. Survivors come aboard.

When it happened we were up on deck looking the wrong way, facing west towards Argentina, waiting for the air attack that never came. Instead they shouted, 'Look east, behind!', where the smoke was spreading. Out of nowhere, with not a sight or sound of an aircraft, the destroyer *Sheffield* had been hit amidships and was ablaze.

Until then I had heard nobody mention the name of the missile that was to become so infamous. The Exocet is made by the French and is what is called a 'fire and forget missile' – that is, once launched it is guided by its own radar to the target, travelling ten feet above the waves at just below the speed of sound. It can knock out the largest ship. Only two in the task force had the means to combat it: the frigates *Broadsword* and *Brilliant* with their short-range Sea Wolf missiles. If an Exocet were fired at any of the others, our two carriers among them, there was little they could do except wait.

This did not cause much alarm among task force captains, because it was confidently assumed the Argentinians did not have the capability to launch Exocets from their aircraft. They had assumed too much; perhaps they should not have trusted the French. Officially, the French government backed Britain during the entire crisis, imposing sanctions against Argentina. It also provided technical information about the French aircraft the Argentinians were flying – the Etendard and the Mirage – and even allowed British Harrier pilots to fly in mock combat against those planes over France to practise shooting them down.

What the British did not know and what the French somehow forgot to tell, was that a specialist French team was already in Argentina, at the base Espora, modifying the Etendard and the Exocet so that the one could carry the other. The team remained and worked throughout the war. They even volunteered to travel with the attack squadron wherever it was based in case things went wrong – such was their enthusiasm!

When it came, it was travelling so fast and so low the officer of the watch did not even have time to call action stations which was probably just as well because when the missile hit, *Sheffield* would have been full of running men and the casualties would have been much higher. All they saw from the bridge was a trail of light grey smoke on the horizon and somebody shouted, 'God! There's a missile!' Four seconds later the Exocet slammed into the starboard side about six feet above the waterline. The blast went upwards and forwards. Those who survived the blast suffocated in the acrid, black, poisonous smoke from the burning electrical cables. The machinery control room and the damage control centre were gutted. Nothing worked, and men tried to put out the fires with buckets of sea water.

A shuttle of helicopters brought the survivors to *Hermes*. We filmed them, and junior officers watching from higher decks shouted 'Ghouls!' at us. The dead were brought on stretchers covered in sodden blankets dripping oil, the living hung limp between the shoulders of their rescuers, their feet dragging across the deck. Some, the just-living, were horribly burnt. I remember wide surprised eyes in a sponge of blistered red that had been a man's face. But no pain seemed to be felt; the suffering came later; shock was the morphine until morphine was injected. One man walked on his own from the Sea King across the deck to the medics and nodded to the camera quite matter-of-factly. He died a few minutes later as the doctors attended him. In the intense heat blast, his nylon clothes, his socks, trousers and shirt, standard Royal Navy issue, had melted and fused with his skin. There was no way to separate the two.

What we did not know then was that two Exocets were fired that afternoon from two Etendards and both were intended for *Hermes*. When the Argentinian pilots returned to their squadron and heard on the BBC World Service that they had hit *Sheffield* they were surprised and puzzled. Both missiles had been targeted on the task force flagship. *Sheffield* had got in the way of the flight path of one; the second simply disappeared.

The sinking of the *Belgrano* was the first test of Argentine resolve, for civilians as much as for the military. The loss of *Sheffield* was ours. Public support for their governments did not waver in either country. Aboard the task force ships there was a different mood. We were clearly more vulnerable than anyone had assumed; the myth of invincibility had been shattered. All the way south we had been told of the Royal Navy's 'protective shield' that no one and nothing could pierce. They boasted about their sophisticated armoury of weapons and counter-attack systems, the Sea Darts, Sea Wolf and Sidewinder missiles, the impenetrable radar surveillance, the all-seeing and ever-searching Harrier combat air patrols. Then we were caught with our trousers down by a daring young man whom we never saw, and who never saw us.

The French armaments industry ignored the spectacular tragedy. A full-page advertisement in the weapons magazine *Heracles* applauded the Exocet and the devastation wrought that Tuesday afternoon.

We, the press, were not allowed to report the *Sheffield* disaster until after it had been announced in the Commons by the defence secretary, John Nott. We were not even allowed to film it until three days later and only then because Sandy Woodward wanted to know how it looked and could not afford the time to fly to see it for himself. He permitted Bernard to fly over it and he watched the video later in his cabin. Then he kept the tape. It reached the television screens via the Ministry of Defence over a month later.

We became more and more depressed at being employed simply to confirm what was being announced by a minister or his spokesman in London. On 6 May two Harriers off *Invincible* collided in fog and both pilots were lost. We were forbidden to report it. That evening we heard it officially announced on the BBC World Service. On the twelfth, HMS *Glasgow* was hit by a bomb which did not explode. The same day a Sea King helicopter crashed and sank, a crewman was lost. *Hermes'* number two, Commander John Locke, piped to the crew: 'You will not refer to these incidents in your letters home. Such information will be invaluable to Argentinian intelligence.' At that time all letters were censored and, anyway, took at least three weeks to reach Britain. However, that same evening, news of *Glasgow*'s escape and of the Sea King crash was broadcast over the BBC World Service, quoting the ministry.

We were taking the risks but the politicians and the military had built in a delay for all news leaving the task force. We could not escape the military's embrace. The senior officers aboard *Hermes* were hypersensitive about us – paranoid, almost – quite ignoring the fundamental truth: we could not report anything that had not been passed by our many naval censors or in any other way than on a navy radio with a minder sitting at our elbows. We were treated by some as if we had found a secret way to transmit information home, or even, I suspect, to Buenos Aires. One evening in the wardroom, a senior air control officer, three gins the worse, loudly accused us of 'giving too much away', of being 'as good as Argentinian intelligence agents'. Our cameraman, Bernard Hesketh, a genial man, exploded. White and quivering with rage, he pulled up a trouser leg to show a long and vivid scar. 'This,' he said, 'I got in the last war fighting for my king and country. Don't you ever dare call me a spy again!'

They suffered from the Vietnam syndrome. The analogy was made frequently and the spectre haunted those in charge of us: the Vietnam war was a television war and it was lost; *ergo* all television wars are lost. It was not possible to indulge in reasonable debate with the military about it: they would not accept that the Americans lost in Vietnam because consecutive American generals got it wrong. The media simply reported the state of affairs; it did not create it. It was North Vietnamese ingenuity and determination that defeated them. Not CBS.

Our censors and our ministry minders saw innuendoes in every *but* and *if*, and quite forgot whose side we were on. After weeks of this, I finally sent a radio message to ITN London telling them that all my reports were being censored and I urged them to make this clear when they were broadcast. But our censor censored the word 'censored' from my message. ITN must have found the text gobbledegook.

Occasionally there was reasonable censorship; when someone took the trouble to explain why we could not report something. For example, there was the day when the entire fleet was enveloped in dense fog, so thick we could not see the stern from the bow. Yet Harriers were lined up on standby for combat air patrol should the alert be given, which thankfully that day it was not. Later I asked one of the pilots how he would ever have found his way back in such weather. He answered that he would not have done, that almost certainly on his return to the task force he would have had to ditch his plane because he would not have been able to find *Hermes*. I asked about radar and homing devices but he explained that they would only help him return to the fleet; they would not help him find his 'mother' ship. If he had gone full range to intercept an enemy plane he would have only two minutes' fuel left when he returned and that would not be enough time to find *Hermes* and land. His whole returning flight would depend almost entirely on luck; without it, aircraft costing over ten million pounds each would simply be pitched into the sea. I thought such a thing worth including in my next report, but the censor said 'no', which did not surprise me – the military were not keen to have such problems emphasised. But there was a different and wholly reasonable explanation why the navy did not want me on the BBC World Service that night talking about the fog and its problems. In the meteorological briefing room I was shown a map of the area we were in, the north-western corner of the total exclusion zone. The area of fog was clearly marked, the only fog in the entire zone. Had I mentioned we were in it, the Argentine air force would have targeted us immediately.

But reasonable censorship and such explanations were not the rule, and the relationship between them and us went from bad to worse. When one of the dead from *Sheffield* was buried at sea, we were not allowed to film the ceremony; it would not, the padre said, be decent. It became more and more difficult to get a helicopter to fly us to the Marisat ships to transmit our reports to London. The officer-in-charge of the flight schedules gave his opinion of us quite directly: 'You bastards are the lowest priority rating – at the bottom of the list, and as long as I'm here, that's where you'll remain!'

From the very first day out of Portsmouth, the mood had been set by *Hermes'* Captain Middleton. He was not the happiest of men and took his responsibilities heavily. He was born in South Africa and when we first met I detected the slightest accent. I have often wondered since whether it worried him that I might use that against him: a South African commanding the task force flagship might not have been ideal publicity for some. With hindsight, he ought never to have been given the extra and onerous responsibility of being our censor. He had more than enough on his plate and I regret much of the *angst* I caused him.

Nor, with the compassion of hindsight, should we be too critical of the way captains and Ministry of Defence minders reacted to our demands, especially the demands of the writing press. On the carrier *Invincible*, where there were five newspapermen, their copy accounted for up to thirty per cent of the daily signal traffic sent to London. Known workaholics like A. J. McIlroy of the *Daily Telegraph* were churning out a thousand and more words a day and no doubt would have doubled that had it been allowed. Often it would take a signals clerk two hours to type and transmit a story, especially when the ship changed course and the satellite link was broken. There were five stories waiting to go every day, and in between the carrier's own service signals had to be sent and received. The farther south we sailed, the testier the navy became. They were particularly angry when their traffic was delayed by the trivial nonsense the reporters from the *Sun* and the *Star* were writing:

> Skinhead Ian Walter Mitty would put the frighteners on anyone. With his close shaved head, tattoo covered body and heavy bovver boots, he looks every inch what he is . . . a hard man. But Walter, 20, from Richmond Yorkshire, was near to tears yesterday when he learnt that his dearest wish to get at an Argie with his bare hands had been denied!

This description of a British soldier was composed by Tony Snow of the *Sun*. It should surprise nobody that Captain Black of *Invincible* considered his signal to Northwood concerning modifications to the Harrier's Sidewinder missiles should take precedence over copy like that. The newspapermen complained that it was taking so long for their stories to get through to London. Given what was on offer, it was astonishing some of it was ever sent.

On 11 May I was in disgrace: I was summoned to Admiral Woodward's day cabin. He had just received a telephone call from the commander-in-chief, Admiral Sir John Fieldhouse in Northwood, who accused me of revealing secret ship movements in a broadcast on ITN. What I had reported, which had been passed by the censor, was that Royal Navy frigates had crept to within a mile of the Falklands, had bombarded Argentine emplacements and steamed away untouched. I ended: 'With that kind of cheek they may well be encouraged to have another go sometime soon.'

That phrase, by Sir John's reckoning, was tantamount to giving the Argentinians a date, a time and a rendezvous. Admiral Woodward had already passed judgement. He said he had ordered a transcript of my report and I should prepare for a rapid departure for Ascension Island and home. 'I'm going to sack you,' were the words he used. The message was then piped to the entire ship. Its effect shocked me; officers and ratings threatened me physically for endangering lives. I stayed in my bunk for the rest of the day and only after much gentle persuasion did Bernard get me to eat in the wardroom that evening.

Eventually the transcript arrived and was read. Nothing more was said. There was no apology from Woodward, piped or otherwise, and to many I must have remained guilty but reprieved. It was a bad day for me, as bad as any of the flak in store.

Now at last we were getting close to the Falklands and to the day when we would land there. Soon we had a preview of what it would be like. We were airlifted to HMS *Glamorgan* and after some of our roughest hours at sea we were taken to witness the SAS attack on Pebble Island off West Falkland. It was so rough – the captain told us it was a force nine gale – we could hear the scream of the propellers as the boat reared above the waterline and, with the crew, we braced ourselves for the shudder as the hull hit the sea again. After an hour of it Brian, Bernard, John Jockell our sound recordist, and I, unable to stand any longer, strapped ourselves into bunks and waited to be called on deck.

I mention the conditions because even aboard *Glamorgan* that night we did not escape the critical eye of someone who would have preferred us not to be there and, for reasons known only to him, was prepared to invent some lies about us. Lieutenant David Tinker kept a meticulous diary and sent many letters home; throughout his writings he showed, like many with the task force, that he was not impressed by the reporting of the British press. On the night of the Pebble Island attack he wrote:

> The BBC [and ITN – *my addition*] were on board and grandiosed everything out of all proportion: Antarctic gales, force nine winds, terrific disruption done, disrupted entire Argentinian war effort etc. Mostly, they sat drinking the wardroom beer and were sick in the heads; the weather was in fact quite good.

Let me say that the weather that night was the worst we had experienced until then, our fifth week at sea. We drank nothing but sugarless tea and, unaccustomed though we were to light, fast frigates, we were not sick that night or any night before or later. Nor did the events Brian and I described in our reports contain any reference to the SAS attack 'disrupting the entire Argentinian war effort, etc.' It was his, not our, fantasy.

Why Lieutenant Tinker should have been so vindictive I cannot know, nor shall we know. He was killed in an air attack on *Glamorgan* two days before the war ended. He was a young man in his first war, a war he despised and wished he had no part in: it made him wretched and ashamed. Considering his aversion to war and its killing, one wonders why he chose such a profession. Perhaps, like so many of his colleagues, he had never expected to go to war.

It was night and we could see only the outline of the land but after so many weeks living the name Falklands, there was a wonderful exhilaration in seeing the first glimpse of it and even catching its scent.

The SAS, in sticks of four, had been landed by helicopter on the northern shores of West Falkland about three miles downwind from a particularly troublesome Argentine radar tracking station. The raiding party had to make its way to the island's grass airstrip which had become a conduit for supplies delivered by light aircraft from the Argentine mainland. The SAS had with them an artillery officer, and once they were in position to attack he called in fire from *Glamorgan* and other ships close by. The salvo was devastating; twenty shells at a time, one every two seconds. Over the radio we could hear the voice of the gunnery officer directing the fire into the Argentinian positions, careful to keep them away from the civilian settlement nearby. We watched the line of explosions move slowly left to right, closer to the airfield, and nearer to where he was crouching. This was how I reported it. I was allowed to refer to the SAS only as 'commandos', though I never understood why.

. . . It was a clear sky and in the bright moonlight we could see the islands rising sharply out of the sea with the shoreline and the mountains beyond quite visible. And between the high ground and the sea I could just make out the small village of Pebble Island settlement – but after so many nights of naval bombardment of the islands no light shone anywhere. Our ship, detached from the main task force, had come as close to the shore as any British ship yet, and its task was to provide cover for a British commando unit: fifty men who'd been landed on the island only a few miles to the left of us. Naval gunfire spotters – a forward observation team led by a young army captain – were already in position, hiding close to the Argentinian positions waiting to direct our fire. Then, on a radio signal from him, we opened fire with rapid salvos from our 4½-inch guns. We let off with twenty shells in a short burst, and then paused as two spotters asked for a concentrated bombardment to push the Argentinian troops farther away from the target the British commandos were after. Then the commandos themselves called for flares. Immediately our guns sent them in – star shells that lit up the sky – and for a moment silhouetting our ship against the sea. But it seemed just what the commandos wanted because immediately afterwards we saw red streaks arcing upwards towards the high ground. It was the commandos' machine-gun tracers showing where they were hitting Argentinian positions. The commandos were after selected targets, among them a small grassy airstrip near the village: and on that strip were Argentinian

Pucara attack and Skyvan short take-off aircraft used by the Argentinians' main garrison near Port Stanley to re-supply their troops around the island. They would also be used, armed, to attack British troops in any seaborne landing. We continued with our bombardment. It was an enormous flow of shells out of each gun, firing sixteen shells a minute – one shell leaving the ship every two seconds. Over a hundred shells were fired by us in five short bursts. A senior gunnery officer aboard told me that the naval bombardment of the Falklands these past few days is the most intensive gunfire action since the second world war: and he insisted that all the fire was carefully sited away from civilian settlements and he showed me the safety lines drawn on his map beyond which fire is forbidden. The flashes from our guns' muzzles lit up the deck around us and in that instant of orange light we could see men throwing empty shell cases into the sea and men crouched behind Oerlikon ack-ack guns scanning the sky. Then the order came from the bridge to stop firing. We could see the first break of light on the eastern horizon, and within half an hour it would be daylight and we ourselves would be targets for Argentinian guns ashore and their aircraft from the mainland. The captain's decision was made even though, as he turned the ship away from the island and towards the open sea, we could still see fighting continuing – with the sky lit up with the commandos' and the Argentinian tracers and mortar explosions. But despite the delay caused by the enormous seas we had to plough through, by the time we got back to the task force we heard the good news: that the commandos had completed their mission, and all fifty men had got back to their helicopters with only minor casualties. They left behind them eleven Argentinian aircraft blown to pieces and an ammunition dump destroyed.

A few days after that attack, the seven of us aboard *Hermes*, including Martin Cleaver, the PA photographer, and Richard Saville, the PA reporter, were summoned to Admiral Woodward's cabin. The date of D-day had been decided, so had the place. We huddled around a map on the floor and Woodward dug his forefinger into the name of a small inlet on East Falkland, not close to Stanley as we had expected, but at the other end of the island some sixty miles away. Ringed in red crayon, at the northern end of the Falkland Sound, was San Carlos Bay.

It had been chosen, we discovered, in a most unmilitary way. No one could agree how upwards of four thousand troops aboard the task force ships should be landed. Woodward had insisted from the start that before he would sanction any amphibious operation, he had to establish air superiority and he wanted an airstrip built at Port North on West Falkland. He was the only one who thought it remotely possible; the rest – the operational planning committee of top brass was called R Group – thought it hare-brained and finally talked him out of it. The SAS commander, the dashing young Colonel Mike Rose, suggested an Entebbe-style attack: landing by night in helicopters and storming the Argentinian garrison, hurling grenades and firing from the hip. The captain of HMS *Fearless*, Jeremy Larkin, reportedly offered to back his ship into Stanley harbour and let the troops simply run off. No one thought him really serious and anyway the Argentinians had probably mined the entrance to the harbour. It was even suggested that troops should climb down ropes from hovering helicopters – which explained why we had watched and filmed marines aboard *Hermes* practising exactly that day after day on the way south.

Nothing came of any of these ideas, which was just as well. The first SAS assessment of the number of Argentinian troops on the islands put the figure in excess of ten thousand, which was three times the number of British and the reverse of the ratio the military textbooks consider the minimum for such an offensive.

The choice of San Carlos was the brainchild not of R Group or of any of the senior officers in the task force. That distinction belongs to an unsung hero of the war: Major Ewen Southby-Tailyour of the Royal Marines. He ought not to have been with the task force at all, but he had an encyclopaedic knowledge of the islands, without which the war might well have gone the other way.

Irrepressible, eccentric, whimsical, capricious, stoic, idiosyncratic, cussed, charming – they all fitted Ewen (and still do) – depending, of course, on the mood. Then in his early forties, he was small and stocky with white wavy hair and a way of speaking seldom heard nowadays except in period television drama. He had seen service in Aden and was awarded a medal by the Sultan of Oman for action against guerrillas. His passion was sailing, preferably on his own. In 1978, while he was serving with a marine guard detachment on the Falklands, he sailed the islands' coastline, diligently charting their bays and inlets. There was an official complaint at the time that he spent more time in his dinghy than he did on guard duties but no one could have guessed how valuable his notebook of depths, tides and sketches would one day be. Except possibly Ewen himself, because four years later, on the weekend the Argentinians invaded, he pulled out the dog-eared exercise book and, even before it had been decided a British force should sail south, marked the spot where he thought the landing should be: San Carlos. Next to it he scribbled: *Sheltered, dominated, good ops, 65 miles to Stanley – 92 by sea.*

Ewen had not been selected to go with the task force, so, true to form, when his commanding officer asked him to hand over his notebook, he said he would – on one condition. If the book went south so would he; if he did not, neither would it. It was brazen blackmail and it worked. Ewen had one final card to play before he sailed south. During his stint in the Falklands he had become friendly with a woman, now married and living in Edinburgh, called Lief Barton. He contacted her with a special request. She needed no persuasion; she understood it and agreed. The following day a special military messenger picked up from her two lists containing the names of certain Falkland Islanders; one was of all on the islands who had two-way radios and their call signs: the other was of all known Argentinian sympathisers. The lists were taken to Royal Navy headquarters at Northwood and copies later sent to British military intelligence and the SAS.

On the evening of 20 May in heavy sleet, bitter winds and a rough sea, the seven of us of the media corps aboard *Hermes* were told to pull on our luminous orange rubber survival suits and stand by to board a Sea King helicopter. We were being transferred to another ship to join the troops who were going ashore the next morning at the place where Ewen had said they should. There was excitement and there was fear; the two blend easily. And there was a third which sat by itself: self-doubt. Possibly Ewen suffered it more than most. In his diary he wrote: *'Didn't sleep well. I am worried about the mines in the Falkland Sound. I am worried about the accuracy of everything I have told them.'*

Fear was well fertilised. Whatever else we lacked, there was no shortage of rumour. It is always so; when things are getting bad there is always someone ready to make them worse. Somebody said there was going to be a last-minute order for everyone to donate a pint of blood – a thousand pints and more would be needed. Then Admiral Woodward was said to be expecting a thousand casualties and somebody had seen a mountain of plastic body bags in the corner of the hangar. They turned out to be ordinary refuse bags for the galley and hardly big enough to hold the smallest dwarf. There was superstition too. *Canberra*, bringing the Parachute Regiment, had sliced through a whale just south of Ascension, turning the sea red, and every seaman knows that is bad luck. And some clever dick had discovered the *Canberra*'s postal code was 666 – the sign of the devil!

But the last film show aboard *Hermes* was the Royal Navy's own special contribution to morale. Wth D-day imminent and the spectre of Argentine machine-gun posts on the beaches waiting for the doors of the landing craft to open what film did they consider the month's best selection? *Gallipoli*! It began with a shout from the back row: 'Three cheers for Mrs T, cover your balls and over the top lads!' as we sat and watched the Turks gunning down the Australians by the score – crimson gore, history on the screen in vivid colour, a touch of fantasy in the dark.

Then the lights were on and the film stuttered to a stop. Ratings were saluting senior officers in the front row and messages were passed along from seat to seat. Men whom I recognised as helicopter pilots got up and left hurriedly. The buzz finally reached my row and, as the lights went out and the Turks resumed their slaughter, our war was real and with us again. A Sea King helicopter with eighteen SAS men aboard – among them many who had fought on Pebble Island – had crashed into the sea. There were no survivors.

We were told that an albatross had flown into the engine air-intake but few believed it. It was also said that the men were being transferred from one ship to another. That too was unlikely. It was rumoured though never confirmed that they were on their way to the Argentine mainland on a sabotage operation and as the heli-copter was to be destroyed there, it made sense to someone to pro-vide the oldest and least valuable machine. It was also carrying the crew plus eighteen heavily-loaded men, twice the maximum payload. Perhaps that better explains why those men died and why a seabird was blamed.

None of us knew, certainly no one was warned, what the likely Argentinian resistance would be on D-day. We assumed nobody knew. We heard that the SAS and SBS had landed their units along the shore of San Carlos Water all the previous week and had reported there were no Argentine emplacements, at least no per-manent ones. But the Argentinian garrison at Stanley was only half an hour away by Chinook helicopter and the smaller one at Goose Green was even closer. Surely, we thought, they must know what we are up to by now. They did not. They would have been there to meet us otherwise.

Like the soldiers, we were ill-prepared to greet the Falklands. The navy had fitted us out with heavy oiled sweaters, heavy seaboots and dark blue anoraks and leggings. We would be about as well camouflaged on the green and brown peatlands as a lump of coal in the snow. After I was winched down on the Royal Fleet Auxiliary ship *Stromness* to join the marine commando, I tried to swop my navy gear for army, but a sergeant explained in the plainest English that I was far better clothed for the Falklands winter than any one of his men and refused me even a cotton khaki scarf.

At one point it looked doubtful whether Brian Hanrahan would get ashore, which would have suited me rather well! A few days after our departure from Portsmouth we had had our photographs taken. The print was enclosed in a clear plastic case and, together with a disc on which our name and blood group had been stamped, we hung them around our necks. When the security officer came to inspect us on the morning of the landing, he looked at Brian, clean-shaven, and then at the bearded Brian in the photograph and shook his head. 'I'm sorry,' he said and he meant it. 'I can't allow you to go ashore. Your face is invalid.'

There were five hundred men below on what was called the tank deck of RFA *Stromness*. They were hardly visible in the faint red emergency lights, but as my eyes adjusted I could see something of their camouflage and the tattered bits of English hedgerow stuck into their helmets. Their faces were blackened, their bodies weighed down by criss-crossing bandoliers of bullets and grenades. They rested against bulging self-survival backpacks, mostly silent, many smoking, their eyes closed and no doubt seeing much the same thing. We could hear the shelling outside but we could not know whether they were ours going out or theirs coming in. I kept hearing myself saying to anyone nearby. 'It's just like the movies,' until I realised how boring and unnecessary it sounded; everyone could see it was.

We had waited too long and we knew things could not be going well. The first units of the Paras should have gone ashore at 1.30 a.m. and everyone else was meant to be in their land positions by first light, six hours later, when the Argentinians could be expected to send their air force at us. We should have been on deck ready for the landing craft to come alongside at four. It was now well after five.

Then news of what was happening and what was going wrong trickled to us. There had been a firefight on Fanning Head, just over a mile away, and Argentinians had been killed. The Paras had had mishaps getting off their ship, the *Norland*, and into their land-ing craft; a man had been injured, a machine-gun had gone off accidentally; one of their landing craft had headed in the wrong direction and Southby-Tailyour had to chase after them and bring them back. The Scorpion light tanks could not be beached and men had to jump into freezing water to wade past them as other men with long poles searched for shallower ground.

On our tank deck the last cigarette had been smoked again and again. The air was heavy and damp, men ached, men had cramp but when they stood to stretch the company sergeant major ordered them down again. No one could keep still. Tempers and tension were rising. There was another boom of guns and a deafening clanging thud in the ship's side. Five hundred anxious faces turned and bodies stiffened. The sergeant-major calmed and comforted the way sergeant-majors do: 'Don't shit yourselves, lads,' he shouted. 'It's only a landing craft fucking up his parking space! Just a bruise!'

Then came a precious piece of unrehearsed farce. I remember

237

every detail, it was so welcome and could not have been better timed. The sergeant-major, looking every bit the casting director's dream, with a shaven head and a lantern jaw, suddenly shouted, and a loud shout it was. Recognising the heaven-sent and making absolutely certain nobody should miss it, he turned sharply and barked in his best parade-ground voice:

'Marine Nowaks!'

'Sir!'

'Stand up!'

'Yes, sir!'

'What is that you're wearing, Nowaks?'

'It's a brassière, sir.'

Nowaks appeared to be a little over five feet tall and so stocky that had he been just a little wider he would have been perfectly square. He had the most enormous grin and, in the dim red glow, it was a beam of white from a blackened face. He was covered in every weapon that had ever been made for an infantryman, topped by a bandolier of bullets for the heavy Browning machine-gun. And stretched across his wide chest was a white and generous bra.

'May I ask, Nowaks,' said the sergeant-major, 'why one of my marine commandos is wearing a brassière?'

Nowaks' sense of timing would have made a professional envious. He paused, turned in a half-circle so that everyone might see, and then replied indignantly, 'It's every marine's right to wear a bra in San Carlos, sir.' There was a great and prolonged roar of approval. The sergeant-major waited. Then he said, without a grin but in an almost kindly way, 'Too bloody right, Nowaks. And when this business is over I'll make it my job to pin a medal on that bra of yours!'

Then, exactly then, as if someone on deck had been waiting for the play-acting to end, a bell rang and it was 'Cigarettes out' and 'On your feet' and 'To the right', and within minutes the tank deck was completely empty and five hundred men, mostly teenagers it seemed to me, were clambering down the side of the ship on rope nets into the waiting landing craft to begin their journey to the beaches.

I did not see Nowaks or his bra again. Nor, sadly, did the sergeant-major have the chance to pin anything to it. Marine

Michael Nowaks was killed on the twelfth of June, two days before the war ended.

When we came on deck it was bright moonlight – a bomber's moon, a familiar phrase that kept repeating itself – and not the kind of weather the commanders had been promised and hoped for. We had been told (though I've heard it disputed since) that the ploy was for the task force to steam towards Stanley in clear weather so that the Argentinians could see us and assume we were coming directly at them. Instead, the skies were black, there was fog, and, later in the day, gales. Then, when the fleet turned sharply into the Falkland Sound towards San Carlos, we prayed for fog to hide us. But the moon shone so brightly we could have been seen twenty miles away. Despite it and the few hiccups that followed, nearly four thousand fully-equipped men and thousands of tons of equipment were dispatched from eleven ships by night without serious mishap.

Six weeks and over ten thousand miles at sea and the British had at last touched the land they had come so far to claim back.

Falkland Islands, 21 May 1982:
It was beginning to get light and we could still hear the naval bombardment on known Argentinian positions on high ground just beyond us. Sixty shells in less than fifteen minutes. The landing forces have established their beach-heads. I can see them quite clearly, the Scorpion light tanks, the helicopter pads, the tents and men fanning out across the open moorlands – it's a little like Scotland – crouching, sometimes running, from one hillock to the next. Flocks of sheep scamper from them. At one of the unopposed landings near a small village, a cluster of white stone buildings, troops found thirty-one Falklanders in their own makeshift shelter, among them fourteen children. All are safe.

After yesterday's fog and force nine gales, the dawn, this very cold morning, was crystal clear with a brilliant sun. There are about twenty ships with us in the long narrow fjord that comes off the Falkland Sound, which divides the two main islands, East and West. Helicopters are flying between the ships and the troops, taking ashore supplies of ammunition, food and water – water is going to be a problem. And so are the air attacks.

Just after ten o'clock here – that's one o'clock British time – with the winter sun still low and dazzling, the Argentinians began their air attacks, the first in a long long day of them.

We called it Bomb Alley and, because of their casualties, the brave and daring Argentinian pilots knew it as Death Valley. By the end of that Friday we, the press, knew the extent of British casualties even if we were not allowed to report them immediately. We were, as we were constantly reminded, there to do a 'good news job – the British tommy goes over the top to give the Argies a black eye'. By the end of that Friday it was quite the other way round.

The warnings came over the pipe: 'Four hostiles . . . 145 degrees . . . four miles and closing'. We looked southwards, scanning the slopes of the hills across the bay, knowing we should not see the planes until a few seconds before they dropped their bombs. Aboard HMS *Fearless*, I watched our missiles swivel on their pods awkwardly as if their controlling computer could not make up its mind which way they should point. It was much more comforting to watch the men – boys, really – at the Bofors guns (made in Halifax in 1943), wheels spinning as the barrels turned across the ship to face the attackers, hands passing shells, hands wrapped in mittens, faces wrapped in anti-flash masks – eyes that had never seen an enemy before, peering into the sun. And their captain, Jeremy Larkin (middle name Shackleton after an ancestor who knew something of the South Atlantic), with the drawling stutter, duffel coat and wellington boots, in a second world war helmet with CAPTAIN chalked on it – he looked more like an air-raid warden.

Left of us and a couple of hundred yards away was *Canberra*, huge and white – the wedding cake, the white whale, the most conspicuous target of all. Beyond us in the narrow channel leading to the Sound were the frigates *Plymouth* and *Yarmouth*, and steaming furiously and protectively around them the cruiser *Antrim*. Out in the Sound on the gun line, our first line of defence, were the five frigates: *Brilliant, Broadsword, Argonaut, Alacrity* and *Ardent*.

The ships began firing together and I followed the line of black explosions in the sky to the silver Skyhawks, two on our port bow, two on our stern, splitting the fire, followed by four Mirages – what the Argentinians called Daggers. I turned to run forward for a better view and tripped over the Ministry of Defence minder who was on his knees praying, eyes closed. The Skyhawks hit *Argonaut* first, and then decided to go for *Antrim*. We could see their shells cutting the water towards her and hitting her bows. They overshot, climbed, banked, then turned again. For an instant we lost them in the blaze of sun and when we looked again they had hit *Ardent*. Two thousand-pounders opened up her aft deck and she went out of control at eighteen knots. Then another pair of Daggers swooped down and dropped more bombs in the blazing hole. It was said later that when Captain Alan West gave the order to abandon ship men cried; West admitted he did. They lined up at the bow in their orange survival suits, waiting for the helicopters to winch them off. The thirty injured went first. They left twenty-four dead behind.

In San Carlos the bombs were dropping so near to us, *Fearless* shuddered with the shock waves. A thousand-pounder dropped so close, the spray covered our decks and the force of its underwater blast turned the ship around a few degrees. The Bofors guns and the lighter Oerlikons were firing nonstop and the marines aboard were even using their automatic rifles, spraying the sky back and forth. Then, every few minutes a whoosh of air as a missile was fired and we watched it chase its target until both went over the hills out of sight. Less than two hundred yards away was the ammunition ship, still fully loaded. Had the Argentinians known it and had they hit her, the blast would have sunk or damaged every ship in the bay. One of us asked the crew whether we ought to be issued with survival suits – just in case she went up. Not suits, they said: best have a parachute!

Up on the slopes overlooking the bay I could see the silhouettes of the Rapier air defence missile batteries. They were intended to be our first means of defence, the faultless, impeccably fast and accurate Rapiers which could bring down a shell in flight; no attacking aircraft could match them. They were unused and useless to us. Saltwater on the voyage had damaged their sensitive mechanisms and the diesel oil for the engines which turned their launch pads had thickened in the cold.

The SBS reconnaissance parties had reported that there were no Argentinians in San Carlos, but they were wrong. The unit on Fanning Head had already been discovered and dealt with – 'taken out' was a euphemism we were to get used to. Three Parachute Regiment found the others – or rather just missed them at Port San Carlos, further along the bay, since they had fled inland when they saw the paras' landing craft approaching. But news of the enemy's presence in the area never reached the helicopter pilots and a Sea King carrying Rapier missiles and its escorting Gazelle were fired at and hit. The Gazelle crashed into the sea and the crewmen struggled in the water trying to keep the pilot afloat, not realising he was already dead. All the while, the Argentinians on the shore continued machine-gunning them. A few minutes later, still unaware of the danger, another Gazelle rounded Cameron's Point on its way to Port San Carlos and the Argentinians turned their guns on it. It exploded and crashed, killing the crew. One of the men who ran to the wreckage and pulled the dead men clear was the same SBS commander who some days before had reported the area clear. The men's chests were soaked in blood from the machine-gun fire and, although it was strictly forbidden to take the dead back to the ships, he helped a naval surgeon load them aboard a rescue helicopter. Despite orders, he would not leave them on the hillside.

The sun sets very early in a Falklands winter and never was darkness more gratefully received than that late Friday afternoon. We sat eating in the wardroom, silent and shocked. We had not expected this. Our troops were safely ashore; at least the day had accomplished that first objective. But now it looked as if the Argentinian air force would, in their time, destroy all our ships and from what we had seen there did not seem to be a great deal we could do about it. The troops could dig in, make shelters and trenches; they were dispersed; they had cover. We had none. We were monumental sitting ducks. As soon as it was dark, *Canberra*, the great white whale, pulled anchor and moved quietly and slowly out of San Carlos and set a course east, away from the war and out of range of the Argentine air force – at least for a while.

The damage in that one day was devastating. HMS *Ardent* sunk; *Argonaut* hit, repaired and set on fire again; *Antrim*, *Brilliant* and

Broadsword hit by bombs which had failed to detonate and were still on board.

It was the bombs which did not explode that saved us. The UXB – the unexploded bomb – became the best-kept secret of the war. Some of them, American-made, had been stored for fifteen years or more and the wiring had deteriorated. The other reason was as simply explained. The Argentinian pilots, despite their undisputed skills, were throwing the bombs at the ships too low and the arming mechanism, a little propeller inside the tail fins that screws in as the bomb falls, was not in the air long enough for the detonator to touch the charge. It would not be long before the pilots realised their mistake, but by then it would be too late.

In another day of air raids HMS *Antelope* close by us was hit by an unexploded bomb and that evening as a bomb disposal expert tried to defuse it, it exploded.

Falkland Islands, May 1982

The entire stern section [of *Antelope*] is on fire right down to the water level. I can see men in white fire suits, asbestos suits, trying to fight the fire. There is water power. I can see water and powder being sprayed on to the fire; they're trying to do what they can. It's dark now. The helicopters from all the other ships are hovering close by, ignoring the flames, trying to take men off her by winch, winching them up; but explosions continue. The fire is lighting up this entire corner of San Carlos Bay. She was hit by a Skyhawk aircraft; it came in from the Falkland Sound, bombed and strafed one ship and then turned sharply on *Antelope*, dropped its second bomb, and then climbed to try and avoid the gunfire from the frigate. But a millisecond afterwards, missiles from the frigate hit it and the plane exploded in a ball of orange.

The following morning I watched her sink:

HMS *Antelope* – our escort into San Carlos Bay two days ago – broke her back and sank some twenty hours after she had been hit. Fuel and shells exploding aboard her finally split her apart. Her bows and stern lifted and enormous white clouds of steam and smoke billowed up across the bay, as the decks and superstructure, red-hot from the fires, touched the water. Then, in a great surge of water and smoke, she went down. Minutes later, when the water had settled, only a few feet of her bows showed, her anchor-chain tied to her, still tight against the tide. Now only orange buoys show where she lies. Men aboard our ship did not watch her die. Just as seamen do not celebrate the sinking of an enemy ship, they will not witness the sinking of their own.

It was relentless that week in Bomb Alley. Courage had been easy in the beginning, but by the fifth day it was different. Our ships moved position around San Carlos Water and those two faithful accompanists, panic and fear, moved with them. It seemed to me only a matter of time, not chance, before we on *Fearless* were hit too. As well as my anti-flash hood and gloves, my flak jacket and helmet, I strapped on a life jacket. I made absolutely sure I was wearing nothing made of nylon and, ignoring orders, I hid my orange rubber survival suit under the starboard side Bofors gun so that if I had to I could get to it quickly. Somebody must have seen me do it because there were two suits there the next day.

The two knights of the fleet, the landing ships *Sir Lancelot* and *Sir Galahad*, were hit together in the same Skyhawk attack. The bombs did not explode. *Galahad*'s was safely defused but *Lancelot* had to be towed and gently pushed by landing craft to an anchorage on the far side of the bay in case she went up and took some of us with her. Her decks were still packed high with vehicles and crates of weapons and ammunition; the two one-thousand pounders had gone through her sides. As she passed us that evening less than a hundred yards away, we could see, through the gaping holes in her hull, men with acetylene torches cutting their way through the bulkheads to get to the bombs and defuse them. We held our breath as she moved by. There was no movement on our deck – as if the slightest hint of it might be our last.

Lieutenant-Commander Bernie Bruen was one of the select and brave men who worked under the title Bomb Disposal Squad. He was a naval salvage diver in peacetime; now in San Carlos he was fully employed detaching the detonator fuse from the inside of bombs that had yet to explode. He was a big man in his early thirties with a red beard, a young James Robertson Justice look-alike. He was never without his pipe and fiddle. No one ever saw him carrying a gun. He was also a poet and supplied me with a daily rhymed commentary of our war in San Carlos. Following the attacks, it took him twenty-two hours to cut a hole in the hold of *Sir Galahad*, the first time she was hit, to get to the one-thousand pounder wedged there. Bruen used a steel toothpick and a tiny dentist's mirror to dismantle its detonator, all the while lying upside-down. When it was done they rolled the bomb into a rubber dinghy and pushed it out to sea away from the ship, and when it was a safe distance they punctured the dinghy with rifle fire, but it would not sink. Finally he had to paddle another dinghy to it and manhandle the bomb overboard. Bruen spent his in-between hours drinking enormous quantities of beer, writing poems and playing his fiddle. The last time I saw him playing it, he was standing in the snow at a military funeral above Ajax Bay.

Towards the end of that week, we had hoped the Argentine air raids would slacken off. How could they keep it up, losing so many men and planes? But on the Thursday they took us by surprise again. Until then, lengthening shadows and a low red sun signalled the end of the day's war. But as late afternoon turned to evening, Captain Larkin piped 'Four hostiles . . . two four zero . . . three miles and closing', and even before the men turned the guns, before we could even pull on our flak jackets, four Skyhawks hurtled over the slopes from the Sound. We saw their silver bellies, then great orange balls of flame, and black smoke on Ajax Bay directly opposite us. Then three were gone; we heard the fourth exploding out of sight and saw the parachute falling into the bay a few hundred yards away. They had hit the marines' beach-head, the ammunition dumps and the field hospital in the disused refrigeration factory nearby.

That night was full of helicopters as the casualties were shared out among the ships and the rescued Argentinian pilot was treated by the doctor aboard *Fearless* as if he were one of our own.

The casualties on both sides were now such that it seemed the war would be decided not on land but in San Carlos Water itself. Had we really expected to suffer so much? Had it been anticipated? Was it a portion of the losses Admiral Sir John Fieldhouse and Mrs

Thatcher's war cabinet considered 'acceptable'? Or was it now a matter of either–or? Would all our ships be destroyed before the Argentinians ran out of aircraft and pilots? And which would come first? The Argentinians had already lost over forty aircraft, including those destroyed on Pebble Island and, by 25 May, we had lost five ships, with as many severely damaged, including the two vital landing ships, *Sir Lancelot* and *Sir Galahad*.

The twenty-fifth was Argentine's National Day and we at the sharp end of their aggression felt they had something to celebrate. That same day the destroyer HMS *Coventry* was sunk at the entrance to the Falkland Sound and the *Atlantic Conveyor*, the container ship bringing supplies and more aircraft and helicopters, was hit and sunk by an Exocet. It was our lowest ebb, the nadir of the entire campaign. That evening, our casualties in the previous five days were announced: fifty-four seamen killed; nearly one hundred wounded, many seriously.

We had been in the Falklands for less than a week but we were beginning to wonder if the unbelievable was happening – that the war was already lost.

The next day, 26 May, I went ashore to stay. The battle of Bomb Alley, the war of planes against ships, was suddenly, unexpectedly over. The Mirages and Skyhawks did not come back again, at least not there. Now the British forces would leave their San Carlos beach-head and fight on land. The push towards Stanley had begun.

The problem for me now was where to go, with whom to go, and for how long. I had made a decision the morning we sailed into San Carlos that I would not go roaming until it was absolutely necessary. I would resist the temptation to be a soldier and go yomping off across the sodden Falklands peatbogs looking for Argies. Gareth Parry of the *Guardian* was one who quickly discovered that the excursions ashore were not worth the risk. One night, having lost his way from one trench to another, he heard the unnerving click of a bolt being slid back in a self-loading rifle, followed by the stern challenge: 'What's the password?' To which Parry replied: 'I'm terribly sorry but I don't know,' and expected to die.

If newspapermen wanted to play soldiers in their camouflage

and smoked cork disguises, if they thought it was worthwhile to spend the night in trenches simply to write about how cold it was and how much the tommies were missing home, they were welcome to it. There was nothing in it for me. The story was where the telephone was and that was aboard the Marisat ship in the bay. Feeding my stories to ITN daily, often hourly, was the first priority, and rather than chasing ashore I waited for reports to come filtering back, which they did.

When I discovered that our video tapes would take weeks to get back to London (and even that turned out to be optimistic), I decided this was going to be a radio war. Television would take second place. It was the first time I had ever done extended radio reports, and it was enormously exciting and gratifying. A television news reporter is often simply a caption writer; the picture is supposed to tell the story. Now with my newly acquired tape recorder – I bought it from a naval rating for £20 and a tin of toffee – I could move on my own, travelling on impulse from unit to unit, hitching lifts on a passing helicopter, standing in the middle of nowhere thumbing the sky – without the hindrance of a camera-recording interviews, capturing the natural sound of an air attack or an artillery bombardment and writing my words around them. Suddenly I was creating word pictures and it was altogether a new sensation.

There was one newspaperman who had also decided never to be so far from a satellite link to London that he could not send a daily report. He was Max Hastings of the *Daily Telegraph*. Many mean things have been said and written about Max's role in the war – some untrue and unfair. He was hugely disliked by most of the Falklands press corps and treated with some suspicion by the junior military; by the former because he was a thoroughly skilled, ruthless, incorrigible and tireless operator; by the latter because of his connections in high military places; they referred to him either as General or Lord Hastings. He was considered an insufferably pompous, bumptious egotist, which of course he was and remains, but as he has since inherited the editor's throne at the *Telegraph*, such things are forgiven, even expected. On the journey to the South Atlantic on *Canberra* he made many enemies among his fellows. They called him Mad Max and sent the ship's doctor and ship's padre to his cabin one evening, having persuaded both that Max was suffering intolerable mental anguish and was in desperate need of their treatment and comfort. Both were given very short shrift.

Max was accused of many things in the Falklands, including deliberately destroying other reporters' copy, which was absurd. He had no need to; there was no competition, at least among the newspapermen, and there were many reasons why. He was not inclined to cooperate or share stories and worked harder and stayed awake longer than most. He also made full and blatant use of his family and class connections: he of Charterhouse and Oxford, son of famous novelist Anne Scott-James and father McDonald Hastings, second world war correspondent and later BBC television reporter. Max was an officer in style and in breeding. Given the pedigree, we would have done the same.

That was the rub! While the rest of us in *Fearless* were sleeping rough night after night under the tables in the wardroom or, if the floor was full, in the gangways, Max was given use of the commodore's cabin, complete with change of sheets and a shower. He was also privy to confidential military information denied the rest of us and even, on one occasion, given access to the SAS secret satellite link to Britain to file a story.

The other reasons why he did so well, besides his bravery and bravado, were his patriotism and (to be kind) his facility for writing things the way he felt his readers thought they ought to be. In one of his earliest stories for the *Telegraph* under the headline NONE OF US CAN BE NEUTRAL IN THIS WAR he wrote: 'Most of us had decided before we landed that our role was simply to report as sympathetically as possible what the British forces were doing – and not file a dispatch that was likely to give the Argentinians any hope or comfort.'

Which was not true. Only Max decided that. Justifying his stance, he quoted his father: 'When one's nation is at war, one's reporting becomes an extension of the war effort.' If the *Telegraph* readers – and that included Margaret Thatcher and her war council – liked what Max was writing, so did the military on the Falklands. So confident was he that he pinned a copy of his dispatches on the ship's notice-board every evening and then waited for the plaudits.

It was just one of the many gambits Mad Max used to win *his* Falklands war.

We – Brian and I – made things especially difficult for the newspapermen. There was a great deal of anger and resentment when they arrived back from their gruelling trips ashore to discover that their stories were out of date and unwanted by their editors in London because they had already been told by us over the Marisat link and broadcast on television. Our reports had even been published word for word in their newspapers the next day.

I was especially lucky in getting my reports widely published. My deadline for *News at Ten* was an hour later than the *BBC Nine O'clock News*. We were often unable to transmit until late because of radio satellite timings and censorship delays at both ends, so reports were often too late for his main news but were cleared in time for me to make mine. This happened so frequently, there was a suspicion that due to the government's growing abhorrence of the BBC's negative and, as they saw it, biased attitude to the war, (especially in the *Newsnight* studio), Brian's reports and those from Robert Fox, the BBC's radio reporter, were deliberately delayed by the Ministry of Defence on a nod and a wink from the prime minister's mischievous press secretary, Bernard Ingham.

Things became particularly bad for Brian and Robert before and after the Paras' attack on Darwin and Goose Green in which Colonel H. and fifteen of his men died. Brigadier Julian Thompson, in command of 3 Brigade (who was so determined to win he gave up drink until we did), was all for the softly-softly advance – prodding the Argentine defences, accumulating intelligence reports on their strengths and locations. But following the disasters of the previous week, Mrs Thatcher and her war council were demanding blood and revenge, fearful that public support would evaporate otherwise. The order to Thompson, via the commander-in-chief in Northwood, was for action and a quick success. The Argentine garrisons at the small settlements at Darwin and Goose Green were the nearest targets.

But then on 26 May, two days before it was due, we heard that the BBC World Service had announced the attack was imminent and even reported that in the Commons that afternoon Mrs Thatcher had confirmed British forces were moving out of their beach-head at San Carlos. As the Argentinians believed what they heard on the BBC, they quickly reinforced both garrisons. The paras were furious and threatened to 'kneecap' any BBC man who came near them, and Colonel H. was reported to have said that when the battle was over he would sue the BBC for manslaughter. It was later reported that he had threatened to sue Mrs Thatcher as well. In this atmosphere then, anything could be believed. Two British tabloids had already fictitiously reported the taking of Goose Green!

Colonel H. died in what now ranks as one of the Parachute Regiment's greatest victories and the legendary H. (it stood for Herbert which was probably why he preferred H.) was awarded a posthumous Victoria Cross.

The Argentinians must anyway have been expecting an attack. The British were obviously not intending to remain in San Carlos and the fact that a reconnaissance patrol lately out of Darwin had not returned (captured by the paras) was evidence that the British were close by. But the attack might never have been attempted had British intelligence been better than it was. The SAS were asked to reconnoitre the area and report back the number of Argentine troops and their fire strength. The SAS patrols estimated there were about five hundred men spread over both garrisons, which meant the paras would be fighting on about a one-to-one basis. The SAS were dreadfully wrong; there were over sixteen hundred Argentine troops there, which made the odds more than three to one. Had that been known, it is doubtful if even Mrs Thatcher would have sanctioned the attack.

The taking of Darwin and Goose Green, like most of the land battles, was done in darkness. In such open sprawling land, without trees or cover, it was suicidal to send infantry forward during daylight. Our television camera too was often redundant because of it. I spent much of my time watching the war at night, which in the Falklands winter stretches from four in the afternoon to after ten o'clock in the morning. In those six hours of light, both sides rested, replenished, took stock of their fortunes and prepared for darkness again. In those hours our indefatigable camera crew, Bernard Hesketh and John Jockell, went urgently about the battlefields recording the gory aftermath and the bloody postmortems of success or defeat. But I, the television reporter, had long changed coats: radio was now my game, and I was doing what a generation of hallowed men had done before me; recording the war's images on a tape-recorder.

Robert Fox was the only reporter with the paras at Darwin and Goose Green and I came across him soon after it was over. He was filthy with mud and oil and shaking with the cold. His eyes were red, which I thought was the effect of cordite and grenade smoke but he said he had been crying: first from fear and then from the shock of survival. He had suffered all those hours of artillery and machine-gun fire with men he knew falling dead around him. I wanted to interview him then and there in all his shocked state, to grab him while the images were still powerful, the emotions running strong and the anger and the fright ready to explode. But camerman Bernard said no; he was, he said, still a BBC employee and he could not film an interview of mine unless Brian Hanrahan were there too. Preposterous then, preposterous still and the only time Bernard and I came close to blows.

That morning, in the bitter sleeting rain and icy wind, I had my first sight ever of British dead in the aftermath of a British victory. The paras had brought their own in from the battlefield and were reverently putting them in body bags for burial the next day. One was a machine-gunner, hit in the head. They found him under the body of his ammunition carrier who had been hit by a sniper as he was tying a dressing to his comrade's head. Another had run under fire to pull a wounded man to safety; then, knowing they were short of ammunition, had gone out again to retrieve a hundred rounds. He was hit in the neck by a single sniper's bullet when he was only a few yards from his own trench again. Three more, a platoon commander and two NCOs, had gone forward when a white flag was waved from a machine-gun post in a schoolhouse. But it was a mistake and as they ran back across open ground and with their own giving them covering fire, the Argentinians shot them down. In their fury the rest of the platoon ran and took the building, killing everybody there, including those with their hands above their heads.

The paras had spent some of that day looking for the body of another British casualty, a Harrier pilot whose plane had exploded above them during an attack on the Argentine positions. Squadron Leader Bob Iveson had made two runs strafing and dropping cluster bombs, when he decided to make a third and last run over trenches he had seen on Darwin Hill – the same trenches that were causing the paras so much trouble and from which Colonel H. was finally shot. Iveson's Harrier was hit as he came off target but he ejected a split second before his plane exploded:

> Things went wrong very quickly . . . the controls stopped working . . . there was smoke in the cockpit and when I saw fire I pulled the ejector handle. But I was going a bit too fast and a bit low . . . about a hundred feet. The chute opened and I found myself going right towards the fireball of my aircraft in front of me. I couldn't tell whether it had hit the ground or not. Seconds later I did.

The Harrier's momentum had taken him well beyond Goose Green. When he came to, he had a fractured back and wind-blast damage to his eyes, but he found his way to a deserted shepherd's house and lived on tins of baked beans he found there until he eventually made contact with a passing helicopter on his survival radio.

The Argentine dead were still out there in the gloom, lying half-submerged in mud and water in the trenches and dugout machine-gun posts. I saw that the paras had killed with bayonets as well as bullets. They had used grenades too, including the white phosphorus grenade which burns a man alive, eating into his flesh; there is nothing he can do to stop it, except cutting it out of the flesh with a knife or bayonet. Nothing I had seen since Vietnam compared to the horror on those small dead young faces. There was another reminder of Vietnam: as others would later, the paras used the Milan guided anti-tank rocket. No one survived it; the Argentinians died the way the Vietcong had in a B-52 bombing attack; not from shrapnel but from concussion in the explosion. Their insides had burst.

We saw the official surrender on the football pitch at Goose Green, but we were not allowed to film it. Major Chris Keeble, who had taken command of 2 Para at the height of the battle when Colonel

H. had been killed, decided that the camera might aggravate the Argentine commander, and pacification was the order of the day. So we did not record for posterity the final scene of the first British victory, the thousand men and more laying down their arms and then being ordered by their commander to sing their national anthem as though that somehow compensated for their defeat.

The prisoners, mostly teenage conscripts, wet and cold and still dazed by the battle, were herded into the settlement's sheep-shearing sheds. Some were taken under armed escort to clear up the ammunition that was everywhere. While some were moving artillery shells, they exploded – we wondered later if they had been booby-trapped. A British medical orderly ran into the fire and pulled out two wounded prisoners. He went back for a third man whose legs had been blown off. Unable to move him and rather than let him burn to death, the orderly shot him through the head.

We were allowed to film the mass burial of the Argentinians who were killed at Darwin and Goose Green. Some had already been buried where they had died, and a stick with a helmet on it marked those graves. In the pouring rain, a British army Roman Catholic chaplain conducted the service and an Argentinian officer by his side repeated his words in Spanish. But the wind took their words away and by the time the Argentinian threw his handful of earth into the hole the bodies were already half-covered in water.

The paras took their dead back to San Carlos, to a site overlooking the sea just beyond Ajax Bay, which had been prepared some days before the attack, such was their aplomb. The sky was low and black, the clouds almost touching the bare heads of those who had come to mourn. Major Keeble marched at the head of the bearers carrying the seventeen bodies wrapped in silver burial sheets, and men stood silently to attention as they were laid in a line side by side. General Jeremy Moore, the newly-arrived Commander of Land Forces, stood stiffly, looking out of place in his neat little forage cap and clean pressed uniform, as the names of the dead were read out. Among them was a Royal Marines helicopter pilot who had gone through fire to provide the paras with support.

It began to snow but the mourners waited, like monuments, until the last body disappeared under the shovelled earth. Behind and a little above them, standing alone on an outcrop of rock,

Bernie Bruen played the Scottish dirge, 'The Dark Island', on his fiddle.

When *Canberra* returned to San Carlos at the end of May bringing the Fifth Infantry Brigade of the Scots and Welsh Guards and the Gurkhas, the war took on another unexpected dimension; the fierce competition, at times open hostility, between the two brigade commanders. Tony Wilson of Fifth arrived knowing he was late into the action and declared he was determined to catch up by hook or by crook. Julian Thompson of the Third had landed on D-day and considered he would continue to make the running. Their competition led to one of the war's most daring initiatives and ultimately its worst tragedy.

Both reported directly to Jeremy Moore. He was a small thin man with a perpetual grin and a habit of standing, arms crossed, staring at nothing; not at all the very model of the modern major-general. He had come prepared for a long hard slog, believing that the Argentine commander in the Falklands, Brigadier-General Mario Menendez, would not abandon the fight willingly. Just as General Montgomery had familiarised himself with Rommel before the start of the North Africa campaign, so General Moore, before he had left England, had asked for a full briefing on Menendez. On his voyage to the South Atlantic, he studied carefully the man's background and character; he even carried a photograph of him. Moore decided that his adversary was a tough paratrooper who could be expected to attempt an aggressive battle and would not easily give in. Unfortunately, there were five General Menendezes in the Argentine army and General Moore had got the wrong one, something he did not realise until he met the real one at the surrender.

It was now approaching midwinter and in that first week of June we had our worst weather yet: low clouds, high winds and sweeping, chilling mists. Everyone was cold and wet and wondering how much longer it would go on. Day temperatures were around freezing, the rain and sleet were constant and became sheets of thin ice on our clothes. At night it dropped well below zero and we all slept (in our sleeping-bags), in dugout or trench or if we were lucky on the earth floor of a sheep-shearing shed, fully clothed in overcoats, gloves and boots. Men and vehicles had turned the camps into mud swamps. Those who were dug in higher up on the mountain slopes lived in snow and arctic winds. No British soldier, except those few who had previously done specialist winter training in Norway, was equipped for such conditions. They were dressed as if they were on exercises on Salisbury Plain in spring. Their light trousers and tunics and anoraks could not properly have protected them from anything more severe than an April shower, their boots leaked and they suffered foot-rot and worse, frostbite. Only later, as they advanced on Argentinian positions, were some British troops better off. The enemy was well and warmly dressed with kapok-lined uniforms and calf-length vulcanised boots which kept their feet dry. Dead, they were often stripped and their clothes and boots worn by those who had killed them in combat.

The weather might easily have halted any British advance and given the Argentine command time to reinforce their garrison at Stanley. But Brigadier Tony Wilson decided he would use it to his advantage, desperate as he was to move the four thousand men of the Fifth forward. What had delayed him was the Argentine observation posts on top of the mountains which were radioing back every British movement. But the clouds that covered those mountains also covered the observation posts, and the men up there with binoculars were now blind.

Wilson decided to send a helicopter-borne force as far forward as he could. But how far forward? The enemy were known to be holding a number of bridges en route to Stanley and he dared not send his men 'a bridge too far'. So he decided to make a telephone call to find out. One of his patrols had discovered that the telephone line connecting one civilian settlement to another had not been cut by the retreating Argentinians, so Wilson promptly rang from a house at Swan Inlet to another at Fitzroy, some way up the coast. To the brigadier's astonishment it was answered by the owner, Reg Binney, who said, 'Yes, the Argies were here yesterday but they're not here today.' Wilson replied, 'Well, in that case I think I'll join you,' and Binney thought that would be a good idea.

It was a heaven-sent opportunity to take a critical enemy position without a fight. With an eye still on the clouds, Wilson launched his first wave of helicopters loaded with paratroopers, the pilots flew less than twenty feet above the ground, with helicopter gunships flying in close formation protecting them from ground attack. They landed at Fitzroy and fanned out in a circle as the next wave of helicopters came in. Not a shot was fired. The black clouds still covered the observation posts high above them. The only people to watch the operation were the villagers of Fitzroy. British troops had that afternoon made a startling leapfrog of nearly forty miles and the Argentinians did not know a thing about it.

It was daring, it was original, it did not endear him to Julian Thompson and Third Brigade, but Wilson's gamble had paid off. Soon the odds would be stacked against him and he would pay dearly for it.

His problem was how to get the rest of his brigade, some twelve hundred men, forward to Fitzroy. Obviously, it could not be done by helicopter. So Ewen Southby-Tailyour was summoned to advise how to do it by sea and it was decided that the first contingent would be taken from San Carlos in *Fearless* and transferred to Ewen's landing craft for the final few miles by sea to the landing point at Bluff Cove.

The first attempt at night succeeded, even though winds were gusting to eighty miles an hour and soldiers in the open craft suffered from exposure. But the weather worsened and the second shuttle the following night failed; the winds were so high and the sea so rough, Ewen could not get his landing craft out of Bluff Cove to make the rendezvous. Aboard *Fearless* we were buffeted by the huge waves as our own two landing craft were filled with men and sent off into the blackness, to what many must have thought was certain drowning.

It was then decided that the remainder of the Guards would go aboard *Sir Galahad*, recently repaired after Bernie Bruen had rid her of her unexploded bomb. Surprisingly, the navy decided she would be sent without escorts and therefore without protection, assuming the men would be ashore long before it was daylight, before the Argentinians could attack. But there was a cock-up: it was discovered too late that *Sir Galahad* could not offload at Bluff Cove because the channel was too shallow. Instead she would have to go to Fitzroy, a settlement four miles away, separated by a deep inlet. But the Argentinians had blown the bridge which meant the

Guards would have a sixteen-mile march to Bluff Cove. If they stayed aboard *Sir Galahad* it was only four hundred yards by water, so they decided to stay put and wait their turn in the landing craft – however long it took.

The off-loading took longer than anyone had feared. The landing craft were too small and the landing sites restricted. By lunchtime, when I arrived there expecting to see the men ashore and the ships safely away, *Sir Galahad* was still anchored with lines of troops queueing on her decks. A hundred yards from her was another knight of the fleet, *Sir Tristram*, which had brought the Fifth's supplies. Ewen was horrified; he found a major from the Fifth and demanded the men be put on land, any land, before it was too late. They were in great danger, he said. But the officers and men of the Fifth knew nothing of Bomb Alley, had never seen the Skyhawks and Mirages in attack, had never seen what their bombs could do to ships and men. So Fifth Brigade continued their casual, almost nonchalant, disembarkation.

Later, at a field gun battery on the slopes overlooking Fitzroy, gunners told me what they had seen that afternoon. They had watched four Argentine aircraft in a line, two Skyhawks and two Mirages, wingtip to wingtip, flying very low towards them in the valley. Chasing them was a single Harrier. As they passed overhead, no more than a hundred feet high, the aircraft broke formation; the two on the right banked east towards Fitzroy, the other two turned left and climbed sharply; the Harrier pilot, in a split-second decision, turned left too and disappeared after them over the mountains.

We were only four hundred yards away but the blast from the explosions took the roof off the shed and we were buried under the debris. We heard bursts of heavy machine-gun fire and the other distinctive sound of heavy cannon and we stayed where we were until it was quiet. When we came running out, the aircraft had gone and *Sir Galahad* and *Sir Tristram* were burning.

Falkland Islands, 9 June 1982 (radio report):
The bombs hit *Sir Galahad* aft through the engine-room and accommodation sections and I watched from the shore less than four hundred yards away as boxes of ammunition aboard

exploded, shaking the ground beneath us, and we crouched as bullets from the ship whistled and whirled past us. I saw hundreds of men rush forward along the decks pulling on their lifejackets, pulling on survival suits, some – the ship's crewmen just off watch – pulling on shirts and trousers. Many trapped in the wrong side of the ship jumped overboard as the flames spread. I saw men swim underwater away from the ship to avoid the burning oil, and I watched other men, men who were safely away forward of the flames, risk their lives to jump into the water with lifejackets to save those men swimming below. Inflatable rubber life-rafts, bright orange, were hurled over the side. Some immediately burst into flames as debris from the explosions hit them, others landed but were blown by the wind into the burning oil. Ropes were thrown over the side of the ship and men clambered down them and despite the wind, despite the heat of the metal on their feet, despite the movement of the ship, they got into their life-rafts. The strong wind fanned the flames, enormous flames, and as the fuel tanks exploded the ship was half-enveloped in thick black smoke. The Royal Navy Sea King and Wessex helicopter pilots and their crews ignored the flames, they ignored the explosions, they ignored the ammunition erupting around them and flew their machines into the smoke to lift the queues of men below. The helicopters waited in turn, steady in the air, to move in over the bow to winch the men off. I watched one pilot steer his machine slowly and deliberately into the black and hover. He was completely blinded, completely enveloped, and then I saw his crewman winching down on a line to pick men out of the sea. Three times I watched him go down, three times he brought men up, to the blackness that covered his helicopter above him. I saw another helicopter almost touch the water, its rotor blades seemed to be spinning through the flames, to pick up a man in a bright orange survival suit who was clinging to the anchor chain. Lifeboats were launched from *Sir Tristram*, whose crew seemed to be containing their fire, and these boats, under power, began taking some of the rubber life-rafts in tow. Other rafts began drifting, taken by the wind away from the inferno, and, as the breeze turned suddenly, towards it again. Pilots in the helicopters waiting at the bow, waiting to bring the men aboard, saw what was happening and immediately four of them took their machines to the stern, by the flames. They came down low and using the downdraught of their rotor blades, began to push the rubber dinghies away, slowly, yard by yard, each helicopter taking care of one dinghy full of men, and pushing them to the safety of the beach. There was much heroism yesterday at Fitzroy but this single tribute must be paid to the helicopter pilots and their winchmen who saved so many. The casualties and survivors – many suffering from shock and burns – were picked up from the beach by soldiers who had run from their trenches to help. Dozens of soldiers waded out into the freezing water up to their chests to pull men to safety. I watched soldiers struggling in the waves, picking the injured out of the life rafts and carrying them back on their shoulders to the shore and then going back for more. It was a day of tragedy, but I vouch it was a day of extraordinary heroism and selflessness by every man who witnessed it.

High above, maybe ten thousand feet up, were the thin vapour trails of our Harriers on their combat air patrols. Over the past few weeks we had grown used to them, felt safe because of them and were cheered whenever we saw their white trails cross, like kisses. It meant all was well and the sky was ours. As the smoke rose from the exploding inferno out in the bay and men without legs and arms and open stomachs were carried past me, I looked up again and saw those same kisses.

We of the Falklands press corps were thrown out of the final briefing for the final offensive. Brigadier Wilson had invited us to attend at his new headquarters, believing it important we should know what was to happen so that we might make our own decisions about which units we should accompany. It was especially important for the television camera to be properly placed with a unit that was 'up front'. But Wilson was now a very different man from the enthusiastic hero of the Fitzroy leapfrog. His flamboyance and his impulsiveness were gone. He now bore the dreadful onus of the *Galahad* disaster, accused, though never publicly, of reckless-ness in jumping too far forward and forcing the pace of events which had resulted in the unnecessary deaths of fifty of his men. He was never forgiven.

When General Moore countermanded his invitation to us, Wilson promptly obeyed and we were left out in the cold. Despite all the general's previously friendly bluster and the promises that we should go everywhere and anywhere we wanted (he had told me he wanted the war properly covered by television so that his son would see what he had done), Moore denied us the opportunity to do exactly that. That afternoon, much against our will, we were helicoptered to the top of Two Sisters to join the Gurkhas. There we would wait until the first-line troops took Mount Tumbledown just ahead of us and Mount Harriet a little below us on our right. We could see Stanley, less than eight miles away.

The four of us – Brian Hanrahan, Bernard Hesketh, John Jockell and I – prepared for what we were warned would be four days at least of bitter fighting. The major in charge of our Gurkha company was not overpleased with the additional burden we obviously were and cheerfully told us our position was in direct line of fire for the Argentine 155mm guns in Stanley. He told us to dig in and not to show our heads above the protective line of rocks at the mountain's summit. Behind and far below us, our own guns began firing, five batteries, six guns apiece, with a reserve of over a thousand shells each. It was reassuring for a little while, but then none of us – not even the Gurkhas I think – quite expected the bombardment that came back.

We had no need to dig ourselves in; we simply took over the holes in the ground vacated by the Argentinians who had had an observation post there, and we thanked them for the bed of moss they had made. But we were on hard rock and you can only con-sider yourself safe from shrapnel if you are below ground level. We were not. Worse, when the shells landed, the explosions sprayed us with rock splinters, as lethal as shrapnel. During that first day, remembering how I had done the same thing in Cyprus, I began to recognise the sound of the guns aimed at us, and when I heard the boom I stretched out as flat as I could on the hard rock, waiting for the most dreadful of all the sounds of war: the whistle of a shell.

It was just before dusk when we saw the Scots Guards, under the cover of British artillery fire, take up their positions among the rocks of Mount Harriet, two miles from the Argentine lines; their objective, Mount Tumbledown, a long sloping mountain covered in shale and pinnacles of rock hiding Argentine machine-gun and mortar positions. The Gurkhas began their move and we followed. They would hold until the Guards had taken Tumbledown and then sweep around them to take Mount William. Harriers began dropping clusters of bombs on to Argentine positions on Tumbledown and Mount Harriet, guided by laser. They could not miss. The casualties were terrible.

The artillery exchange went on all that day. Come darkness, a little after four, the infantry war began. The sky was suddenly lit with flares and in that eerie light we saw battalions on the move. With smoke around them like the thick mist of dawn, young soldiers were moving forward in line, bayonets fixed. Many men that night were killed by those bayonets. It could have been an advance at the Somme.

Bernard was sick and we decided not to wake him. The camera anyway would not be able to record what only the eye could see. Bernard had been superhuman and uncomplaining from the very beginning and whatever was wrong with him would not be put right by robbing him of sleep simply to record the war's night-time pyrotechnics. Despite his sickness, despite the sub-zero temperature, he had wrapped his camera in his overcoat to prevent the lubricating oil inside it from thickening in the cold and not working the next day. It was so true to form.

Brian and I went to separate points to watch the war on the slopes below us. I lay at the sheer edge of the mountain to record the sounds, describing what I saw in a freewheeling commentary – half in disbelief: the arcing red tracers marking their targets, the heavy thump of the Browning machine-guns, the flash and crump of mortars, the echo rebounding as a Milan anti-tank rocket exploded: then another Argentine flare floating in the sky and sudden daylight, with men running like rabbits caught out of cover, and more tracers as a machine-gunner tried to put out the light.

A little after 3 a.m. it began snowing, which made the flares doubly dangerous, highlighting the British troops in their dark camouflage against the white. For a while our artillery stopped firing and we heard Argentine aircraft overhead, looking for the muzzle flashes of our field guns to drop their bombs. There was soon another hazard. Knowing that thousands of men were now spread out and advancing across the valleys, the Argentinians began using air-burst shells which, like fragmentation bombs, explode just above the ground, spraying shrapnel and thousands of tiny white-hot steel balls.

But there was no stopping the British advance. By midmorning, as it was getting light and the snow was still falling, we could see Argentine troops throwing down their rifles and running from their positions along the ridge that led to Stanley. And as proof that our men had taken Tumbledown and Mount William, Sea King and Wessex helicopters flew towards them carrying enormous slings full of ammunition. Then, shortly afterwards, small army Scout helicopters came to pick up the dead and wounded.

We waited for the artillery to begin again, waited for air attacks; but except for the drone of the helicopters all was quiet. We stood on the edge of our mountain peering through the snow, and began to wonder, began to think of one marvellous possibility. Perhaps it really was all over. Perhaps the Argentinians had given up.

We sat listening to the field radio for news from below, but the network was silent too. We heated our tins of combat rations over tiny fires, did our ablutions and waited. For two hours and more we waited. Then suddenly the snow clouds were gone and there was a shout from our lookout on the summit and he was pointing towards Stanley. We climbed to some higher rocks and could see the town clearly. Buildings close to the waterfront were on fire, so was an area on the slopes beyond the town where we knew the Argentinians had their big guns. We saw their hospital ship come slowly into the harbour and small boats going out to meet it. And beyond that the airfield. We watched for movement but there was none.

At five to four that afternoon, our major came running excitedly out of his bunker towards us: the radio message had just come through.

'There's a white flag flying over Stanley. It's all over. Bloody marvellous . . . bloody, bloody marvellous!'

It was a wonderful way to end the war, but it had happened so suddenly that Bernard had not captured it on camera. At this juncture, that could not be allowed to happen. So we asked our major to go back inside his bunker and do it all over again. Which he did . . . four times and three times something went wrong, first with the camera, then with the microphone, then he fluffed his lines. On the final attempt, with his Gurkhas cheering him, we had a take.

Faked or not it did not matter, then or now. There was a white flag over Stanley, and it *was* absolutely bloody marvellous!

At eight o'clock that same evening, Monday 14 June, General Jeremy Moore flew by helicopter from his field headquarters at Bluff Cove to Stanley to accept the Argentine surrender. I tried to hitch a lift with him, there was room, but he said no . . . no press . . . absolutely no press! Nothing and no one should jeopardise the final negotiations and so fearful was he that not even an official naval photographer was allowed into the room to record the signing ceremony. Perhaps Moore, who had once wanted everything recorded, believed that even at this late hour, General Menendez, furious at being filmed or photographed in his moment of defeat, would still change his mind.

If we were disappointed about that, worse was to come. I thumbed a lift on a Scout from Bluff Cove to Fitzroy, from there a Sea King to Darwin and another to San Carlos. There I 'borrowed' a small outboard dinghy that was tied up on the shore and took myself to *Olna*, a ship out in the bay which I knew had Marisat. I walked into the radio room full of my own victory. It was ten minutes to *News at Ten* and I had the scoop of my life. I knew Brian Hanrahan was still in Bluff Cove, and no one else could have made it back so fast. I had the story to myself and ITN would break it to the world.

I was wrong on all counts! The Ministry of Defence had imposed a news blackout. Nothing was to leave the Falklands that night. Mrs Thatcher had decided that she alone would deliver the good news to the nation; it would not come firsthand from the front. To console me, the captain of *Olna* invited me to his private dining-room for food and whisky. Already there at the table, some many whiskies ahead, was Kim Sabido of Independent Radio News, and by his side was the inevitable Max Hastings. The way it had happened, we represented the three arms of the media – television, radio and the printed word – so each of us would, in his own right, have been able to claim his scoop. It had been decided we should not.

There was much whisky, gloom and bitterness at the table that night, with Max the gloomiest and most bitter. The war had been won, we had witnessed it and we had survived, so let us be thankful. But Max had, had he not, the best story of all to tell. When the paras had stopped to regroup by the tiny racecourse outside Stanley, he had thrown off his camouflage and calmly walked into Stanley on his own: an hour ahead of the victorious British army!

We were jubilant. We had survived the war on sea and on land. But, having witnessed the first marathon bouts of beer and jollity at the bar of the 'Upland Goose' in Stanley, I was beginning to doubt if some of the press corps would survive the peace. The humour generated by victory did not last long. The press were not a happy bunch. Few allies had been made and fewer friends, which was surprising. We were more friendly with the military than we were with one another. Someone suggested our offices should pay for an enormous binge together when it was all over. Someone else said; 'Fools – we shan't ever want to see each other again.' And he was right.

To make things a great deal more dangerous, our friends the soldiers, who might have been able to maintain some goodwill among us, were banned from the bar by the town's magistrate, who also happened to be the owner of the 'Upland Goose'. We never did discover why: perhaps, unlike the press, they might have queried his new increased prices; perhaps he preferred the Argentinians; perhaps army boots might have ruined the carpets. As it happened, the carpets were very nearly ruined by the blood of what was almost the first and only death in our corps. Had it succeeded it would have been murder and Max Hastings would have had a lively obituary.

In a press bar, bonhomie fades and recriminations generally begin after the fourth gin. So it was that night in the 'Upland Goose'. Because of his good connections and seeming ability to get a helicopter whenever he needed one, Max had been entrusted with carrying the newspapermen's pooled dispatches back to San Carlos for Marisat transmission to London. What the hacks could not understand or forgive was that although Max's copy invariably got through, the pool copy did not or was delayed. That meant, of course, that as Max's story was the first and often the only story to arrive in London, he appeared in all the newspapers the next day. That famous night in the bar, the newspapermen thought they understood why and were not in a forgiving mood. There is probably no more dangerous an assignment than to be among newspapermen when they read how little their stories have been used and why.

Bob McGowan of the *Daily Express* had just called his office and, instead of receiving a hero's welcome as he had expected, was roundly criticised for not providing enough stories. Many had not reached London, at least not on time. McGowan accused Max in front of everyone: 'You've deliberately buggered our copy.'

Max replied: 'Fuck you!' He said it too casually, considering the allegation and the mood.

Derek Hudson of the *Yorkshire Post* barked across the bar that Max should have filed the pooled dispatches before he sent his own. Max replied again just as casually, emphasising the upper-class drawl that so infuriates: 'Then fuck you both!'

Ian Bruce, a tough little Scot from the *Glasgow Herald*, joined in. He too had been talking to his office and, like McGowan, was not pleased with what they had to say. They told him he sounded very bitter and he had replied: 'That's because I am fucking bitter – bitter about people I know who are dead. And for what? We've liberated 700,000 sheep and 1800 sheep shaggers. Terrific!' He was still trembling with anger as Max, whom he of all of us liked the least, stood nonchalantly in front of him. Bruce slammed down his whisky glass and shouted: 'Yes or no, you bastard. Have you been sending my copy back?'

He did not wait for an answer. Instead he grabbed a bayonet, one of the many captured war trophies, and charged. Hudson grabbed him just in time and held him with only inches to spare because Max had not moved. Then Hudson immortalised the scene with the words, 'This is neither the time nor the place to kill Max

Hastings.' Then someone shouted that McGowan had gone upstairs for his gun (many had them, again captured bounty) and the bar cleared in seconds.

It had been ten weeks and one day since we had sailed from Portsmouth and the British task force, so hastily put together and against all the odds, had done what it had come eight thousand miles to accomplish. In the words of the surrender document, the Falkland Islands were once again under the government desired by its inhabitants and God Save the Queen! Now, it seemed, the biggest threat to life and limb was to be knifed or shot by a drunken reporter. It scarcely seemed worth it for the beer!

No. We had all done what we had been sent to do.

Now it was time to go home.

INDEX